C-2398   CAREER EXAMINATION SERIES

This is your
PASSBOOK for...

Office Manager

Test Preparation Study Guide
Questions & Answers

NATIONAL LEARNING CORPORATION®

COPYRIGHT NOTICE

This book is SOLELY intended for, is sold ONLY to, and its use is RESTRICTED to individual, bona fide applicants or candidates who qualify by virtue of having seriously filed applications for appropriate license, certificate, professional and/or promotional advancement, higher school matriculation, scholarship, or other legitimate requirements of education and/or governmental authorities.

This book is NOT intended for use, class instruction, tutoring, training, duplication, copying, reprinting, excerption, or adaptation, etc., by:

1) Other publishers
2) Proprietors and/or Instructors of "Coaching" and/or Preparatory Courses
3) Personnel and/or Training Divisions of commercial, industrial, and governmental organizations
4) Schools, colleges, or universities and/or their departments and staffs, including teachers and other personnel
5) Testing Agencies or Bureaus
6) Study groups which seek by the purchase of a single volume to copy and/or duplicate and/or adapt this material for use by the group as a whole without having purchased individual volumes for each of the members of the group
7) Et al.

Such persons would be in violation of appropriate Federal and State statutes.

PROVISION OF LICENSING AGREEMENTS – Recognized educational, commercial, industrial, and governmental institutions and organizations, and others legitimately engaged in educational pursuits, including training, testing, and measurement activities, may address request for a licensing agreement to the copyright owners, who will determine whether, and under what conditions, including fees and charges, the materials in this book may be used them. In other words, a licensing facility exists for the legitimate use of the material in this book on other than an individual basis. However, it is asseverated and affirmed here that the material in this book CANNOT be used without the receipt of the express permission of such a licensing agreement from the Publishers. Inquiries re licensing should be addressed to the company, attention rights and permissions department.

All rights reserved, including the right of reproduction in whole or in part, in any form or by any means, electronic or mechanical, including photocopying, recording, or by any information storage and retrieval system, without permission in writing from the Publisher.

Copyright © 2024 by
National Learning Corporation

212 Michael Drive, Syosset, NY 11791
(516) 921-8888 • www.passbooks.com
E-mail: info@passbooks.com

PUBLISHED IN THE UNITED STATES OF AMERICA

PASSBOOK® SERIES

THE *PASSBOOK® SERIES* has been created to prepare applicants and candidates for the ultimate academic battlefield – the examination room.

At some time in our lives, each and every one of us may be required to take an examination – for validation, matriculation, admission, qualification, registration, certification, or licensure.

Based on the assumption that every applicant or candidate has met the basic formal educational standards, has taken the required number of courses, and read the necessary texts, the *PASSBOOK® SERIES* furnishes the one special preparation which may assure passing with confidence, instead of failing with insecurity. Examination questions – together with answers – are furnished as the basic vehicle for study so that the mysteries of the examination and its compounding difficulties may be eliminated or diminished by a sure method.

This book is meant to help you pass your examination provided that you qualify and are serious in your objective.

The entire field is reviewed through the huge store of content information which is succinctly presented through a provocative and challenging approach – the question-and-answer method.

A climate of success is established by furnishing the correct answers at the end of each test.

You soon learn to recognize types of questions, forms of questions, and patterns of questioning. You may even begin to anticipate expected outcomes.

You perceive that many questions are repeated or adapted so that you can gain acute insights, which may enable you to score many sure points.

You learn how to confront new questions, or types of questions, and to attack them confidently and work out the correct answers.

You note objectives and emphases, and recognize pitfalls and dangers, so that you may make positive educational adjustments.

Moreover, you are kept fully informed in relation to new concepts, methods, practices, and directions in the field.

You discover that you are actually taking the examination all the time: you are preparing for the examination by "taking" an examination, not by reading extraneous and/or supererogatory textbooks.

In short, this PASSBOOK®, used directedly, should be an important factor in helping you to pass your test.

OFFICE MANAGER

DUTIES
This position is responsible for supervising, overseeing, scheduling and monitoring the activities of clerical and technical staff, engaged in the performance of various clerical, administrative and technical tasks in an assigned department, bureau or agency. While the ability to exercise independent judgment and make independent decisions is a requirement, direct supervision is received from a department head or management personnel. Does related work as required.

TYPICAL WORK ACTIVITIES
Supervises, oversees, schedules and monitors the work of departmental employees engaged in performing administrative, clerical and/or technical tasks; trains and provides orientation for new employees and conducts ongoing work performance evaluations; coordinates work with other city departments, agencies, bureaus and outside vendors; makes recommendations regarding the purchase of office supplies and materials, reviews various requisitions and maintains an inventory; conducts studies and prepares reports and manuals regarding departmental operations, procedures and policies; operates a computer or word processor, copier and other office machinery and equipment; interviews prospective employees and makes recommendations; prepares financial reports, department operational budget, payroll and maintains statistics and records; oversees collection of fees and processing.

SCOPE OF THE EXAMINATION
The written test will cover knowledge, skills and abilities in such areas as:

1. Office management;
2. Office record keeping;
3. Preparing written material;
4. Supervision; and
5. Understanding and interpreting written material.

HOW TO TAKE A TEST

I. YOU MUST PASS AN EXAMINATION

A. *WHAT EVERY CANDIDATE SHOULD KNOW*

Examination applicants often ask us for help in preparing for the written test. What can I study in advance? What kinds of questions will be asked? How will the test be given? How will the papers be graded?

As an applicant for a civil service examination, you may be wondering about some of these things. Our purpose here is to suggest effective methods of advance study and to describe civil service examinations.

Your chances for success on this examination can be increased if you know how to prepare. Those "pre-examination jitters" can be reduced if you know what to expect. You can even experience an adventure in good citizenship if you know why civil service exams are given.

B. *WHY ARE CIVIL SERVICE EXAMINATIONS GIVEN?*

Civil service examinations are important to you in two ways. As a citizen, you want public jobs filled by employees who know how to do their work. As a job seeker, you want a fair chance to compete for that job on an equal footing with other candidates. The best-known means of accomplishing this two-fold goal is the competitive examination.

Exams are widely publicized throughout the nation. They may be administered for jobs in federal, state, city, municipal, town or village governments or agencies.

Any citizen may apply, with some limitations, such as the age or residence of applicants. Your experience and education may be reviewed to see whether you meet the requirements for the particular examination. When these requirements exist, they are reasonable and applied consistently to all applicants. Thus, a competitive examination may cause you some uneasiness now, but it is your privilege and safeguard.

C. *HOW ARE CIVIL SERVICE EXAMS DEVELOPED?*

Examinations are carefully written by trained technicians who are specialists in the field known as "psychological measurement," in consultation with recognized authorities in the field of work that the test will cover. These experts recommend the subject matter areas or skills to be tested; only those knowledges or skills important to your success on the job are included. The most reliable books and source materials available are used as references. Together, the experts and technicians judge the difficulty level of the questions.

Test technicians know how to phrase questions so that the problem is clearly stated. Their ethics do not permit "trick" or "catch" questions. Questions may have been tried out on sample groups, or subjected to statistical analysis, to determine their usefulness.

Written tests are often used in combination with performance tests, ratings of training and experience, and oral interviews. All of these measures combine to form the best-known means of finding the right person for the right job.

II. HOW TO PASS THE WRITTEN TEST

A. *NATURE OF THE EXAMINATION*

To prepare intelligently for civil service examinations, you should know how they differ from school examinations you have taken. In school you were assigned certain definite pages to read or subjects to cover. The examination questions were quite detailed and usually emphasized memory. Civil service exams, on the other hand, try to discover your present ability to perform the duties of a position, plus your potentiality to learn these duties. In other words, a civil service exam attempts to predict how successful you will be. Questions cover such a broad area that they cannot be as minute and detailed as school exam questions.

In the public service similar kinds of work, or positions, are grouped together in one "class." This process is known as *position-classification*. All the positions in a class are paid according to the salary range for that class. One class title covers all of these positions, and they are all tested by the same examination.

B. *FOUR BASIC STEPS*

1) Study the announcement

How, then, can you know what subjects to study? Our best answer is: "Learn as much as possible about the class of positions for which you've applied." The exam will test the knowledge, skills and abilities needed to do the work.

Your most valuable source of information about the position you want is the official exam announcement. This announcement lists the training and experience qualifications. Check these standards and apply only if you come reasonably close to meeting them.

The brief description of the position in the examination announcement offers some clues to the subjects which will be tested. Think about the job itself. Review the duties in your mind. Can you perform them, or are there some in which you are rusty? Fill in the blank spots in your preparation.

Many jurisdictions preview the written test in the exam announcement by including a section called "Knowledge and Abilities Required," "Scope of the Examination," or some similar heading. Here you will find out specifically what fields will be tested.

2) Review your own background

Once you learn in general what the position is all about, and what you need to know to do the work, ask yourself which subjects you already know fairly well and which need improvement. You may wonder whether to concentrate on improving your strong areas or on building some background in your fields of weakness. When the announcement has specified "some knowledge" or "considerable knowledge," or has used adjectives like "beginning principles of..." or "advanced ... methods," you can get a clue as to the number and difficulty of questions to be asked in any given field. More questions, and hence broader coverage, would be included for those subjects which are more important in the work. Now weigh your strengths and weaknesses against the job requirements and prepare accordingly.

3) Determine the level of the position

Another way to tell how intensively you should prepare is to understand the level of the job for which you are applying. Is it the entering level? In other words, is this the position in which beginners in a field of work are hired? Or is it an intermediate or advanced level? Sometimes this is indicated by such words as "Junior" or "Senior" in the class title. Other jurisdictions use Roman numerals to designate the level – Clerk I, Clerk II, for example. The word "Supervisor" sometimes appears in the title. If the level is not indicated by the title, check the description of duties. Will you be working under very close supervision, or will you have responsibility for independent decisions in this work?

4) Choose appropriate study materials

Now that you know the subjects to be examined and the relative amount of each subject to be covered, you can choose suitable study materials. For beginning level jobs, or even advanced ones, if you have a pronounced weakness in some aspect of your training, read a modern, standard textbook in that field. Be sure it is up to date and has general coverage. Such books are normally available at your library, and the librarian will be glad to help you locate one. For entry-level positions, questions of appropriate difficulty are chosen – neither highly advanced questions, nor those too simple. Such questions require careful thought but not advanced training.

If the position for which you are applying is technical or advanced, you will read more advanced, specialized material. If you are already familiar with the basic principles of your field, elementary textbooks would waste your time. Concentrate on advanced textbooks and technical periodicals. Think through the concepts and review difficult problems in your field.

These are all general sources. You can get more ideas on your own initiative, following these leads. For example, training manuals and publications of the government agency which employs workers in your field can be useful, particularly for technical and professional positions. A letter or visit to the government department involved may result in more specific study suggestions, and certainly will provide you with a more definite idea of the exact nature of the position you are seeking.

III. KINDS OF TESTS

Tests are used for purposes other than measuring knowledge and ability to perform specified duties. For some positions, it is equally important to test ability to make adjustments to new situations or to profit from training. In others, basic mental abilities not dependent on information are essential. Questions which test these things may not appear as pertinent to the duties of the position as those which test for knowledge and information. Yet they are often highly important parts of a fair examination. For very general questions, it is almost impossible to help you direct your study efforts. What we can do is to point out some of the more common of these general abilities needed in public service positions and describe some typical questions.

1) General information

Broad, general information has been found useful for predicting job success in some kinds of work. This is tested in a variety of ways, from vocabulary lists to questions about current events. Basic background in some field of work, such as sociology or economics, may be sampled in a group of questions. Often these are principles which have become familiar to most persons through exposure rather than through formal training. It is difficult to advise you how to study for these questions; being alert to the world around you is our best suggestion.

2) Verbal ability

An example of an ability needed in many positions is verbal or language ability. Verbal ability is, in brief, the ability to use and understand words. Vocabulary and grammar tests are typical measures of this ability. Reading comprehension or paragraph interpretation questions are common in many kinds of civil service tests. You are given a paragraph of written material and asked to find its central meaning.

3) Numerical ability

Number skills can be tested by the familiar arithmetic problem, by checking paired lists of numbers to see which are alike and which are different, or by interpreting charts and graphs. In the latter test, a graph may be printed in the test booklet which you are asked to use as the basis for answering questions.

4) Observation

A popular test for law-enforcement positions is the observation test. A picture is shown to you for several minutes, then taken away. Questions about the picture test your ability to observe both details and larger elements.

5) Following directions

In many positions in the public service, the employee must be able to carry out written instructions dependably and accurately. You may be given a chart with several columns, each column listing a variety of information. The questions require you to carry out directions involving the information given in the chart.

6) Skills and aptitudes

Performance tests effectively measure some manual skills and aptitudes. When the skill is one in which you are trained, such as typing or shorthand, you can practice. These tests are often very much like those given in business school or high school courses. For many of the other skills and aptitudes, however, no short-time preparation can be made. Skills and abilities natural to you or that you have developed throughout your lifetime are being tested.

Many of the general questions just described provide all the data needed to answer the questions and ask you to use your reasoning ability to find the answers. Your best preparation for these tests, as well as for tests of facts and ideas, is to be at your physical and mental best. You, no doubt, have your own methods of getting into an exam-taking mood and keeping "in shape." The next section lists some ideas on this subject.

IV. KINDS OF QUESTIONS

Only rarely is the "essay" question, which you answer in narrative form, used in civil service tests. Civil service tests are usually of the short-answer type. Full instructions for answering these questions will be given to you at the examination. But in case this is your first experience with short-answer questions and separate answer sheets, here is what you need to know:

1) Multiple-choice Questions

Most popular of the short-answer questions is the "multiple choice" or "best answer" question. It can be used, for example, to test for factual knowledge, ability to solve problems or judgment in meeting situations found at work.

A multiple-choice question is normally one of three types—

- It can begin with an incomplete statement followed by several possible endings. You are to find the one ending which *best* completes the statement, although some of the others may not be entirely wrong.
- It can also be a complete statement in the form of a question which is answered by choosing one of the statements listed.

- It can be in the form of a problem – again you select the best answer.

Here is an example of a multiple-choice question with a discussion which should give you some clues as to the method for choosing the right answer:

When an employee has a complaint about his assignment, the action which will *best* help him overcome his difficulty is to
- A. discuss his difficulty with his coworkers
- B. take the problem to the head of the organization
- C. take the problem to the person who gave him the assignment
- D. say nothing to anyone about his complaint

In answering this question, you should study each of the choices to find which is best. Consider choice "A" – Certainly an employee may discuss his complaint with fellow employees, but no change or improvement can result, and the complaint remains unresolved. Choice "B" is a poor choice since the head of the organization probably does not know what assignment you have been given, and taking your problem to him is known as "going over the head" of the supervisor. The supervisor, or person who made the assignment, is the person who can clarify it or correct any injustice. Choice "C" is, therefore, correct. To say nothing, as in choice "D," is unwise. Supervisors have and interest in knowing the problems employees are facing, and the employee is seeking a solution to his problem.

2) True/False Questions

The "true/false" or "right/wrong" form of question is sometimes used. Here a complete statement is given. Your job is to decide whether the statement is right or wrong.

SAMPLE: A roaming cell-phone call to a nearby city costs less than a non-roaming call to a distant city.

This statement is wrong, or false, since roaming calls are more expensive.

This is not a complete list of all possible question forms, although most of the others are variations of these common types. You will always get complete directions for answering questions. Be sure you understand *how* to mark your answers – ask questions until you do.

V. RECORDING YOUR ANSWERS

Computer terminals are used more and more today for many different kinds of exams.
For an examination with very few applicants, you may be told to record your answers in the test booklet itself. Separate answer sheets are much more common. If this separate answer sheet is to be scored by machine – and this is often the case – it is highly important that you mark your answers correctly in order to get credit.
An electronic scoring machine is often used in civil service offices because of the speed with which papers can be scored. Machine-scored answer sheets must be marked with a pencil, which will be given to you. This pencil has a high graphite content which responds to the electronic scoring machine. As a matter of fact, stray dots may register as answers, so do not let your pencil rest on the answer sheet while you are pondering the correct answer. Also, if your pencil lead breaks or is otherwise defective, ask for another.

Since the answer sheet will be dropped in a slot in the scoring machine, be careful not to bend the corners or get the paper crumpled.

The answer sheet normally has five vertical columns of numbers, with 30 numbers to a column. These numbers correspond to the question numbers in your test booklet. After each number, going across the page are four or five pairs of dotted lines. These short dotted lines have small letters or numbers above them. The first two pairs may also have a "T" or "F" above the letters. This indicates that the first two pairs only are to be used if the questions are of the true-false type. If the questions are multiple choice, disregard the "T" and "F" and pay attention only to the small letters or numbers.

Answer your questions in the manner of the sample that follows:

32. The largest city in the United States is
    A. Washington, D.C.
    B. New York City
    C. Chicago
    D. Detroit
    E. San Francisco

1) Choose the answer you think is best. (New York City is the largest, so "B" is correct.)
2) Find the row of dotted lines numbered the same as the question you are answering. (Find row number 32)
3) Find the pair of dotted lines corresponding to the answer. (Find the pair of lines under the mark "B.")
4) Make a solid black mark between the dotted lines.

VI. BEFORE THE TEST

Common sense will help you find procedures to follow to get ready for an examination. Too many of us, however, overlook these sensible measures. Indeed, nervousness and fatigue have been found to be the most serious reasons why applicants fail to do their best on civil service tests. Here is a list of reminders:

- Begin your preparation early – Don't wait until the last minute to go scurrying around for books and materials or to find out what the position is all about.
- Prepare continuously – An hour a night for a week is better than an all-night cram session. This has been definitely established. What is more, a night a week for a month will return better dividends than crowding your study into a shorter period of time.
- Locate the place of the exam – You have been sent a notice telling you when and where to report for the examination. If the location is in a different town or otherwise unfamiliar to you, it would be well to inquire the best route and learn something about the building.
- Relax the night before the test – Allow your mind to rest. Do not study at all that night. Plan some mild recreation or diversion; then go to bed early and get a good night's sleep.
- Get up early enough to make a leisurely trip to the place for the test – This way unforeseen events, traffic snarls, unfamiliar buildings, etc. will not upset you.
- Dress comfortably – A written test is not a fashion show. You will be known by number and not by name, so wear something comfortable.

- Leave excess paraphernalia at home – Shopping bags and odd bundles will get in your way. You need bring only the items mentioned in the official notice you received; usually everything you need is provided. Do not bring reference books to the exam. They will only confuse those last minutes and be taken away from you when in the test room.
- Arrive somewhat ahead of time – If because of transportation schedules you must get there very early, bring a newspaper or magazine to take your mind off yourself while waiting.
- Locate the examination room – When you have found the proper room, you will be directed to the seat or part of the room where you will sit. Sometimes you are given a sheet of instructions to read while you are waiting. Do not fill out any forms until you are told to do so; just read them and be prepared.
- Relax and prepare to listen to the instructions
- If you have any physical problem that may keep you from doing your best, be sure to tell the test administrator. If you are sick or in poor health, you really cannot do your best on the exam. You can come back and take the test some other time.

VII. AT THE TEST

The day of the test is here and you have the test booklet in your hand. The temptation to get going is very strong. Caution! There is more to success than knowing the right answers. You must know how to identify your papers and understand variations in the type of short-answer question used in this particular examination. Follow these suggestions for maximum results from your efforts:

1) Cooperate with the monitor

The test administrator has a duty to create a situation in which you can be as much at ease as possible. He will give instructions, tell you when to begin, check to see that you are marking your answer sheet correctly, and so on. He is not there to guard you, although he will see that your competitors do not take unfair advantage. He wants to help you do your best.

2) Listen to all instructions

Don't jump the gun! Wait until you understand all directions. In most civil service tests you get more time than you need to answer the questions. So don't be in a hurry. Read each word of instructions until you clearly understand the meaning. Study the examples, listen to all announcements and follow directions. Ask questions if you do not understand what to do.

3) Identify your papers

Civil service exams are usually identified by number only. You will be assigned a number; you must not put your name on your test papers. Be sure to copy your number correctly. Since more than one exam may be given, copy your exact examination title.

4) Plan your time

Unless you are told that a test is a "speed" or "rate of work" test, speed itself is usually not important. Time enough to answer all the questions will be provided, but this does not mean that you have all day. An overall time limit has been set. Divide the total time (in minutes) by the number of questions to determine the approximate time you have for each question.

5) Do not linger over difficult questions

If you come across a difficult question, mark it with a paper clip (useful to have along) and come back to it when you have been through the booklet. One caution if you do this – be sure to skip a number on your answer sheet as well. Check often to be sure that you have not lost your place and that you are marking in the row numbered the same as the question you are answering.

6) Read the questions

Be sure you know what the question asks! Many capable people are unsuccessful because they failed to *read* the questions correctly.

7) Answer all questions

Unless you have been instructed that a penalty will be deducted for incorrect answers, it is better to guess than to omit a question.

8) Speed tests

It is often better NOT to guess on speed tests. It has been found that on timed tests people are tempted to spend the last few seconds before time is called in marking answers at random – without even reading them – in the hope of picking up a few extra points. To discourage this practice, the instructions may warn you that your score will be "corrected" for guessing. That is, a penalty will be applied. The incorrect answers will be deducted from the correct ones, or some other penalty formula will be used.

9) Review your answers

If you finish before time is called, go back to the questions you guessed or omitted to give them further thought. Review other answers if you have time.

10) Return your test materials

If you are ready to leave before others have finished or time is called, take ALL your materials to the monitor and leave quietly. Never take any test material with you. The monitor can discover whose papers are not complete, and taking a test booklet may be grounds for disqualification.

VIII. EXAMINATION TECHNIQUES

1) Read the general instructions carefully. These are usually printed on the first page of the exam booklet. As a rule, these instructions refer to the timing of the examination; the fact that you should not start work until the signal and must stop work at a signal, etc. If there are any *special* instructions, such as a choice of questions to be answered, make sure that you note this instruction carefully.

2) When you are ready to start work on the examination, that is as soon as the signal has been given, read the instructions to each question booklet, underline any key words or phrases, such as *least, best, outline, describe* and the like. In this way you will tend to answer as requested rather than discover on reviewing your paper that you *listed without describing*, that you selected the *worst* choice rather than the *best* choice, etc.

3) If the examination is of the objective or multiple-choice type – that is, each question will also give a series of possible answers: A, B, C or D, and you are called upon to select the best answer and write the letter next to that answer on your answer paper – it is advisable to start answering each question in turn. There may be anywhere from 50 to 100 such questions in the three or four hours allotted and you can see how much time would be taken if you read through all the questions before beginning to answer any. Furthermore, if you come across a question or group of questions which you know would be difficult to answer, it would undoubtedly affect your handling of all the other questions.

4) If the examination is of the essay type and contains but a few questions, it is a moot point as to whether you should read all the questions before starting to answer any one. Of course, if you are given a choice – say five out of seven and the like – then it is essential to read all the questions so you can eliminate the two that are most difficult. If, however, you are asked to answer all the questions, there may be danger in trying to answer the easiest one first because you may find that you will spend too much time on it. The best technique is to answer the first question, then proceed to the second, etc.

5) Time your answers. Before the exam begins, write down the time it started, then add the time allowed for the examination and write down the time it must be completed, then divide the time available somewhat as follows:
    - If 3-1/2 hours are allowed, that would be 210 minutes. If you have 80 objective-type questions, that would be an average of 2-1/2 minutes per question. Allow yourself no more than 2 minutes per question, or a total of 160 minutes, which will permit about 50 minutes to review.
    - If for the time allotment of 210 minutes there are 7 essay questions to answer, that would average about 30 minutes a question. Give yourself only 25 minutes per question so that you have about 35 minutes to review.

6) The most important instruction is to *read each question* and make sure you know what is wanted. The second most important instruction is to *time yourself properly* so that you answer every question. The third most important instruction is to *answer every question*. Guess if you have to but include something for each question. Remember that you will receive no credit for a blank and will probably receive some credit if you write something in answer to an essay question. If you guess a letter – say "B" for a multiple-choice question – you may have guessed right. If you leave a blank as an answer to a multiple-choice question, the examiners may respect your feelings but it will not add a point to your score. Some exams may penalize you for wrong answers, so in such cases *only*, you may not want to guess unless you have some basis for your answer.

7) Suggestions
    a. Objective-type questions
        1. Examine the question booklet for proper sequence of pages and questions
        2. Read all instructions carefully
        3. Skip any question which seems too difficult; return to it after all other questions have been answered
        4. Apportion your time properly; do not spend too much time on any single question or group of questions

5. Note and underline key words – *all, most, fewest, least, best, worst, same, opposite,* etc.
6. Pay particular attention to negatives
7. Note unusual option, e.g., unduly long, short, complex, different or similar in content to the body of the question
8. Observe the use of "hedging" words – *probably, may, most likely,* etc.
9. Make sure that your answer is put next to the same number as the question
10. Do not second-guess unless you have good reason to believe the second answer is definitely more correct
11. Cross out original answer if you decide another answer is more accurate; do not erase until you are ready to hand your paper in
12. Answer all questions; guess unless instructed otherwise
13. Leave time for review

  b. Essay questions
    1. Read each question carefully
    2. Determine exactly what is wanted. Underline key words or phrases.
    3. Decide on outline or paragraph answer
    4. Include many different points and elements unless asked to develop any one or two points or elements
    5. Show impartiality by giving pros and cons unless directed to select one side only
    6. Make and write down any assumptions you find necessary to answer the questions
    7. Watch your English, grammar, punctuation and choice of words
    8. Time your answers; don't crowd material

8) Answering the essay question

Most essay questions can be answered by framing the specific response around several key words or ideas. Here are a few such key words or ideas:

M's: manpower, materials, methods, money, management
P's: purpose, program, policy, plan, procedure, practice, problems, pitfalls, personnel, public relations

  a. Six basic steps in handling problems:
    1. Preliminary plan and background development
    2. Collect information, data and facts
    3. Analyze and interpret information, data and facts
    4. Analyze and develop solutions as well as make recommendations
    5. Prepare report and sell recommendations
    6. Install recommendations and follow up effectiveness

  b. Pitfalls to avoid
    1. *Taking things for granted* – A statement of the situation does not necessarily imply that each of the elements is necessarily true; for example, a complaint may be invalid and biased so that all that can be taken for granted is that a complaint has been registered

2. *Considering only one side of a situation* – Wherever possible, indicate several alternatives and then point out the reasons you selected the best one
3. *Failing to indicate follow up* – Whenever your answer indicates action on your part, make certain that you will take proper follow-up action to see how successful your recommendations, procedures or actions turn out to be
4. *Taking too long in answering any single question* – Remember to time your answers properly

IX. AFTER THE TEST

Scoring procedures differ in detail among civil service jurisdictions although the general principles are the same. Whether the papers are hand-scored or graded by machine we have described, they are nearly always graded by number. That is, the person who marks the paper knows only the number – never the name – of the applicant. Not until all the papers have been graded will they be matched with names. If other tests, such as training and experience or oral interview ratings have been given, scores will be combined. Different parts of the examination usually have different weights. For example, the written test might count 60 percent of the final grade, and a rating of training and experience 40 percent. In many jurisdictions, veterans will have a certain number of points added to their grades.

After the final grade has been determined, the names are placed in grade order and an eligible list is established. There are various methods for resolving ties between those who get the same final grade – probably the most common is to place first the name of the person whose application was received first. Job offers are made from the eligible list in the order the names appear on it. You will be notified of your grade and your rank as soon as all these computations have been made. This will be done as rapidly as possible.

People who are found to meet the requirements in the announcement are called "eligibles." Their names are put on a list of eligible candidates. An eligible's chances of getting a job depend on how high he stands on this list and how fast agencies are filling jobs from the list.

When a job is to be filled from a list of eligibles, the agency asks for the names of people on the list of eligibles for that job. When the civil service commission receives this request, it sends to the agency the names of the three people highest on this list. Or, if the job to be filled has specialized requirements, the office sends the agency the names of the top three persons who meet these requirements from the general list.

The appointing officer makes a choice from among the three people whose names were sent to him. If the selected person accepts the appointment, the names of the others are put back on the list to be considered for future openings.

That is the rule in hiring from all kinds of eligible lists, whether they are for typist, carpenter, chemist, or something else. For every vacancy, the appointing officer has his choice of any one of the top three eligibles on the list. This explains why the person whose name is on top of the list sometimes does not get an appointment when some of the persons lower on the list do. If the appointing officer chooses the second or third eligible, the No. 1 eligible does not get a job at once, but stays on the list until he is appointed or the list is terminated.

X. HOW TO PASS THE INTERVIEW TEST

The examination for which you applied requires an oral interview test. You have already taken the written test and you are now being called for the interview test – the final part of the formal examination.

You may think that it is not possible to prepare for an interview test and that there are no procedures to follow during an interview. Our purpose is to point out some things you can do in advance that will help you and some good rules to follow and pitfalls to avoid while you are being interviewed.

What is an interview supposed to test?

The written examination is designed to test the technical knowledge and competence of the candidate; the oral is designed to evaluate intangible qualities, not readily measured otherwise, and to establish a list showing the relative fitness of each candidate – as measured against his competitors – for the position sought. Scoring is not on the basis of "right" and "wrong," but on a sliding scale of values ranging from "not passable" to "outstanding." As a matter of fact, it is possible to achieve a relatively low score without a single "incorrect" answer because of evident weakness in the qualities being measured.

Occasionally, an examination may consist entirely of an oral test – either an individual or a group oral. In such cases, information is sought concerning the technical knowledges and abilities of the candidate, since there has been no written examination for this purpose. More commonly, however, an oral test is used to supplement a written examination.

Who conducts interviews?

The composition of oral boards varies among different jurisdictions. In nearly all, a representative of the personnel department serves as chairman. One of the members of the board may be a representative of the department in which the candidate would work. In some cases, "outside experts" are used, and, frequently, a businessman or some other representative of the general public is asked to serve. Labor and management or other special groups may be represented. The aim is to secure the services of experts in the appropriate field.

However the board is composed, it is a good idea (and not at all improper or unethical) to ascertain in advance of the interview who the members are and what groups they represent. When you are introduced to them, you will have some idea of their backgrounds and interests, and at least you will not stutter and stammer over their names.

What should be done before the interview?

While knowledge about the board members is useful and takes some of the surprise element out of the interview, there is other preparation which is more substantive. It *is* possible to prepare for an oral interview – in several ways:

1) Keep a copy of your application and review it carefully before the interview

This may be the only document before the oral board, and the starting point of the interview. Know what education and experience you have listed there, and the sequence and dates of all of it. Sometimes the board will ask you to review the highlights of your experience for them; you should not have to hem and haw doing it.

2) Study the class specification and the examination announcement

Usually, the oral board has one or both of these to guide them. The qualities, characteristics or knowledges required by the position sought are stated in these documents. They offer valuable clues as to the nature of the oral interview. For example, if the job involves supervisory responsibilities, the announcement will usually indicate that knowledge of modern supervisory methods and the qualifications of the candidate as a supervisor will be tested. If so, you can expect such questions, frequently in the form of a hypothetical situation which you are expected to solve. NEVER go into an oral without knowledge of the duties and responsibilities of the job you seek.

3) Think through each qualification required

Try to visualize the kind of questions you would ask if you were a board member. How well could you answer them? Try especially to appraise your own knowledge and background in each area, *measured against the job sought*, and identify any areas in which you are weak. Be critical and realistic – do not flatter yourself.

4) Do some general reading in areas in which you feel you may be weak

For example, if the job involves supervision and your past experience has NOT, some general reading in supervisory methods and practices, particularly in the field of human relations, might be useful. Do NOT study agency procedures or detailed manuals. The oral board will be testing your understanding and capacity, not your memory.

5) Get a good night's sleep and watch your general health and mental attitude

You will want a clear head at the interview. Take care of a cold or any other minor ailment, and of course, no hangovers.

What should be done on the day of the interview?

Now comes the day of the interview itself. Give yourself plenty of time to get there. Plan to arrive somewhat ahead of the scheduled time, particularly if your appointment is in the fore part of the day. If a previous candidate fails to appear, the board might be ready for you a bit early. By early afternoon an oral board is almost invariably behind schedule if there are many candidates, and you may have to wait. Take along a book or magazine to read, or your application to review, but leave any extraneous material in the waiting room when you go in for your interview. In any event, relax and compose yourself.

The matter of dress is important. The board is forming impressions about you – from your experience, your manners, your attitude, and your appearance. Give your personal appearance careful attention. Dress your best, but not your flashiest. Choose conservative, appropriate clothing, and be sure it is immaculate. This is a business interview, and your appearance should indicate that you regard it as such. Besides, being well groomed and properly dressed will help boost your confidence.

Sooner or later, someone will call your name and escort you into the interview room. *This is it.* From here on you are on your own. It is too late for any more preparation. But remember, you asked for this opportunity to prove your fitness, and you are here because your request was granted.

What happens when you go in?

The usual sequence of events will be as follows: The clerk (who is often the board stenographer) will introduce you to the chairman of the oral board, who will introduce you to the other members of the board. Acknowledge the introductions before you sit down. Do not be surprised if you find a microphone facing you or a stenotypist sitting by. Oral interviews are usually recorded in the event of an appeal or other review.

Usually the chairman of the board will open the interview by reviewing the highlights of your education and work experience from your application – primarily for the benefit of the other members of the board, as well as to get the material into the record. Do not interrupt or comment unless there is an error or significant misinterpretation; if that is the case, do not hesitate. But do not quibble about insignificant matters. Also, he will usually ask you some question about your education, experience or your present job – partly to get you to start talking and to establish the interviewing "rapport." He may start the actual questioning, or turn it over to one of the other members. Frequently, each member undertakes the questioning on a particular area, one in which he is perhaps most competent, so you can expect each member to participate in the examination. Because time is limited, you may also expect some rather abrupt switches in the direction the questioning takes, so do not be upset by it. Normally, a board member will not pursue a single line of questioning unless he discovers a particular strength or weakness.

After each member has participated, the chairman will usually ask whether any member has any further questions, then will ask you if you have anything you wish to add. Unless you are expecting this question, it may floor you. Worse, it may start you off on an extended, extemporaneous speech. The board is not usually seeking more information. The question is principally to offer you a last opportunity to present further qualifications or to indicate that you have nothing to add. So, if you feel that a significant qualification or characteristic has been overlooked, it is proper to point it out in a sentence or so. Do not compliment the board on the thoroughness of their examination – they have been sketchy, and you know it. If you wish, merely say, "No thank you, I have nothing further to add." This is a point where you can "talk yourself out" of a good impression or fail to present an important bit of information. Remember, *you close the interview yourself*.

The chairman will then say, "That is all, Mr. _____, thank you." Do not be startled; the interview is over, and quicker than you think. Thank him, gather your belongings and take your leave. Save your sigh of relief for the other side of the door.

How to put your best foot forward

Throughout this entire process, you may feel that the board individually and collectively is trying to pierce your defenses, seek out your hidden weaknesses and embarrass and confuse you. Actually, this is not true. They are obliged to make an appraisal of your qualifications for the job you are seeking, and they want to see you in your best light. Remember, they must interview all candidates and a non-cooperative candidate may become a failure in spite of their best efforts to bring out his qualifications. Here are 15 suggestions that will help you:

1) Be natural – Keep your attitude confident, not cocky

If you are not confident that you can do the job, do not expect the board to be. Do not apologize for your weaknesses, try to bring out your strong points. The board is interested in a positive, not negative, presentation. Cockiness will antagonize any board member and make him wonder if you are covering up a weakness by a false show of strength.

2) Get comfortable, but don't lounge or sprawl

Sit erectly but not stiffly. A careless posture may lead the board to conclude that you are careless in other things, or at least that you are not impressed by the importance of the occasion. Either conclusion is natural, even if incorrect. Do not fuss with your clothing, a pencil or an ashtray. Your hands may occasionally be useful to emphasize a point; do not let them become a point of distraction.

3) Do not wisecrack or make small talk

This is a serious situation, and your attitude should show that you consider it as such. Further, the time of the board is limited – they do not want to waste it, and neither should you.

4) Do not exaggerate your experience or abilities
In the first place, from information in the application or other interviews and sources, the board may know more about you than you think. Secondly, you probably will not get away with it. An experienced board is rather adept at spotting such a situation, so do not take the chance.

5) If you know a board member, do not make a point of it, yet do not hide it
Certainly you are not fooling him, and probably not the other members of the board. Do not try to take advantage of your acquaintanceship – it will probably do you little good.

6) Do not dominate the interview
Let the board do that. They will give you the clues – do not assume that you have to do all the talking. Realize that the board has a number of questions to ask you, and do not try to take up all the interview time by showing off your extensive knowledge of the answer to the first one.

7) Be attentive
You only have 20 minutes or so, and you should keep your attention at its sharpest throughout. When a member is addressing a problem or question to you, give him your undivided attention. Address your reply principally to him, but do not exclude the other board members.

8) Do not interrupt
A board member may be stating a problem for you to analyze. He will ask you a question when the time comes. Let him state the problem, and wait for the question.

9) Make sure you understand the question
Do not try to answer until you are sure what the question is. If it is not clear, restate it in your own words or ask the board member to clarify it for you. However, do not haggle about minor elements.

10) Reply promptly but not hastily
A common entry on oral board rating sheets is "candidate responded readily," or "candidate hesitated in replies." Respond as promptly and quickly as you can, but do not jump to a hasty, ill-considered answer.

11) Do not be peremptory in your answers
A brief answer is proper – but do not fire your answer back. That is a losing game from your point of view. The board member can probably ask questions much faster than you can answer them.

12) Do not try to create the answer you think the board member wants
He is interested in what kind of mind you have and how it works – not in playing games. Furthermore, he can usually spot this practice and will actually grade you down on it.

13) Do not switch sides in your reply merely to agree with a board member
Frequently, a member will take a contrary position merely to draw you out and to see if you are willing and able to defend your point of view. Do not start a debate, yet do not surrender a good position. If a position is worth taking, it is worth defending.

14) Do not be afraid to admit an error in judgment if you are shown to be wrong

The board knows that you are forced to reply without any opportunity for careful consideration. Your answer may be demonstrably wrong. If so, admit it and get on with the interview.

15) Do not dwell at length on your present job

The opening question may relate to your present assignment. Answer the question but do not go into an extended discussion. You are being examined for a *new* job, not your present one. As a matter of fact, try to phrase ALL your answers in terms of the job for which you are being examined.

Basis of Rating

Probably you will forget most of these "do's" and "don'ts" when you walk into the oral interview room. Even remembering them all will not ensure you a passing grade. Perhaps you did not have the qualifications in the first place. But remembering them will help you to put your best foot forward, without treading on the toes of the board members.

Rumor and popular opinion to the contrary notwithstanding, an oral board wants you to make the best appearance possible. They know you are under pressure – but they also want to see how you respond to it as a guide to what your reaction would be under the pressures of the job you seek. They will be influenced by the degree of poise you display, the personal traits you show and the manner in which you respond.

ABOUT THIS BOOK

This book contains tests divided into Examination Sections. Go through each test, answering every question in the margin. We have also attached a sample answer sheet at the back of the book that can be removed and used. At the end of each test look at the answer key and check your answers. On the ones you got wrong, look at the right answer choice and learn. Do not fill in the answers first. Do not memorize the questions and answers, but understand the answer and principles involved. On your test, the questions will likely be different from the samples. Questions are changed and new ones added. If you understand these past questions you should have success with any changes that arise. Tests may consist of several types of questions. We have additional books on each subject should more study be advisable or necessary for you. Finally, the more you study, the better prepared you will be. This book is intended to be the last thing you study before you walk into the examination room. Prior study of relevant texts is also recommended. NLC publishes some of these in our Fundamental Series. Knowledge and good sense are important factors in passing your exam. Good luck also helps. So now study this Passbook, absorb the material contained within and take that knowledge into the examination. Then do your best to pass that exam.

EXAMINATION SECTION

EXAMINATION SECTION
TEST 1

DIRECTIONS: Each question or incomplete statement is followed by several suggested answers or completions. Select the one that BEST answers the question or completes the statement. *PRINT THE LETTER OF THE CORRECT ANSWER IN THE SPACE AT THE RIGHT.*

1. A certain system for handling office supplies requires that supplies be issued to the various agency offices only on a bi-weekly basis and that all supply requisitions be authorized by the unit supervisor.
   The BEST reason for establishing this supplies system is to
   A. standardize ordering descriptions and stock identification codes
   B. prevent the disordering of stock shelves and cabinets by unauthorized persons searching for supplies
   C. ensure that unit supervisors properly exercise their right to make determinations on supply orders
   D. encourage proper utilization of supplies to control the workload

   1.____

2. It is important that every office have a retention and disposal program for filing material. Suppose that you have been appointed administrative assistant in an office with a poorly organized records-retention program.
   In establishing a revised program for the transfer or disposal of records, the step which would logically be taken THIRD in the process is
   A. preparing a safe and inexpensive storage area and setting up an indexing system for records already in storage
   B. determining what papers to retain and for how long a period
   C. taking an inventory of what is filed, where it is filed, how much is filed, and how often it is used
   D. moving records from active to inactive files and destroying useless records

   2.____

3. In the effective design of office forms, the FIRST step to take is to
   A. decide what information should be included
   B. decide the purpose for which the form will be used
   C. identify the form by name and number
   D. identify the employees who will be using the form

   3.____

4. Some designers of office forms prefer to locate the instructions on how to fill out the form at the bottom of it.
   The MOST logical objection to placing such instructions at the bottom of the form is that
   A. instructions at the bottom require an excess of space
   B. all form instructions should be outlined with a separate paragraph
   C. the form may be partly filled out before the instructions are seen
   D. the bottom of the form should be reserved only for authorization and signature

   4.____

5. A formal business report may consist of many parts, including the following:
   I. Table of Contents
   II. List of References
   III. Preface
   IV. Index
   V. List of Tables
   VI. Conclusions or Recommendations

   Of the following, in setting up a formal report, the PROPER order of the six parts listed is
   A. I, III, VI, V, II, IV
   B. IV, III, II, V, VI, I
   C. III, I, V, VI, II, IV
   D. II, V, III, I, IV, VI

6. Three of the basic functions of office management are considered to be planning, controlling, and organizing.
   Of the following, the one which might BEST be considered ORGANIZING activity is
   A. assigning personnel and materials to work units to achieve agreed-upon objectives
   B. determining future objectives and indicating conditions affecting the accomplishment of the goals
   C. evaluating accomplishments and applying necessary corrective measures to insure results
   D. motivating employees to perform their work in accordance with objectives

7. The following four statements relate to office layout.
   I. Position supervisors' desks at the front of their work group so that they can easily be recognized as persons in authority.
   II. Arrange file cabinets and frequently used equipment near the employees who utilize them most often.
   III. Locate the receptionist's desk near the entrance of the office so that visitor traffic will not distract other workers.
   IV. Divide a large office area into many smaller offices by using stationary partitions so that all employees may have privacy and prestige.

   According to authorities in office management and administration, which of these statements are generally recommended guides to effective office layout?
   A. I, II, III   B. II, III, IV   C. II, III   D. All of the above

8. For which of the following purposes would a flow chart have the GREATEST applicability?
   A. Training new employees in performance of routine duties
   B. Determining adequacy of performance of employees
   C. Determining the accuracy of the organization chart
   D. Locating causes of delays in carrying out an operation

9. Office work management concerns tangible accomplishment or production. It has to do with results; it does not deal with the amount of energy expended by the individual who produces the results.
   According to this statement, the production in which of the following kinds of jobs would be MOST difficult to measure accurately?

A(n)
- A. file clerk
- B. secretary
- C. computer operator
- D. office administrator

10. The FIRST step in the statistical analysis of a great mass of data secured from a survey is to
    - A. scan the data to determine which is atypical of the survey
    - B. determine the number of deviations from the average
    - C. arrange the data into groups on the basis of likenesses and differences
    - D. plot the drama on a graph to determine trends

11. Suppose that, as an administrative assistant in charge of an office, you are required to change the layout of your office to accommodate expanding functions.
    The LEAST important factor to be considered in planning the revised layout is the
    - A. relative productivity of individuals in the office
    - B. communication and work flow needs
    - C. need for screening confidential activities from unauthorized persons
    - D. areas of noise concentration

12. Suppose you have instructed a new employee to follow a standardized series of steps to accomplish a job. He is to use a rubber stamp, then a red pencil on the first paper, and a numbering machine on the second. Then, he is to staple the two sheets of paper together and put them to one side. You observe, however, that he sometimes uses the red pencil first, sometimes the numbering machine first. At other times, he does the stapling before using the numbering machine.
    For you as supervisor to suggest that the clerk use the standardized method when doing this job would be
    - A. *bad*, because the clerk should be given a chance to use his independent judgment on the best way to do his job
    - B. *good*, because the clerk's sequence of actions results in a loss of efficiency
    - C. *bad*, because it is not wise to interrupt the work habit the clerk has already developed
    - D. *good*, because the clerk should not be permitted to make unauthorized changes in standard office routines

13. Suppose study of the current records management system for students' transcripts reveals needless recopying of transcript data throughout various offices within the university. On this basis, a recommendation is made that this unnecessary recopying of information be eliminated.
    This decision to eliminate waste in material, time, and space is an application of the office management principle of
    - A. work simplification
    - B. routing and scheduling
    - C. job analysis
    - D. cost and budgetary control

14. It is generally LEAST practical for an office manager to prepare for known peak work periods by
    A. putting job procedures into writing so that they can be handled by more than one person
    B. arranging to make assignments of work on a short-interval scheduling basis
    C. cleaning up as much work as possible ahead of known peak periods
    D. rotating jobs and assignments among different employees to assure staff flexibility

14.____

15. The four statements below are about office manuals used for various purposes. If you had the job of designing and controlling several kinds of office manuals to be used in your agency, which one of these statements would BEST apply as a general rule for you to follow?
    A. Office manual content should be classified into main topics with proper subdivisions arranged in strict alphabetical order.
    B. Manual additions and revisions should be distributed promptly to all holders of manuals for their approval, correction, and criticism.
    C. The language used in office manuals should be simple, and charts and diagrams should be interspersed within the narrative material for further clarity.
    D. Office manual content should be classified into main topics arranged in strict alphabetical order with subtopics in sequence according to importance.

15.____

16. Suppose that, as an administrative assistant, you have been assigned to plan the reorganization of an office which has not been operating efficiently because of the uncoordinated manner in which new functions have been assigned to it over the past year.
    The FIRST thing you should so is
    A. call a meeting of the office staff and explain the purposes of the planned reorganization
    B. make a cost-value analysis of the present operations to determine what should be changed or eliminated
    C. prepare a diagram of the flow of work as you think it should be
    D. define carefully the current objectives to be achieved by this reorganization

16.____

17. Effective organization requires that specific actions be taken in proper sequence. The following are four actions essential to effective organization:
    I. Group activities on the basis of human and material resources
    II. Coordinate functions and provide for good communications
    III. Formulate objectives, policies, and plans
    IV. Determine activities necessary to accomplish goals

    The PROPER sequence of these four actions is:
       A. III, II, IV, I   B. IV, III, I, II   C. III, IV, I, II   D. IV, I, III, II

17.____

18. For an administrative assistant to give each of his subordinates exactly the same type of supervision is
    A. *advisable*, because he will gain a reputation for being fair and impartial
    B. *inadvisable*, because subordinates work more diligently when they think they are receiving preferential treatment
    C. *advisable*, because most human problems can be classified into categories which make them easier to handle
    D. *inadvisable*, because people differ and there is no one supervisory procedure that applies in every case to dealing with individuals

18.____

19. Suppose that, as an administrative assistant, you find that some of your subordinates are coming to you with complaints you think are trivial.
    For you to hear them through is
    A. *poor practice*; subordinates should be trained to come to you only with major grievances
    B. *good practice*; major grievances sometimes are the underlying cause of minor complaints
    C. *poor practice*; you should delegate this kind of matter and spend your time on more important problems
    D. *good practice*; this will make you more popular with your subordinates

19.____

20. Suppose that a new departmental policy has just been established which you feel may be resented by your subordinates, but which they must understand and follow.
    Which would it be MOST advisable for you as their supervisory to do FIRST?
    A. Make clear to your subordinates that you are not responsible for making this policy.
    B. Tell your subordinates that you agree with the policy whether you do or not.
    C. Explain specifically to your subordinates the reasons for the policy and how it is going to affect them.
    D. Distribute a memo outlining the new policy and require your subordinates to read it.

20.____

21. An office assistant under your supervision tells you that she is reluctant to speak to one of her subordinates about poor work habits because this subordinate is strong-willed, and she does not want to antagonize her.
    For you to refuse the office assistant's request that you speak to her subordinate about this matter is
    A. *inadvisable*, since you are in a position of greater authority
    B. *advisable*, since supervision of his subordinate is a basic responsibility of that office assistant
    C. *inadvisable*, since the office assistant must work more closely with her subordinate than you do
    D. *advisable*, since you should not risk antagonizing her subordinate yourself

21.____

22. The GREATEST advantage to a supervisor of using oral communication as compared to written is the
    A. opportunity provided for immediate feedback
    B. speed with which orders can be given and carried out
    C. reduction in amount of paper work
    D. establishment of an informal atmosphere

22.____

23. Of the following, the MOST important reason for an administrative assistant to have private, face-to-face discussions with subordinates about their performance is
    A. encourage a more competitive spirit among employees
    B. give special praise to employees who perform well
    C. discipline employees who perform poorly
    D. help employees improve their work

23.____

24. For a supervisor to keep records of reprimands to subordinates about violations of rules is
    A. *poor practice*; such records are evidence of the supervisor's inability to maintain discipline
    B. *good practice*; these records are valuable to support disciplinary actions recommended or taken
    C. *poor practice*; the best way to prevent recurrences is to apply penalties without delay
    D. *good practice*; such records are evidence that the supervisor is doing a good job

24.____

25. As an administrative assistant supervising a small office, you decide to hold a staff meeting to try to find an acceptable solution to s problem that is causing serious conflicts within the group.
    At this meeting, your role should be to prevent the problem and
    A. see that the group keeps the problem in focus and does not discuss irrelevant matters
    B. act as chairman of the meeting, but take no other part in the discussion
    C. see to it that each member of the group offers a suggestion for its solution
    D. state you views on the matter before any discussion gets under way

25.____

KEY (CORRECT ANSWERS)

1.	D	11.	A
2.	A	12.	B
3.	B	13.	A
4.	C	14.	B
5.	C	15.	C
6.	A	16.	D
7.	C	17.	C
8.	D	18.	D
9.	D	19.	B
10.	C	20.	C

21. B
22. A
23. D
24. B
25. A

TEST 2

DIRECTIONS: Each question or incomplete statement is followed by several suggested answers or completions. Select the one that BEST answers the question or completes the statement. *PRINT THE LETTER OF THE CORRECT ANSWER IN THE SPACE AT THE RIGHT.*

1. Suppose that one of your subordinates who supervises two young office assistants has been late for work a number of times and you have decided to talk to him about it.
   In your discussion, it would be MOST constructive for you to emphasize that
   A. personal problems cannot be used as an excuse for these latenesses
   B. the department suffers financially when he is late
   C. you will be forced to give him a less desirable assignment if his latenesses continue
   D. his latnesses set a bad example to those he supervises

   1.____

2. Suppose that, as a newly-appointed administrative assistant, you are in charge of a small but very busy office. Your four subordinates are often required to make quick decisions on a wide range of matters while answering telephone or in-person inquiries.
   You can MOST efficiently help your subordinates meet such situations by
   A. delegating authority to make such decisions to only one or two trusted subordinates
   B. training each subordinate in the proper response for each kind of inquiry that might be made
   C. making certain that subordinates understand clearly the basic policies that affect these decisions
   D. making each subordinate an expert in one area

   2.____

3. Of the following, the MOST recent development in methods of training supervisors that involves the human relations approach is
   A. conference training   B. the lecture method
   C. the case method   D. sensitivity training

   3.____

4. Which of the following is MOST likely to result in failure as a supervisor?
   A. Showing permissiveness in relations with subordinates
   B. Avoiding delegation of tasks to subordinates
   C. Setting high performance standards for subordinates
   D. Using discipline only when necessary

   4.____

5. The MOST important long-range benefit to an organization of proper delegation of work by supervisors is generally that
   A. subordinates will be developed to assume greater responsibilities
   B. subordinates will perform the work as their supervisors would
   C. errors in delegated work will be eliminated
   D. more efficient communication among organizational components will result

   5.____

6. Which of the following duties would it be LEAST appropriate for an administrative assistant in charge of an office to delegate to an immediate subordinate?
    A. Checking of figures to be used in a report to the head of the department
    B. On-the-job training of newly appointed college office assistants
    C. Reorganization of assignments for higher level office staff
    D. Contacting other school offices for needed information

7. Decisions should be delegated to the lowest point in the organization at which they can be made effectively.
   The one of the following which is MOST likely to be a result of the application of this accepted management principle is that
    A. upward communications will be facilitated
    B. potential for more rapid decisions and implementation is increased
    C. coordination of decisions that are made will be simplified
    D. no important factors will be overlooked in making decisions

8. The lecture-demonstration method would be LEAST desirable in a training program set up for
    A. changing the attitudes of long-term employees
    B. informing subordinates about new procedures
    C. explaining how a new office machine works
    D. orientation of new employees

9. Which one of the following conditions would be LEAST likely to indicate a need for employee training?
    A. Large number of employee suggestions
    B. Large amount of overtime
    C. High number of chronic latenesses
    D. Low employee morale

10. An administrative assistant is planning to make a recommendation to change a procedure which would substantially affect the work of his subordinates. For this supervisor to consult with his subordinates about the recommendation before sending it through would be
    A. *undesirable*; subordinates may lose respect for a supervisor who evidences such indecisiveness
    B. *desirable*; since the change in procedure would affect their work, subordinates should decide whether the change should be made
    C. *undesirable*; since subordinates would not receive credit if the procedure were changed, their morale would be lowered
    D. *desirable*; the subordinates may have some worthwhile suggestions concerning the recommendation

11. The BEST way to measure improvement in a selected group of office assistants who have undergone a training course in the use of specific techniques is to
    A. have the trainees fill out questionnaires at the completion of the course as to what they have learned and giving their opinions as to the value of the course

B. compare the performance of the trainees who completed the course with the performance of office assistants who did not take the course
C. compare the performance of the trainees in these techniques before and after the training course
D. compare the degree of success on the next promotion examination of trainees and non-trainees

12. When an administrative assistant finds it necessary to call in a subordinate for a disciplinary interview, his MAIN objective should be to
    A. use techniques which can penetrate any deception and get at the truth
    B. stress correction of, rather than punishment for, past errors
    C. maintain a reputation for being an understanding superior
    D. decide on disciplinary action that is consistent with penalties applied for similar infractions

12.____

13. Suppose that a newly promoted office assistant does satisfactory work during the first five months of her probationary period. However, her supervisor notices shortly after this time that her performance is falling below acceptable standards. The supervisor decides to keep records of this employee's performance, and if there is no significant improvement by the end of 11 months, to recommend that this employee not be given tenure in the higher title.
    This, as the sole course of action, is
    A. *justified*; employees who do not perform satisfactorily should not be promoted
    B. *unjustified*; the supervisor should attempt to determine the cause of the poor performance as soon as possible
    C. *justified*; the supervisor will have given the subordinate the full probationary period to improve herself
    D. *unjustified*; the subordinate should be demoted to her previous title as soon as her work becomes unsatisfactory

13.____

14. Suppose that you are conducting a conference-style training course for a group of 12 office assistants. Miss Jones is the only conferee who has not become involved in the discussion.
    The BEST method of getting Miss Jones to participate is to
    A. ask her to comment on remarks made by the best-informed participant
    B. ask her to give a brief talk at the next session on a topic that interests her
    C. set up a role-play situation and assign her to take a part
    D. ask her a direct questions which you know she can answer

14.____

15. Which of the following is NOT part of the *control* function of office management?
    A. Deciding on alternative courses of action
    B. Reporting periodically on productivity
    C. Evaluating performance against the standards
    D. Correcting deviations when required

15.____

16. Which of the following is NOT a principal aspect of the process of delegation? 16._____
    A. Developing improvements in methods used to carry out assignments
    B. Granting of permission to do what is necessary to carry out assignments
    C. Assignment of duties by a supervisor to an immediate subordinate
    D. Obligation on the part of a subordinate to carry out his assignment

17. Reluctance of a supervisor to delegate work effectively may be due to any or 17._____
    all of the following EXCEPT the supervisor's
    A. unwillingness to take calculated risks
    B. lack of confidence in subordinates
    C. inability to give proper directions as to what he wants done
    D. retention of ultimate responsibility for delegated work

18. A man cannot serve two masters. 18._____
    This statement emphasizes the importance in an organization of following the
    principle of
    A. specialization of work   B. unity of command
    C. uniformity of assignment   D. span of control

19. In general, the number of subordinates an administrative assistant can 19._____
    supervise effectively tends to vary
    A. *directly* with both similarity and complexity of their duties
    B. *directly* with similarity of their duties and *inversely* with complexity of their duties
    C. *inversely* with both similarity and complex of their duties
    D. *inversely* with similarity of their duties and *directly* with complexity of their duties

20. When an administrative assistant practices *general* rather than *close* 20._____
    supervision, which one of the following is MOST likely to happen?
    A. His subordinates will not be as well-trained as employees who are supervised more closely.
    B. Standards are likely to be lowered because subordinates will be under pressures and will not be motivated to work toward set goals.
    C. He will give fewer specific orders and spend more time on planning and coordinating than those supervisors who practice close supervision.
    D. This supervisor will spend more time checking and correcting mistakes made by subordinates than would one who supervises closely.

Questions 21-25.

DIRECTIONS: Questions 21 through 25 are to be answered SOLELY on the basis of the information contained in the following paragraph.

Since an organization chart is pictorial in nature, there is a tendency for it to be drawn in an artistically balanced and appealing fashion, regardless of the realities of actual organizational structure. In addition to being subject to this distortion, there is the difficulty of communicating in any organization chart the relative importance or the relative size of various component parts of an organizational structure. Furthermore, because of the need for simplicity of design, an organization chart can never indicate the full extent of the interrelationships among the component parts of an organization. These interrelationships are often just as vital as the specifications which an organization chart endeavors to indicate. Yet, if an organization chart were to be drawn with all the wide variety of criss-crossing communication and cooperation networks existent within a typical organization, the chart would probably be much more confusing than informative. It is also obvious that no organization chart as such can "prove" or "disprove" that the organizational structure it represents is effective in realizing the objectives of the organization. At best, an organization chart can only illustrate some of the various factors to be taken into consideration in understanding, devising, or altering organizational arrangements.

21. According to the above paragraph, an organization chart can be expected to portray the
    A. structure of the organization along somewhat ideal lines
    B. relative size of the organizational units quite accurately
    C. channels of information distribution within the organization graphically
    D. extent of the obligation of each unit to meet the organizational objectives

22. According to the above paragraph, those aspects of internal functioning which are NOT shown on an organization chart
    A. can be considered to have little practical application in the operations of the organization
    B. might well be considered to be as important as the structural relationships which a chart does present
    C. could be the cause of considerable confusion in the operation of an organization which is quite large
    D. would be most likely to provide the information needed to determine the overall effectiveness of an organization

23. In the above paragraph, the one of the following conditions which is NOT implied as being a defect of an organization chart is that an organization chart may
    A. present a picture of the organizational structure which is different from the structure that actually exists
    B. fail to indicate the comparative size of various organizational units
    C. be limited in its ability to convey some of the meaningful aspects of organizational relationships
    D. become less useful over a period of time during which the organizational facts which it illustrated have changed

24. The one of the following which is the MOST suitable title for the above paragraph is
    A. The Design and Construction of an Organization Chart
    B. The Informal Aspects of an Organization Chart
    C. The Inherent Deficiencies of an Organization Chart
    D. The Utilization of a Typical Organization Chart

25. It can be INFERRED from the above paragraph that the function of an organization chart is to
    A. contribute to the comprehension of the organization form and arrangements
    B. establish the capabilities of the organization to operate effectively
    C. provide a balanced picture of the operations of the organization
    D. eliminate the need for complexity in the organization's structure

KEY (CORRECT ANSWERS)

1. D
2. C
3. D
4. B
5. A

6. C
7. B
8. A
9. A
10. D

11. C
12. B
13. B
14. D
15. A

16. A
17. D
18. B
19. B
20. C

21. A
22. B
23. D
24. C
25. A

TEST 3

DIRECTIONS: Each question or incomplete statement is followed by several suggested answers or completions. Select the one that BEST answers the question or completes the statement. *PRINT THE LETTER OF THE CORRECT ANSWER IN THE SPACE AT THE RIGHT.*

1. Of the following problems that might affect the conduct and outcome of an interview, the MOST troublesome and usually the MOST difficult for the interviewer to control is the
   A. tendency of the interviewee to anticipate the needs and preferences of the interviewer
   B. impulse to cut the interviewee off when he seems to have reached the end of an idea
   C. tendency of interviewee attitudes to bias the results
   D. tendency of the interviewer to do most of the talking

   1.____

2. The administrative assistant MOST likely to be a good interviewer is one who
   A. is adept at manipulating people and circumstances toward his objectives
   B. is able to put himself in the position of the interviewee
   C. gets the more difficult questions out of the way at the beginning of the interview
   D. develops one style and technique that can be used in any type of interview

   2.____

3. A good interviewer guards against the tendency to form an overall opinion about an interviewee on the basis of a single aspect of the interviewee's make-up
   A. assumption error   B. expectancy error
   C. extension effect   D. halo effect

   3.____

4. In conducting an exit interview with an employee who is leaving voluntarily, the interviewer's MAIN objective should be to
   A. see that the employee leaves with a good opinion of the organization
   B. learn the true reasons for the employee's resignation
   C. find out if the employee would consider a transfer
   D. try to get the employee to remain on the job

   4.____

5. During an interview, an interviewee discloses a relevant but embarrassing personal fact.
   It would be BEST for the interviewer to
   A. listen calmly, avoiding any gesture or facial expression that would suggest approval or disapproval of what is related
   B. change the subject, since further discussion in this area may reveal other embarrassing, but irrelevant, personal facts
   C. apologize to the interviewee for having led him to reveal such a fact and promise not to do so again
   D. bring the interview to a close as quickly as possible in order to avoid a discussion which may be distressful to the interviewee

   5.____

6. Suppose that while you are interviewing an applicant for a position in your office, you notice a contradiction in facts in two of his responses.
For you to call the contradictions to his attention would be
    A. *inadvisable*, because it reduces the interviewee's level of participation
    B. *advisable*, because getting the facts is essential to a successful interview
    C. *inadvisable*, because the interviewer should use more subtle techniques to resolve any discrepancies
    D. *advisable*, because the interviewee should be impressed with the necessity for giving consistent answers

6.____

7. An interviewer should be aware that an undesirable result of including *leading questions* in an interview is to
    A. cause the interviewee to give *yes* or *no* answers with qualification or explanation
    B. encourage the interviewee to discuss irrelevant topics
    C. encourage the interviewee to give more meaningful information
    D. reduce the validity of the information obtained from the interviewee

7.____

8. The kind of interview which is PARTICULARLY helpful in getting an employee to tell about his complaints and grievances is one in which
    A. a pattern has been worked out involving a sequence of exact questions to be asked
    B. the interviewee is expected to support his statements with specific evidence
    C. the interviewee is not made to answer specific questions but is encouraged to talk freely
    D. the interviewer has specific items on which he wishes to get or give information

8.____

9. Suppose you are scheduled to interview a student aide under your supervision concerning a health problem. You know that some of the questions you will be asked him will seem embarrassing to him, and that he may resist answering these questions.
In general, to hold these questions for the last part of the interview would be
    A. *desirable*; the intervening time period gives the interviewer an opportunity to plan how to ask these sensitive questions
    B. *undesirable*; the student aide will probably feel that he has been tricked when he suddenly must answer embarrassing questions
    C. *desirable*; the student aide will probably have increased confidence in the interviewer and be more willing to answer these questions
    D. *undesirable*; questions that are important should not be deferred until the end of the interview

9.____

10. The House passed an amendment to delete from the omnibus higher education bill a section that would have prohibited coeducational colleges and universities from considering sex as a factor in their admissions policy.
According to the above passage, consideration of sex as a factor in the admissions policy of coeducational colleges and universities would

10.____

A. be permitted by the omnibus higher education bill if passed without further amendment
B. be prohibited by the amendment to the omnibus higher education bill
C. have been prohibited by the deletion of a section from the omnibus higher education bill
D. have been permitted if the house had failed to pass the amendment

Questions 11-14.

DIRECTIONS: Questions 11 through 14 are to be answered SOLELY according to the information given in the following passage.

The proposition that administrative activity is essentially the same in all organizations appears to underlie some of the practices in the administration of private higher education. Although the practice is unusual in public education, there are numerous instances of industrial, governmental, or military administrators being assigned to private institutions of higher education and, to a lesser extent, of college and university presidents assuming administrative positions in other types of organizations. To test this theory that administrators are interchangeable, there is a need for systematic observation and classification. The myth that an educational administrator must first have experience in the teaching profession is firmly rooted in a long tradition that has historical prestige. The myth is bound up in the expectations of the public and personnel surrounding the administrator. Since administrative success depends significantly on how well an administrator meets the expectations others have of him, the myth may be more powerful than the special experience in helping the administrator attain organizational and educational objectives. Educational administrators who have risen through the teaching profession have often expressed nostalgia for the life of a teacher or scholar, but there is no evidence that this nostalgia contributes to administrative success.

11. Which of the following statements as completed is MOST consistent with the above passage?
The greatest number of administrators has moved from
   A. industry and the military to government and universities
   B. government and universities to industry and the military
   C. government, the armed forces, and industry to colleges and universities
   D. colleges and universities to government, the armed forces, and industry

12. Of the following, the MOST reasonable inference from the above passage is that a specific area requiring research is the
   A. place of myth in the tradition and history of the educational profession
   B. relative effectiveness of educational administrators from inside and outside the teaching profession
   C. performance of administrators in the administration of public colleges
   D. degree of reality behind the nostalgia for scholarly pursuits often expressed by educational administrators

13. According to the above passage, the value to an educational administrator of experience in the teaching profession
    A. lies in the first-hand knowledge he has acquired of immediate educational problems
    B. may lie in the belief of his colleagues, subordinates, and the public that such experience is necessary
    C. has been supported by evidence that the experience contributes to administrative success in educational fields
    D. would be greater if the administrator were able to free himself from nostalgia for his former duties

14. Of the following, the MOST appropriate title for the above passage is
    A. Educational Administration, Its problems
    B. The Experience Needed for Educational Administration
    C. Administration in Higher Education
    D. Evaluating Administrative Experience

Questions 15-20.

DIRECTIONS: Questions 15 through 20 are to be answered SOLELY according to the information contained in the following paragraph.

Methods of administration of office activities, much of which consists of providing information and "know-how" needed to coordinate both activities within that particular office and other offices, have been among the last to come under the spotlight of management analysis. Progress has been rapid during the past decade, however, and is now accelerating at such a pace that an "information revolution" in office management appears to be in the making. Although triggered by technological breakthroughs in electronic computers and other giant steps in mechanization, this information revolution must be attributed to underlying forces, such as the increased complexity of both governmental and private enterprise, and ever-keener competition. Size, diversification, specialization of function, and decentralization are among the forces which make coordination of activities both more imperative and more difficult. Increased competition, both domestic and international, leaves little margin for error in managerial decisions. Several developments during recent years indicate an evolving pattern. In 1960, the American Management Association expanded the scope of its activities and changed the name of its Office Management Division to Administrative Service Division. Also in 1960, the magazine Office Management merged with the magazine American Business, and this new publication was named Administrative Management.

15. A REASONABLE inference that can be made from the information in the above paragraph is that an important role of the office manager today is to
    A. work toward specialization of functions performed by his subordinates
    B. inform and train subordinates regarding any new developments in computer technology and mechanization
    C. assist the professional management analysts with the management analysis work in the organization
    D. supply information that can be used to help coordinate and manager the other activities of the organization

16. An IMPORTANT reason for the "information revolution" that has been taking place in office management is the
    A. advance made in management analysis in the past decade
    B. technological breakthrough in electronic computers and mechanization
    C. more competitive and complicated nature of private business and government
    D. increased efficiency of office management techniques in the past ten years

17. According to the above paragraph, specialization of function in an organization is MOST likely to result in
    A. the elimination of errors in managerial decisions
    B. greater need to coordinate activities
    C. more competition with other organizations, both domestic and international
    D. a need for office managers with greater flexibility

18. The word *evolving*, as used in the third from last sentence in the above paragraph, means MOST NEARLY
    A. developing by gradual changes
    B. passing on to others
    C. occurring periodically
    D. breaking up into separate, constituent parts

19. Of the following, the MOST reasonable implication of the changes in names mentioned in the last part of the above paragraph is that these groups are attempting to
    A. professionalize the field of office management and the title of Office Manager
    B. combine two publications into one because of the increased costs of labor and materials
    C. adjust to the fact that the field of office management is broadening
    D. appeal to the top managerial people rather than the office management people in business and government

20. According to the above paragraph, intense competition among domestic and international enterprises makes it MOST important for an organization's managerial staff to
    A. coordinate and administer office activities with other activities in the organization
    B. make as few errors in decision-making as possible
    C. concentrate on decentralization and reduction of size of the individual divisions of the organization
    D. restrict decision-making only to top management officials

KEY (CORRECT ANSWERS)

1.	A	11.	C
2.	B	12.	B
3.	D	13.	B
4.	B	14.	B
5.	A	15.	D
6.	B	16.	C
7.	D	17.	B
8.	C	18.	A
9.	C	19.	C
10.	A	20.	B

———

EXAMINATION SECTION
TEST 1

DIRECTIONS: Each question or incomplete statement is followed by several suggested answers or completions. Select the one that BEST answers the question or completes the statement. *PRINT THE LETTER OF THE CORRECT ANSWER IN THE SPACE AT THE RIGHT.*

1. Records of one type or another are kept in every office. The MOST important of the following reasons for the supervisor of a clerical or stenographic unit to keep statistical records of the work done in his unit is generally to
    A. supply basic information needed in planning the work of the unit
    B. obtain statistics for comparison with other units
    C. serve as the basis for unsatisfactory employee evaluation
    D. provide the basis for special research projects on program budgeting

    1.____

2. It is better for an employee to report and be responsible directly to several supervisors than to report and be responsible to only one supervisor.
    This statement directly CONTRADICTS the supervisory principle generally known as
    A. span of control
    B. unity of command
    C. delegation of authority
    D. accountability

    2.____

3. The one of the following which would MOST likely lead to friction among clerks in a unit is for the unit supervisor to
    A. defend the actions of his clerks when discussing them with his own supervisor
    B. praise each of his clerks in confidence as the best clerk in the unit
    C. get his men to work together as a team in completing the work of the unit
    D. consider the point of view of the rank and file clerks when assigning unpleasant tasks

    3.____

4. You become aware that one of the employees you supervise has failed to follow correct procedure and has been permitting various reports to be prepared, typed, and transmitted improperly.
    The BEST action for you to take FIRST in this situation is to
    A. order the employee to review all departmental procedures and reprimand him for having violated them
    B. warn the employee that he must obey regulations because uniformity is essential for effective departmental operation
    C. confer with the employee both about his failure to follow regulations and his reasons for doing so
    D. watch the employee's work very closely in the future but say nothing about this violation

    4.____

5. The supervisory clerk who would be MOST likely to have poor control over his subordinates is the one who
   A. goes to unusually great lengths to try to win their approval
   B. pitches in with the work they are doing during periods of heavy workload when no extra help can be obtained
   C. encourages and helps his subordinates toward advancement
   D. considers suggestions from his subordinates before establishing new work procedures involving them

6. Suppose that a clerk who has been transferred to your office from another division in your agency because of difficulties with his supervisor has been placed under your supervision.
   The BEST course of action for you to take FIRST is to
   A. instruct the clerk in the duties he will be performing in your office and make him feel wanted in his new position
   B. analyze the clerk's past grievance to determine if the transfer was the best solution to the problem
   C. advise him of the difficulties his former supervisor had with other employees and encourage him not to feel bad about the transfer
   D. warn him that you will not tolerate any nonsense and that he will be under continuous surveillance while assigned to you

7. A certain office supervisor takes the initiative to represent his employees' interests related to working conditions, opportunities for advancement, etc. to his own supervisor and the administrative levels of the agency.
   This supervisor's actions will MOST probably have the effect of
   A. preventing employees from developing individual initiative in their work goals
   B. encouraging employees to compete openly for the special attention of their supervisor
   C. depriving employees of the opportunity to be represented by persons and/or unions of their own choosing
   D. building employee confidence in their supervisor and a spirit of cooperation in their work

8. Suppose that you have been promoted, assigned as a supervisor of a certain unit, and asked to reorganize its functions so that specific routine procedures can be established.
   Before deciding which routines to establish, the FIRST of the following steps you should take is to
   A. decide who will perform each task in the routine
   B. determine the purpose to be served by each routine procedure
   C. outline the sequence of steps in each routine to be established
   D. calculate if more staff will be needed to carry out the new procedures

9. When routine procedures covering the ordinary work of an office are established, the supervisor of the office tends to be relieved of the need to
   A. make repeated decisions on the handling of recurring similar situations
   B. check the accuracy of the work completed by his subordinates
   C. train his subordinates in new work procedures
   D. plan and schedule the work of his office

10. Of the following, the method which would be LEAST helpful to a supervisor in effectively applying the principles of on-the-job safety to the daily work of his unit is for him to
    A. initiate corrections of unsafe layouts of equipment and unsafe work processes
    B. take charge of operations that are not routine to make certain that safety precautions are established and observed
    C. continue to talk safety and promote safety consciousness in his subordinates
    D. figure the cost of all accidents which could possibly occur on the job

11. A clerk is assigned to serve as receptionist for a large and busy office. Although many members of the public visit this office, the clerk often experiences periods of time in which he has nothing to do.
    In these circumstances, the MOST advisable of the following actions for the supervisor to take is to
    A. assign a number of relatively low priority clerical jobs to the receptionist to do in the slow periods
    B. regularly rotate this assignment so that all of the clerks experience this lighter work load
    C. assign the receptionist job as part of the duties of a number of clerks whose desks are nearest the reception room
    D. overlook the situation since most of the receptionist's time is spent in performing a necessary and meaningful function

12. For a supervisor to require all stenographers in a stenographic pool to produce the same amount of work on a particular day is
    A. advisable since it will prove that the supervisor plays no favorites
    B. fair since all stenographers are receiving approximately the same salary, their output should be equivalent
    C. not necessary since the fast workers will compensate for the slow workers
    D. not realistic since individual differences in abilities and work assignment must be taken into consideration

13. The establishment of a centralized typing pool to service the various units in an organization is MOST likely to be worthwhile when there is
    A. wide fluctuation from time to time in the needs of the various units for typing service
    B. a large volume of typing work to be done in each of the units
    C. a need by each unit for different kinds of typing service
    D. a training program in operation to develop and maintain typing skills

14. A newly appointed supervisor should learn as much as possible about the backgrounds of his subordinates. This statement is GENERALLY correct because
    A. knowing their backgrounds assures they will be treated objectively, equally, and without favor
    B. effective handling of subordinates is based upon knowledge of their individual differences
    C. subordinates perform more efficiently under one supervisor than under another
    D. subordinates have confidence in a supervisor who knows all about them

14.____

15. The use of electronic computers in modern businesses has produced many changes in office and information management.
    Of the following, it would NOT be correct to state that computer utilization
    A. broadens the scope of managerial and supervisory authority
    B. establishes uniformity in the processing and reporting of information
    C. cuts costs by reducing the personnel needed for efficient office operation
    D. supplies management rapidly with up-to-date data to facilitate decision-making

15.____

16. The CHIEF advantage of having a single, large open office instead of small partitioned ones for a clerical unit or stenographic pool is that the single, large open office
    A. afford privacy without isolation for all office workers not directly dealing with the public
    B. assures the smoother, more continuous inter-office flow of work that is essential for efficient work production
    C. facilitates the office supervisor's visual control over and communication with his subordinates
    D. permits a more decorative and functional arrangement of office furniture and machines

16.____

17. When a supervisor provides a new employee with the information necessary for a basic knowledge and a general understanding of practices and procedures of the agency, he is applying the type of training generally known as _____ training.
    A. pre-employment   B. induction
    C. on-the-job   D. supervisory

17.____

18. Many government agencies require the approval by a central forms control unit of the design and reproduction of new office forms.
    The one of the following results of this procedure that is a DISADVANTAGE is that requiring prior approval of a central forms control unit usually
    A. limits the distribution of forms to those offices with justifiable reasons for receiving them
    B. permits checking whether existing forms or modifications of them are in line with current agency needs

18.____

C. encourages reliance on only the central office to set up all additional forms when needed
D. provides for someone with a specialized knowledge of forms design to review and criticize new and revised forms

19. Suppose that a large quantity of information is in the files which are located a good distance from your desk. Almost every worker in your office must use these files constantly. Your duties in particular require that you refer daily to about 25 of the same items. They are short, one-page items distributed throughout the files.
In this situation, your BEST course would be to
    A. take the items that you use daily from the files and keep them on your desk, inserting out cards in their place
    B. go to the files each time you need the information so that the items will be there when other workers need them
    C. make Xerox copies of the information you use most frequently and keep them in your desk for ready reference
    D. label the items you use most often with different colored tabs for immediate identification

20. Of the following, the MOST important advantage of preparing manuals of office procedures in loose-leaf form is that this form
    A. permits several employees to use different sections simultaneously
    B. facilitates the addition of new material and the removal of obsolete material
    C. is more readily arranged in alphabetical order
    D. reduces the need for cross-references to locate material carried under several headings

21. Suppose that you establish a new clerical procedure for the unit you supervise. Your keeping a close check on the time required by your staff to handle the new procedure is WISE mainly because such a check will find out
    A. whether your subordinates know how to handle the new procedure
    B. whether a revision of the unit's work schedule will be necessary as a result of the new procedure
    C. what attitude your employees have toward the new procedure
    D. what alterations in job descriptions will be necessitated by the new procedure

22. From the viewpoint of an office supervisor, the BEST of the following reasons for distributing the incoming mail before the beginning of the regular work day is that
    A. distribution can be handled quickly and most efficiently at that time
    B. distribution later in the day may be distracting to or interfere with other employees
    C. the employees who distribute the mail can then perform other tasks during the rest of the day
    D. office activities for the day based on the mail may then be started promptly

23. Suppose you are the head of a unit with ten staff members who are located in several different rooms.
If you want to inform your staff of a minor change in procedure, the BEST and LEAST expensive way of doing so would usually be to
   A. send a copy to each staff member
   B. call a special staff meeting and announce the change
   C. circulate a memo, having each staff member initial it
   D. have a clerk tell each member of the staff about the change

24. The numbered statements below relate to the stenographic skill of taking dictation. According to authorities on secretarial practices, which of these are generally recommended guides to development of efficient stenographic skills?
   I. A stenographer should date her notebook daily to facilitate locating certain notes at a later time.
   II. A stenographer should make corrections of grammatical mistakes while her boss is dictating to her.
   III. A stenographer should draw a line through the dictated matter in her notebook after she has transcribed it
   IV. A stenographer should write in longhand unfamiliar names and addresses dictated to her.

   The CORRECT answer is:
   A. Only Statements I, II, and III are generally recommended guides.
   B. Only Statements II, III, and IV are generally recommended guides.
   C. Only Statements I, III, and IV are generally recommended guides.
   D. All four statements are generally recommended guides.

25. A bureau of a city agency is about to move to a new location.
Of the following, the FIRST step that should be taken in order to provide a good layout for the office at the new location is to
   A. decide the exact amount of space to be assigned to each unit of the bureau
   B. decide whether to lay out a single large open office or one consisting of small partitioned units
   C. ask each unit chief in the bureau to examine the new location and submit a request for the amount of space he needs
   D. prepare a detailed plan of the dimensions of the floor space to be occupied by the bureau at the new location

26. Of the following, the BEST reason for discarding a sheet of carbon paper is that
   A. some carbon rubs off on your fingers when handled
   B. there are several creases in the sheet
   C. the short edge of the sheet is curled
   D. the finish on the sheet is smooth and shiny

27. Suppose you are the supervisor of a mailroom of a large city agency where the mail received daily is opened by machine, sorted by hand for delivery, and time-stamped. Letters and any enclosures are removed from envelopes and stapled together before distribution. One of your newest clerks asks you what should be done when a letter makes reference to an enclosure but no enclosure is in the envelope.
You should tell him that, in this situation, the BEST procedure is to
    A. make an entry of the sender's name and address in the missing enclosures file and forward the letter to its proper destination
    B. return the letter to its sender, attaching a request for the missing enclosure
    C. put the letter aside until a proper investigation may be made concerning the missing enclosure
    D. route the letter to the person for whom it is intended, noting the absence of the enclosure on the letter-margin

28. The term *work flow*, when used in connection with office management or the activities in an office, GENERALLY means the
    A. use of charts in the analysis of various office functions
    B. rate of speed at which work flows through a single section of an office
    C. step-by-step physical routing of work through its various procedures
    D. number of individual work units which can be produced by the average employee

29. Physical conditions can have a definite effect on the efficiency and morale of an office. Which of the following statements about physical conditions in an office is CORRECT?
    A. Hard, non-porous surfaces reflect more noise than linoleum on the top of a desk.
    B. Painting in tints of bright yellow is more appropriate for sunny, well-lit offices than for dark, poorly-lit offices.
    C. Plate glass is better than linoleum for the top of a desk.
    D. The central typing room needs less light than a conference room does.

30. In a certain filing system, documents are consecutively numbered as they are filed, a register is maintained of such consecutively numbered documents, and a record is kept of the number of each document removed from the files and its destination.
This system will NOT help in
    A. finding the present whereabouts of a particular document
    B. proving the accuracy of the data recorded on a certain document
    C. indicating whether observed existing documents were ever filed
    D. locating a desired document without knowing what its contents are

31. In deciding the kind and number of records an agency should keep, the administrative staff must recognize that records are of value in office management PRIMARILY as
    A. informational bases for agency activities
    B. data for evaluating the effectiveness of the agency
    C. raw material on which statistical analyses are to be based
    D. evidence that the agency is carrying out its duties and responsibilities

32. Complaints are often made by the public about the government's procedures. Although in most cases such procedures cannot be changed since various laws and regulations require them, it may still be possible to reduce the number of complaints.
    Which one of the following actions by personnel dealing with applicants for city services is LEAST likely to reduce complaints concerning city procedures?
    A. Treating all citizens alike and explaining to them that no exceptions to required procedures can be made.
    B. Explaining briefly to the citizen why he should comply with regulations.
    C. Being careful to avoid mistakes which may make additional interviews or correspondence necessary.
    D. Keeping the citizen informed of the progress of his correspondence when immediate disposition cannot be made.

33. Persons whose native language is not English sometimes experience difficulty in communication when visiting public offices.
    The MOST common method used by such persons to overcome the difficulty in communication is to
    A. write in their own language whatever they wish to say
    B. hire a professional interpreter
    C. ask a patrolman for assistance
    D. bring with them an English-speaking friend or relative

34. In answering a complaint made by a member of the public that a certain essential procedure required by your agency is difficult to follow, it would be BEST for you to stress most
    A. that a change in the rules may be considered if enough complaints are received
    B. why the operation of a large agency sometimes proves a hardship in individual cases
    C. the necessity for the procedure
    D. the origin of the procedure

35. When talking to a citizen, it is BEST for an employee of government to
    A. use ordinary conversational phrases and a natural manner
    B. try to copy the pronunciation and level of education shown by the citizen
    C. try to speak in a very cultured manner and tone
    D. use technical terms to show his familiarity with his own work

36. Employees who service the public should maintain an attitude which is both sympathetic and objective. An unsympathetic and subjective attitude would be shown by a public employee who
    A. says *no* with a smile when a citizen's request must be denied
    B. listens attentively to a long complaint from a citizen about government's *red tape*
    C. responds with sarcasm when a citizen asks a question which has an obvious manner
    D. suggests a definite solution to a citizen's problems

37. Of the following methods of conducting an interview, the BEST is to
    A. ask questions with *yes* or *no* answers
    B. listen carefully and ask only questions that are pertinent
    C. fire questions at the interviewee so that he must answer sincerely and briefly
    D. read standardized questions to the person being interviewed

38. An interviewer should begin with topics which are easy to talk about and which are not threatening. This procedure is useful MAINLY because it
    A. allows the applicant a little time to get accustomed to the situation and leads to freer communication
    B. distracts the attention of the person being interviewed from the main purpose of the questioning
    C. is the best way for the interviewer to show that he is relaxed and confident on the job
    D. causes the interviewee to feel that the interviewer is apportioning valuable questioning time

39. The initial interview will normally be more of a problem to the interviewer than any subsequent interviews he may have with the same person because
    A. the interviewee is likely to be hostile
    B. there is too much to be accomplished in one session
    C. he has less information about the client than he will have later
    D. some information may be forgotten when later making record of this first interview

40. You are a supervisor in an agency and are holding your first interview with a new employee. In this interview, you should strive MAINLY to
    A. show the new employee that you are an efficient and objective supervisor, with a completely impersonal attitude toward your subordinate
    B. complete the entire orientation process including the giving of detailed job-duty instructions
    C. make it clear to the employee that all your decisions are based on your many years of experience
    D. lay the groundwork for a good employee-supervisor relationship by gaining the new employee's confidence

41. Most successful interviews are those in which the interviewer shows a genuine interest in the person he is questioning. This attitude would MOST likely cause the individual being interviewed to
    A. feel that the interviewer already knows all the facts in his case
    B. act more naturally and reveal more of his true feelings
    C. request that the interviewer give more attention to his problems, not his personality
    D. react defensively, suppress his negative feelings, and conceal the real facts in his case

42. Questions worded so that the person being interviewed has some hint of the desired answer can modify the person's response. The result of the inclusion of such questions in an interview, even when they are used inadvertently, is to
    A. have no effect on the basic content of the information given by the person interviewed
    B. have value in convincing the person that the suggested plan is the best for him
    C. cause the person to give more meaningful information
    D. reduce the validity of the information obtained from the person

43. The person MOST likely to be a good interviewer is one who
    A. is able to outguess the person being interviewed
    B. tries to change the attitudes of the persons he interviews
    C. controls the interview by skillfully dominating the conversation
    D. is able to imagine himself in the position of the person being interviewed

44. The *halo effect* is an overall impression on the interviewer, whether favorable or unfavorable, usually created by a single trait. This impression then influences the appraisal of all other factors.
    A *halo effect* is LEAST likely to be created at an interview where the interviewee is a
    A. person of average appearance and ability
    B. rough-looking man who uses abusive language
    C. young attractive woman being interviewed by a man
    D. person who demonstrates an exceptional ability to remember facts

45. Of the following, the BEST way for an interviewer to calm a person who seems to have become emotionally upset as a result of a question asked is for the interviewer to
    A. talk to the person about other things for a short time
    B. ask that the person control himself
    C. probe for the cause of his emotional upset
    D. finish the questioning as quickly as possible

46. Of the following, a centralized filing system is LEAST suitable for filing
    A. material which is confidential in nature
    B. routine correspondence
    C. periodic reports of the divisions of the department
    D. material used by several divisions of the department

47. Form letters should be used MAINLY when
    A. an office has to reply to a great many similar inquiries
    B. the type of correspondence varies widely
    C. it is necessary to have letters which are well-phrased and grammatically correct
    D. letters of inquiry have to be answered as soon as possible after they are received

48. Suppose that you are assigned to prepare a form from which certain information will be posted in a ledger. It would be MOST helpful to the person posting the information in the ledger is, in designing the form, you were to
    A. use the same color paper for both the form and the ledger
    B. make the form the same size as the pages of the ledger
    C. have the information on the form in the same order as that used in the ledger
    D. include in the form a box which is to be initialed when the data on the form have been posted in the ledger

49. A misplaced record is a lost record. Of the following, the MOST valid implication of this statement in regard to office work is that
    A. all records in an office should be filed in strict alphabetical order
    B. accuracy in filing is essential
    C. only one method of filing should be used throughout the office
    D. files should be locked when not in use

50. James Jones is applying for a provisional appointment as a clerk in your department. He presents a letter of recommendation from a former employer stating: *James Jones was rarely late or absent; he has a very pleasing manner and never got into an argument with his fellow employees.*
    The above information concerning this applicant
    A. proves clearly that he produces more work than the average employee
    B. indicates that he was probably attempting to conceal his inefficiency from his former employer
    C. presents no conclusive evidence of his ability to do clerical work
    D. indicates clearly that with additional training he will make a good supervisor

KEY (CORRECT ANSWERS)

1. A	11. A	21. B	31. A	41. B
2. B	12. D	22. D	32. A	42. D
3. B	13. A	23. C	33. D	43. D
4. C	14. B	24. C	34. C	44. A
5. A	15. A	25. D	35. A	45. A
6. A	16. C	26. B	36. C	46. A
7. D	17. B	27. D	37. B	47. A
8. B	18. C	28. C	38. A	48. C
9. A	19. C	29. A	39. C	49. B
10. D	20. B	30. B	40. D	50. C

TEST 2

DIRECTIONS: Each question or incomplete statement is followed by several suggested answers or completions. Select the one that BEST answers the question or completes the statement. *PRINT THE LETTER OF THE CORRECT ANSWER IN THE SPACE AT THE RIGHT.*

Questions 1-10.

DIRECTIONS: In each of Questions 1 through 10, there is a quotation which contains a word (one of those underlined) that is either incorrectly used because it is not in keeping with the meaning the quotation is evidently intended to convey, or is misspelled. There is only one incorrect word in each quotation. Of the four underlined words in each question, determine if the first one should be replaced by the word lettered A, the second replaced by the word lettered B, the third replaced by the word lettered C, or the fourth replaced by the word lettered D. Print the letter of the replacement word you have selected in the space at the right.

1. Whether one depends on flourescent or artificial light or both, adequate standards should be maintained by means of systematic tests. 1.____
   A. natural   B. safeguards   C. established   D. routine

2. A policeman has to be prepared to assume his knowledge as a social scientist in the community. 2.____
   A. forced   B. role   C. philosopher   D. street

3. It is practically impossible to tell whether a sentence is very long simply by measuring its length. 3.____
   A. almost   B. mark   C. too   D. denoting

4. By using carbon paper, the typist easily is able to insert as many as six copies of a report. 4.____
   A. adding   B. seldom   C. make   D. forms

5. Although all people have many traits in common, a receptionist in her agreements with people learns quickly how different each person is from every other person. 5.____
   A. impressions   B. associations   C. decides   D. various

6. Strong leaders are required to organize a community for delinquency prevention and for dissemination of organized crime and drug addiction. 6.____
   A. tactics   B. important   C. control   D. meetings

7. The demonstrators, who were taken to the Criminal Courts building in Manhattan (because it was large enough to accommodate them), contended that the arrests were unwarrented. 7.____
   A. demonstraters   B. Manhatten   C. accomodate   D. unwarranted

33

8. When two or more forms for spelling a word exist, it is advisable to use the preferred spelling indicated in the dictionary, and to use it consistantly.
   A. adviseable   B. prefered   C. dictionery   D. consistently

9. If you know the language of the foreign country you are visiting, your embarassment will disappear and you will learn a lot more about the customs and characteristics.
   A. foriegn   B. embarrassment
   C. dissappear   D. charactaristics

10. Material consisting of government bulletins, adverticements, catalogues, announcements of address changes and any other periodical material of this nature, may be filed alphabetically according to subject.
    A. advertisements   B. cataloges
    C. announcments   D. pereodical

Questions 11-14.

DIRECTIONS: Each of the two sentences in Questions 11 through 14 may contain errors in punctuation, capitalization, or grammar.
If there is an error in only Sentence I, mark your answer A.
If there is an error in only Sentence II, mark you answer B.
If there is an error in both Sentences I and II, mark your answer C.
If both Sentences I and II are correct, mark your answer D.

11. I. It is very annoying to have a pencil sharpener, which is not in proper working order.
    II. The building watchman checked the door of Charlie's office and found that the lock has been jammed.

12. I. Since he went on the New York City council a year ago, one of his primary concerns has been safety in the streets.
    II. After waiting in the doorway for about 15 minutes, a black sedan appeared.

13. I. When you are studying a good textbook is important.
    II. He said he would divide the money equally between you and me.

14. I. The question is, "How can a large number of envelopes be sealed rapidly without the use of a sealing machine?"
    II. The administrator assigned two stenographers, Mary and I, to the new bureau.

Questions 15-16.

DIRECTIONS: In each of Questions 15 and 16, the four sentences are from a paragraph in a report. They are not in the right order. Which of the following arrangements is the BEST one?

15. I. An executive may answer a letter by writing his reply on the face of the letter itself instead of having a return letter typed.
    II. This procedure is efficient because it saves the executive's time, the typist's time, and saves office file space.
    III. Copying machines are used in small offices as well as large offices to save time and money in making brief replies to business letters.
    IV. A copy is made on a copying machine to go into the company files, while the original is mailed back to the sender.

   The CORRECT answer is:
   A. I, II, IV, III   B. I, IV, II, III   C. III, I, IV, II   D. III, IV, II, I

16. I. Most organizations favor one of the types but always include the others to a lesser degree.
    II. However, we can detect a definite trend toward greater uses of symbolic control.
    III. We suggest that our local police agencies are today primarily utilizing material control.
    IV. Control can be classified into three types: physical, material, and symbolic.

   The CORRECT answer is:
   A. IV, II, III, I   B. II, I, IV, III   C. III, IV, II, I   D. IV, I, III, II

17. Of the following, the MOST effective report writing style is usually characterized by
    A. covering all the main ideas in the same paragraph
    B. presenting each significant point in a new paragraph
    C. placing the least important points before the most important points
    D. giving all points equal emphasis throughout the report

18. Of the following, which factor is COMMON to all types of reports?
    A. Presentation of information
    B. Interpretation of findings
    C. Chronological ordering of the information
    D. Presentation of conclusions and recommendations

19. When writing a report, the one of the following which you should do FIRST is
    A. set up a logical work schedule
    B. determine your objectives in writing the report
    C. select your statistical material
    D. obtain the necessary data from the files

20. Generally, the frequency with which reports are to be submitted or the length of the interval which they cover should depend MAINLY on the
    A. amount of time needed to prepare the reports
    B. degree of comprehensiveness required in the reports
    C. availability of the data to be included in the reports
    D. extent of the variations in the data with the passage of time

21. The objectiveness of a report is its unbiased presentation of the facts.
    If this be so, which of the following reports listed below is likely to be the MOST objective?
    A. The Best Use of an Electronic Computer in Department Z
    B. The Case for Raising the Salaries of Employees in Department A
    C. Quarterly Summary of Production in the Duplicating Unit of Department Y
    D. Recommendation to Terminate Employee X's Services Because of Misconduct

Questions 22-27.

DIRECTIONS: Questions 22 through 27 are to be answered SOLELY on the basis of the information contained in the charts below which relate to the budget allocations of City X, a small suburban community. The charts depict the annual budget allocations by Department and by Expenditures over a five-year period.

CITY X BUDGET IN MILLIONS OF DOLLARS

TABLE I. Budget Allocations By Department

Department	2012	2013	2014	2015	2016
Public Safety	30	45	50	40	50
Health and Welfare	50	75	90	60	70
Engineering	5	8	10	5	8
Human Resources	10	12	20	10	22
Conversation and Environment	10	15	20	20	15
Education and Development	15	25	35	15	15
TOTAL BUDGET	120	180	225	150	180

TABLE II. Budget Allocations by Expenditures

Category	2012	2013	2014	2015	2016
Raw Materials and Machinery	36	63	68	30	98
Capital Outlay	12	27	56	15	18
Personal Services	72	90	101	105	65
TOTAL BUDGET	120	180	225	150	180

22. The year in which the SMALLEST percentage of the total annual budget was allocated to the Department of Education and Development is
    A. 2012   B. 2013   C. 2015   D. 2016

23. Assume that, in 2015, the Department of Conservation and Environment divided its annual budget into the three categories of expenditures and in exactly the same proportion as the budget shown in Table II for the year 2015. The amount allocated for capital outlay in the Department of Conservation and Environment's 2015 budget was MOST NEARLY _____ million.
    A. $2   B. $4   C. $6   D. $10

24. From the year 2013 to the year 2015, the sum of the annual budgets for the Departments of Public Safety and Engineering showed an overall _____ of _____ million.
    A. decline; $8   B. increase; $7   C. decline; $15   D. increase; $22

25. The LARGEST dollar increase in departmental budget allocations from one year to the next was in
    A. Public Safety from 2012 to 2013
    B. Health and Welfare from 2012 to 2013
    C. Education and Development from 2014 to 2015
    D. Human Resources from 2014 to 2015

26. During the five-year period, the annual budget of the Department of Human Resources was GREATER than the annual budget for the Department of Conservation and Environment in _____ of the years.
    A. none   B. one   C. two   D. three

27. If the total City X budget increases at the same rate from 2016 to 2017 as it did from 2015 to 2016, the total City X budget for 2017 will be MOST NEARLY _____ million.
    A. $180   B. $200   C. $210   D. $215

Questions 28-34.

DIRECTIONS: Questions 28 through 34 are to be answered SOLELY on the basis of the information contained in the graph below which relates to the work of a public agency.

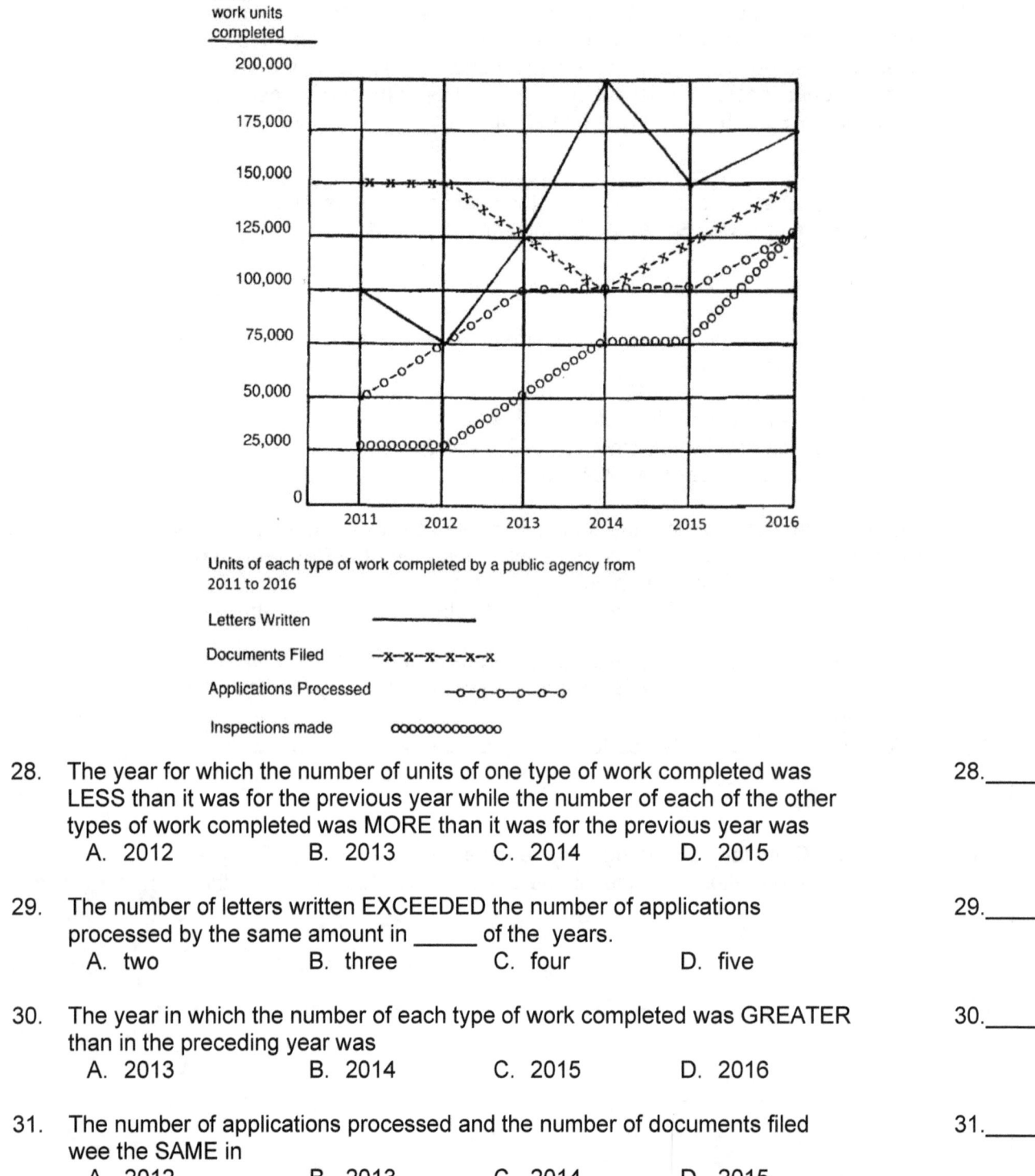

Units of each type of work completed by a public agency from 2011 to 2016

Letters Written ———————
Documents Filed —x—x—x—x—x—x
Applications Processed —o—o—o—o—o—o
Inspections made ooooooooooo

28. The year for which the number of units of one type of work completed was LESS than it was for the previous year while the number of each of the other types of work completed was MORE than it was for the previous year was
  A. 2012   B. 2013   C. 2014   D. 2015

29. The number of letters written EXCEEDED the number of applications processed by the same amount in _____ of the years.
  A. two   B. three   C. four   D. five

30. The year in which the number of each type of work completed was GREATER than in the preceding year was
  A. 2013   B. 2014   C. 2015   D. 2016

31. The number of applications processed and the number of documents filed wee the SAME in
  A. 2012   B. 2013   C. 2014   D. 2015

32. The TOTAL number of units of work completed by the agency   32.____
    A. increased in each year after 2011
    B. decreased from the prior year in two of the years after 2011
    C. was the same in two successive years from 2011 to 2016
    D. was less in 2011 than in any of the following years

33. For the year in which the number of letters written was twice as high as it   33.____
    was in 2011, the number of documents filed was _____ it was in 2011.
    A. the same as   B. two-thirds of what
    C. five-sixths of what   D. 1½ times what

34. The variable which was the MOST stable during the period 2011 through   34.____
    2016 was
    A. Inspections Made   B. Letters Written
    C. Documents Filed   D. Applications Processed

Questions 35-41.

DIRECTIONS: Questions 35 through 41 are to be answered SOLELY on the basis of the information in the following passage.

Job evaluation and job rating systems are intended to introduce scientific procedures. Any type of approach, when properly used, will give satisfactory results. The Point System, when properly validated by actual use, is more likely to be suitable for general use than the ranking system. In many aspects, the Factor Comparison Plan is a point system tied to money values. Of course, there may be another system that combines the ranking system with the point system, especially during the initial stages of the development of the program. After the program has been in use for some time, the tendency is to drop off the ranking phrase and continue the use of the point system.

In the ranking system of rating of jobs, every job within the plant is arranged in some order, either from the one with the simplest qualifications to the one with maximum requirements, or in the reverse order. This system should be preceded by careful job analysis and the writing of accurate job descriptions before the rating process is undertaken. It is possible, of course, to take the jobs as they are found in the business enterprise and use the names as they are without any attempt at standardization, and merely rank them according to the general overall impression of the raters. Such a procedure is certain to fall short of what may reasonably be expected of job rating. Another procedure that is in reality merely a modification of the simple rating described above is to establish a series of grades or zones and arrange all the jobs in the plant into groups within these grades and zones. The practice in most common use is to arrange all the jobs in the plant according to their requirements by rating them and then to establish the classifications or groups.

The actual ranking of jobs may be done by one individual, several individuals, or a committee. If several individuals are working independently on the task, it will usually be found that, in general, they agree but that their rankings vary in certain details. A conference between the individuals, with each person giving his reasons why he rated one way or another, usually produces agreement. The detailed job descriptions are particularly helpful when there is disagreement among raters as to the rating of certain jobs. It is not only possible but desirable to have workers participate in the construction of the job description and in rating the job.

35. The MAIN theme of this passage is
    A. the elimination of bias in job rating
    B. the rating of jobs by the ranking system
    C. the need for accuracy in allocating points in the point system
    D. pitfalls to avoid in selecting key jobs in the Factor Comparison Plan

36. The ranking system of rating jobs consists MAINLY of
    A. attaching a point value to each ratable factor of each job prior to establishing an equitable pay scale
    B. arranging every job in the organization in descending order and then following this up with a job analysis of the key jobs
    C. preparing accurate job descriptions after a job analysis and then arranging all jobs either in ascending or descending order based on job requirements
    D. arbitrarily establishing a hierarchy of job classes and grades and then fitting each job into a specific class and grade based on the opinions of unit supervisors

37. The above passage states that the system of classifying jobs MOST used in an organization is to
    A. organize all jobs in the organization in accordance with their requirements and then create categories or clusters of jobs
    B. classify all jobs in the organization according to the titles and ranks by which they are currently known in the organization
    C. establish a pre-arranged series of grades or zones and then fit all jobs into one of the grades or zones
    D. determine the salary currently being paid for each job, and then rank the jobs in order according to salary

38. According to the above passage, experience has shown that when a group of raters is assigned to the job evaluation task and each individual rates independently of the others, the raters GENERALLY
    A. *agree* with respect to all aspects of their rankings
    B. *disagree* with respect to all or nearly all aspects of the rankings
    C. *disagree* on overall ratings but agree on specific rating factors
    D. *agree* on overall rankings but have some variance in some details

39. The above passage states that the use of a detailed job description is of SPECIAL value when
    A. employees of an organization have participated in the preliminary steps involved in actual preparation of the job description
    B. labor representatives are not participating in ranking of the jobs
    C. an individual rater who is unsure of himself is ranking the jobs
    D. a group of raters is having difficulty reaching unanimity with respect to ranking a certain job

40. A comparison of the various rating systems as described in the above passage shows that
    A. the ranking system is not as appropriate for general use as a properly validated point system
    B. the point system is the same as the Factor Comparison Plan except that it places greater emphasis on money
    C. no system is capable of combining the point system and the Factor Comparison Plan
    D. the point system will be discontinued last when used in combination with the Factor Comparison System

41. The above passage implies that the PRINCIPAL reason for creating job evaluation and rating systems was to help
    A. overcome union opposition to existing salary plans
    B. base wage determination on a more objective and orderly foundation
    C. eliminate personal bias on the part of the trained scientific job evaluators
    D. management determine if it was overpricing the various jobs in the organizational hierarchy

42. As a general rule, in a large office it is desirable to have more than one one employee who is able to operate any one machine and more than one office machine capable of performing any one type of required operation. According to this statement, there USUALLY should be
    A. fewer office machines in an office than are necessary for efficient job performance
    B. more office machines in an office than there are employees able to operate them
    C. more types of required operations to be performed than there are machines necessary to their performance
    D. fewer types of required operations to be performed than there are machines capable of performing them

43. The plan of an organization's structure and procedures may appear to be perfectly sound, but the organization may still operate wastefully and with a great amount of friction because of the failure of the people in the organization to work together.
    The MOST valid implication of this statement is that
    A. inefficiency within an organization may be caused by people being directed to do the wrong things
    B. an organization which operates inefficiently might be improved by revising its systems and methods of operations
    C. use of the best methods an organization can devise may not prevent an organization from being inefficient
    D. the people in an organization may not have an appreciation of the high quality of the organization's plan of operations

44. If an employee is to be held responsible for obtaining results, he should be given every reasonable freedom to exercise his own intelligence and initiative to achieve the results expected.
The MOST valid implication of this statement is that
    A. the authority delegated should match the responsibility assigned
    B. achieving results depends upon the individual's willingness to work
    C. the most important aspect of getting a job done is to know how to do it
    D. understanding the requirements of a task is essential to its accomplishment

44.____

45. Essentially, an organization is defined as any group of individuals who are cooperating under the direction of executive leadership in an attempt to accomplish certain common objectives.
The one of the following which this statement does NOT include as an essential characteristic of an organization is _____ the members of the group.
    A. cooperation among   B. proficiency of
    C. authoritative guidance of   D. goals common to

45.____

46. A supervisor, in organizing the work activities of the staff of an office, should recognize that one of the conditions which is expected to promote a high level of interest on the part of an office worker in his job is to assign him to perform a variety of work.
The MOST valid implication of this statement is that
    A. each worker should be taught to perform each type of work in the office
    B. workers should be assigned to perform types of work in which they have expressed interest
    C. a worker who is assigned to perform a single type of work is likely to become bored
    D. some workers are likely to perform several types of work better than other workers are able to

46.____

47. Of the following basic guides to effective letter writing, which one would NOT be recommended as a way of improving the quality of business letters?
    A. Use emphatic phrases like *close proximity* and *first and foremost* to round out sentences.
    B. Break up complicated sentences by making short sentences out of dependent clauses.
    C. Replace old-fashioned phrases like *enclosed please find* and *recent date* with a more direct approach.
    D. Personalize letters by using your reader's name at least once in the body of the message.

47.____

11 (#2)

48. Suppose that you must write a reply letter to a citizen's request for a certain pamphlet printed by your agency. The pamphlet is temporarily unavailable but a new supply will be arriving by December 8 or 9.
Of the following four sentences, which one expresses the MOST positive business letter writing approach?
A. We cannot send the materials you requested until after December 8.
B. May we assure you that the materials you requested will be sent as quickly as possible.
C. We will be sending the materials you requested as soon as our supply is replenished.
D. We will mail the materials you requested on or shortly after December 8.

48.____

49. Using form letters in business correspondence is LEAST effective when
A. answering letters on a frequently recurring subject
B. giving the same information to many addresses
C. the recipient is only interested in the routine information contained in the form letter
D. a replay must be keyed to the individual requirements of the intended reader

49.____

50. The ability to write memos and letters is very important in clerical and administrative work. Methodical planning of a reply letter usually involves the following basic steps which are arranged in random order:
I. Determine the purpose of the letter you are about to write.
II. Make an outline of what information your reply letter should contain.
III. Read carefully the letter to be answered to find out its main points.
IV. Assemble the facts to be included in your reply letter.
V. Visualize your intended reader and adapt your letter writing style to him.
If the above-numbered steps were arranged in their proper logical order, the one which would be THIRD in the sequence is
A. II   B. III   C. IV   D. V

50.____

KEY (CORRECT ANSWERS)

1.	A	11.	C	21.	C	31.	C	41.	B
2.	B	12.	C	22.	D	32.	C	42.	D
3.	C	13.	A	23.	A	33.	B	43.	C
4.	C	14.	B	24.	A	34.	D	44.	A
5.	B	15.	C	25.	B	35.	B	45.	B
6.	C	16.	D	26.	B	36.	C	46.	C
7.	D	17.	B	27.	D	37.	A	47.	A
8.	D	18.	A	28.	B	38.	D	48.	D
9.	B	19.	B	29.	B	39.	D	49.	D
10.	A	20.	D	30.	D	40.	A	50.	A

EXAMINATION SECTION
TEST 1

DIRECTIONS: Each question or incomplete statement is followed by several suggested answers or completions. Select the one that BEST answers the question or completes the statement. *PRINT THE LETTER OF THE CORRECT ANSWER IN THE SPACE AT THE RIGHT.*

1. As the supervisor of a staff of clerical employees performing various types of work, you are responsible for the accuracy and efficiency with which their work is performed.
   Of the following actions you may take to insure the accuracy of their work, the MOST practical one is for you to

    A. review each operation completed by a staff member before permitting the employee to proceed to the next operation
    B. keep a record of every error made by an employee and use this record to determine whether a careless employee should be transferred or discharged
    C. assign work in such a way that every operation is performed independently by two employees
    D. determine what errors are likely to occur and set up safeguards to prevent the occurrence of these errors

    1.____

2. Assume that you are the supervisor of a small clerical unit. One of your subordinates has violated a staff regulation by failing to inform you that he will be absent on a certain day.
   Of the following, the MOST appropriate action for you to take first is to

    A. discuss this matter with your immediate superior
    B. find out the reason for his failure to obey this staff regulation
    C. determine what disciplinary action other supervisors have taken in similar cases
    D. take no action if his absence did not interfere with the work of the unit; reprimand him if it did

    2.____

3. A newly appointed clerk is assigned to a unit of an agency at a time when the supervisor of the unit is very busy and has little time to devote to instructing the new employee in the work he is to perform.
   Of the following, the MOST appropriate method of training this employee is for the supervisor to

    A. instruct the new employee to observe several experienced clerks at work and question them regarding any aspect of the work he does not understand
    B. delegate the job of training this employee to an employee in the unit who is qualified to instruct him
    C. assign the new employee a simple task and inform him that more complex and varied duties will be given him when the supervisor is less busy
    D. have the employee spend his time reading the agency's annual reports and the laws, rules, and regulations governing its work

    3.____

4. As a supervisor, you may find it necessary to consult with your superior before taking action on some matters.
   Of the following, the action for which it is MOST important that you obtain the prior approval of your superior is one that involves

    4.____

A. assuming additional functions for your unit
B. rotating assignments among your staff members
C. initiating regular meetings of your staff
D. assigning certain members of your staff to work overtime on an emergency job

5. Suppose that a clerk who is employed in a unit under your supervision performs his work quickly but carelessly. He is about to be transferred to another unit in your department. The chief of this other unit asks you for your opinion of this employee's work habits.
Of the following, the MOST appropriate reply for you to make is to

   A. point out this employee's good qualities only since he may correct his bad qualities after his transfer is effected
   B. say nothing good or bad about this employee, thus permitting him to start his new assignment with a clean slate
   C. inform the unit chief that this clerk performed his work speedily but was careless
   D. emphasize this employee's good points and minimize his bad points

6. When subordinates request his advice in solving problems encountered in their work, a certain bureau chief occasionally answers the request by first asking the subordinate what he thinks should be done.
This action by the bureau chief is, on the whole,

   A. *desirable* because it stimulates subordinates to give more thought to the solution of problems encountered
   B. *undesirable* because it discourages subordinates from asking questions
   C. *desirable* because it discourages subordinates from asking questions
   D. *undesirable* because it undermines the confidence of subordinates in the ability of their supervisor

7. Of the following factors that may be considered by a unit head in dealing with the tardy subordinate, the one which should be given LEAST consideration is the

   A. frequency with which the employee is tardy
   B. effect of the employee's tardiness upon the work of other employees
   C. willingness of the employee to work overtime when necessary
   D. cause of the employee's tardiness

8. Of the following, the action that is likely to contribute MOST to the prestige of a supervisor is for him to

   A. expect all his subordinates to perform with equal efficiency any tasks assigned to them
   B. observe the same rules of conduct that he expects his subordinates to observe
   C. seek their advice on his personal problems and offer them his advice on their personal problems
   D. be always frank and outspoken to his subordinates in pointing out their faults

9. Although an employee under your supervision frequently protests when receiving a monotonous assignment, he nevertheless performs the assigned task efficiently. His protests, however, disturb the other employees and interfere with their work.
Of the following actions you may take in handling this employee, the MOST desirable one is for you to

A. point out to him the effect of his conduct on the staff's work and request his cooperation in accepting such assignments
B. arrange to issue such assignments to him when the other members of his staff are not present
C. inform him that you will request his transfer to another unit unless he puts a halt to his unjustifiable protests
D. ask other members of the staff to tell him that he is disturbing them by his protests

10. Assume that you are the supervisor of a small clerical unit which tabulates data prepared by another unit. One of your employees calls your attention to what appears to be an erroneous figure.
    Of the following, the MOST acceptable advice for you to give this employee is to tell him to

    A. omit the figure containing the apparent error and continue with the tabulation
    B. make whatever change in the erroneous figure that appears warranted and notify the supervisor of the unit which prepared the data that errors are being made by his staff
    C. accept the questionable figure as correct and continue with the tabulation since there is no certainty that an error has been made
    D. ask the supervisor of the unit that prepared the data to have the questionable figure checked for accuracy and corrected if it is erroneous

10.____

11. A clerk in an agency informs Mr. Brown, an applicant for a license issued by the agency, that the application filed by him was denied because he lacks a year and six months of required experience. Shortly after the applicant leaves the agency's office, the clerk realizes that Mr. Brown lacks only six months of required experience rather than a year and six months.
    Of the following, the MOST desirable procedure to be followed in connection with this matter is that

    A. a printed copy of the requirements should be sent to Mr. Brown
    B. a letter explaining and correcting the error should be sent to Mr. Brown
    C. no action should be taken because Mr. Brown is not qualified at the present time for the license
    D. a report of this matter should be prepared and attached to Mr. Brown's application for reference if Mr. Brown should file another application

11.____

12. Mr. Stone, who has been recently placed in charge of a clerical unit staffed with ten employees, plans to institute several radical changes in the procedures of his unit.
    Of the following actions he may take before adopting any of the revisions, the MOST desirable one is for Mr. Stone to

    A. distribute to each staff member a memorandum describing the revised procedures and requesting the staff's cooperation in giving the revised procedures a fair trial
    B. issue to each staff member a memorandum describing the proposed changes and inviting him to submit his written criticism of these proposed changes
    C. issue to each staff member a memorandum describing the proposed changes and notifying him of the time and date of a staff conference to be held on the merits of the proposed changes
    D. discuss the proposed changes with each staff member independently and obtain his opinion of the proposed changes

12.____

13. An assignment completed by Frank King is returned to him by his unit supervisor for certain changes. Frank King objects to making these changes.
    Of the following, the MOST appropriate action for the unit supervisor to take first is to

    A. permit Frank King to present his arguments against making these changes
    B. inform Frank King that he is free to take the matter up with a higher authority
    C. reprimand Frank King for objecting and assign another employee to make these changes
    D. state briefly that his decision is final and indicate by his manner that further discussion would be useless

14. A properly conducted job analysis will reveal the qualities essential for efficient job performance.
    Of the following, the MOST accurate implication of this statement is that job analysis

    A. enables the supervisor to standardize procedures
    B. aids the supervisor in fitting the man to the job
    C. is helpful to the supervisor in scheduling work
    D. assists the supervisor in estimating costs of jobs

15. All of us who are employed by a government agency are, figuratively speaking, living in glass houses.
    Of the following, this quotation MOST nearly means that employees of government agencies are

    A. basically secure in their positions
    B. more closely supervised than are those in private industry
    C. not free to exercise initiative
    D. subject to constant surveillance

16. So important to good supervision is effective leadership that some supervisors who are well equipped in this respect have compensated for deficiencies in other supervisory qualities.
    On the basis of this statement, the MOST accurate of the following statements is that

    A. supervisory ability is the most valuable attribute a leader can have
    B. effective leaders are generally deficient in other supervisory qualities
    C. other supervisory qualities may be substituted for leadership ability
    D. good leaders may make good supervisors even though lacking in other supervisory qualities

17. The improvement in skill and the development of proper attitudes are essential factors in the building of correct work habits.
    Of the following, the MOST valid implication of this statement for a supervisor is that

    A. the more skilled an employee is, the better will be his attitude toward his work
    B. developing proper attitudes in subordinates toward their work is more time-consuming for the supervisor than improving their skill
    C. the improvement of a worker's skill is only part of a supervisor's job
    D. correct work habits are established in order to either improve the skill of workers or develop in them a proper attitude toward their work

Questions 18-21.

DIRECTIONS: Questions 18 through 21 are based upon the situation described below. Consider the facts given in this situation when answering these questions.

SITUATION: You are the supervisor of a small unit in a large department. In order to assist your staff in handling a peak work load, ten temporary clerks have been hired for a period of two months.

18. Of the following actions you may take before assigning specific tasks to these temporary employees, the MOST appropriate action is for you to 18.____

   A. designate one of their number as your supervisory assistant
   B. find out what clerical experience and training each one has had
   C. ask each member of this group to indicate the type of work he prefers to do
   D. escort this group throughout the department, introducing each temporary employee to all the unit heads in the department

19. The ten temporary employees have been grouped into two teams of five employees each, and the two teams have been given different assignments. After working with his group for several days, an employee in one group asks to be transferred to the other group. 19.____
Of the following reasons for transferring this employee to the other group, the LEAST acceptable one is that

   A. there is a clash in temperament between him and some of the other members of his group
   B. he can perform the work assigned to the other group more efficiently than he can perform the work assigned to his group
   C. the work assigned to the other group is less monotonous than that assigned to his group
   D. the work assigned to his present group compels him to take frequent rest periods because of a physical disability

20. One of the temporary employees informs you that he has a suggestion for improving the method of performing the work assigned to his group. 20.____
Of the following actions, the MOST desirable one for you to take is to

   A. ignore his suggestion since he knows little about the purpose of the assignment
   B. ask him to try out the suggestion before submitting it to you
   C. have him discuss it with his co-workers before submitting it to you
   D. listen to his suggestion and take appropriate action

21. A temporary clerk who had been decreasing the amount of work he performed and who had also been attempting to induce other temporary clerks to reduce their production was twice cautioned by you to cease these practices. On each occasion, he promised to discontinue these improper practices and to perform his work conscientiously and cooperatively. Soon thereafter, he is detected for the third time attempting to persuade the other temporary clerks to shirk their duties. 21.____
Of the following, the MOST appropriate action for you to take is to

A. reprimand him for his improper conduct and have him transferred immediately to another unit
B. remind him that he may not be employed again as a temporary clerk if he continues his unethical practices
C. call a meeting of the temporary staff and warn them that anyone whose production falls below average will be discharged
D. report his improper practices to your immediate superior and recommend that this employee's services be terminated

22. As a supervisor in an agency, you receive a letter from the head of a civic organization requesting information which you are not permitted to divulge.
In preparing your letter of reply, it is MOST desirable that you

    A. begin with a pleasant phrase or statement and conclude with a brief statement denying the request
    B. limit your reply to a brief statement denying the request
    C. place the denial of the request between a pleasant opening phrase or statement and a cordial closing statement
    D. begin with a denial of the request and conclude with a pleasant closing statement

23. Of the following, it is LEAST essential for a supervisor, in assigning work to a subordinate, to issue written instructions when the

    A. supervisor will be on hand to check the work
    B. instructions are to be passed on to other employees
    C. assignment involves many details
    D. subordinate is to be held strictly accountable for the work performed

24. The suggestion is made that all the secretaries assigned to the bureau chiefs of a certain agency can be transferred to a newly established central transcribing unit which is to be staffed with stenographers and typists. Of the following, the MOST probable effect of reassigning these secretaries would be that

    A. the quality of the stenographic and typing work performed by the secretaries would deteriorate
    B. the bureau chiefs would be burdened with much of the routine work that is now performed by their secretaries
    C. typing and stenographic work would be performed less expeditiously and with frequent delays
    D. the development of understudies for bureau chiefs would be greatly hampered

25. In a large agency where both men and women are employed as clerks, certain duties may be assigned more appropriately to women than to men.
Of the following, the assignment that is generally MOST appropriate for a woman clerk is

    A. sorting and filing 3x5 index cards
    B. issuing supplies from the agency's stockroom to employees presenting requisitions
    C. serving at an information desk during the hours from 7:00 P.M. to 11:00 P.M. for a period of two months
    D. collecting outgoing mail from the various offices of the agency and delivering incoming mail to these offices

26. A unit supervisor discovers several errors in the work performed by a subordinate. 26.____
In dealing with this subordinate, it is LEAST desirable for the supervisor to

   A. give his criticism immediately rather than at a later date
   B. make it clear to the subordinate that he is criticizing the subordinate and not the subordinate's work
   C. praise, when possible, some commendable aspect of the subordinate's work before making the adverse criticism
   D. make sure that his criticism is not overheard by other employees

27. The status of the morale of a staff is usually a good indication of the quality of the leadership displayed by the supervisor of the staff. 27.____
Of the following, the BEST indication of the existence of high morale among a staff is that

   A. the employees are prompt in reporting for work
   B. the staff is always willing to subordinate personal desires to attain group objectives
   C. it is seldom necessary for the staff to work overtime
   D. the subordinates and their superior meet socially after working hours

28. The use of standard practices and procedures in large organizations is often essential in order to insure a smooth, efficient, and controlled flow of work. A strict adherence to standard practices and procedures to the extent that unnecessary delay is created is known, in general, as *red tape*. 28.____
On the basis of this statement, the MOST accurate of the following statements is that

   A. although the use of standard practices and procedures promotes efficiency, it also creates unnecessary delays and *red tape*
   B. in order to insure a smooth, efficient, and controlled plan of work, *red tape* should be eliminated by a strict adherence to standard practices and procedures
   C. *red tape* is a necessary evil which invariably creeps into any large organization which uses standard practices and procedures
   D. *red tape* exists when delay takes place as a result of a too rigid conformity with standard practices and procedures

29. The tasks of government are imposed not only by law but also by public opinion, which at any time may be made into law. Government agencies must, therefore, strive to anticipate and fulfill the needs of the public. 29.____
Of the following, the MOST valid implication of this statement is that the

   A. satisfaction of the needs of the public is one of the obligations of a government agency
   B. law prescribes what tasks government agencies should perform and public opinion determines how these tasks should be performed
   C. tasks imposed by law on a government agency have priority over those imposed by public opinion
   D. functions of a government agency should be carried out in accordance with the letter, rather than the spirit, of the law

30. The manner in which an employee performs on the job rather than his potential ability is the true test of his value to his employer. 30.____
The one of the following which is NOT an implication of the above statement is a(n)

A. employee of great potential ability may be of little or no value to his employer
B. supervisor should observe the manner in which his subordinates perform their work
C. employee's potential ability is of no significance in determining his fitness for a specific job
D. employee should attempt to perform his work to the best of his ability

31. No routine will automatically bring itself into proper relation with changing conditions. Of the following situations, the one which MOST NEARLY exemplifies the truth of this statement is a

    A. change in the rules governing the submission or reports by employees working in the field is found to be impractical and the previous procedure is reinstituted
    B. long established method of filing papers in a bureau is found to be inadequate because of changes in the functions of the bureau
    C. long established method of distributing orders to the staff is found to work effectively when the size of the staff is considerably increased
    D. change in the rules governing hours of attendance at work proves distasteful to many employees

32. Interest is essentially an attitude of continuing attentiveness, found where activity is satisfactorily self-expressive. Whenever work is so circumscribed that the chance for self-expression or development is denied, monotony is present.
    On the basis of this statement, it is MOST accurate to state that

    A. tasks which are repetitive in nature do not permit self-expression and, therefore, create monotony
    B. interest in one's work is increased by financial and non-financial incentives
    C. jobs which are monotonous can be made self-expressive by substituting satisfactory working conditions
    D. workers whose tasks afford them no opportunity for self-expression find such tasks to be monotonous

33. The first step in an organizational study is the reading of the basic documents. There is some documentary basis for any governmental organization, outlining the purposes for which it was established, conferring certain powers, and imposing certain limitations on the conferred powers. This statement indicates that in making an organization study, one should FIRST

    A. review all the authoritative material in the field of government administration and organization
    B. arrange the functions of the organization on a functional chart in accordance with the official documents
    C. study the laws and authorities under which the organization operates
    D. outline the purposes for which the organization study was originally established

34. His attitude is as provincial as an isolationist country's unwillingness to engage in any international trade whatever, on the ground that it will be required to buy something from outsiders which could possibly be produced by local talent, although not as well and not as cheaply. This statement is MOST descriptive of the attitude of the division chief in a government agency who

A. wishes to restrict promotions to supervisory positions in his division exclusively to employees in his division
B. refuses to delegate responsible tasks to subordinates qualified to perform these tasks
C. believes that informal on-the-job training of new staff members is superior to formal training methods
D. frequently makes personal issues out of matters that should be handled on an impersonal basis

35. A trainee was paid a weekly wage of $480.00 for a 40-hour work week. As a result of a new labor contract, he is paid $494.00 a week for a 38-hour work week with time-and-one-half pay for time worked in excess of 38 hours in any work week.
If he continues to work 40 hours weekly under the new contract, the amount by which his average hourly rate for a 40-hour work week under the new contract exceeds the hourly rate previously paid him lies between _____ and _____, inclusive.

    A. $1.02; $1.06   B. $1.08; $1.16   C. $1.18; $1.26   D. $1.28; $1.36

36. The problem of inadequate storage space arising from the large number of inactive records stored in city agencies can be solved MOST satisfactorily with the aid of _____ equipment.

    A. photostat   B. microfilm
    C. IBM sorting   D. digital printing

37. To say that an employee is *erudite* means MOST NEARLY that he is

    A. scholarly
    B. insecure
    C. efficient
    D. punctual

38. The forms design section of a city agency recommended that the sizes of forms used by the agency be limited to the sizes that can be cut with the least amount of waste from either 17" x 22" or 17" x 28" sheets.
Of the following, the size that does NOT comply with this recommendation is

    A. 4 1/2" x 5 1/2"   B. 3 3/4" x 4 1/4"
    C. 3 1/2" x 4 1/4"   D. 4 1/4" x 2 3/4"

39. The number of investigations conducted by an agency in 2007 was 3,600. In 2008, the number of investigations conducted was one-third more than in 2007. The number of investigations conducted in 2009 was three-fourths of the number conducted in 2008. It is anticipated that the number of investigations conducted in 2010 will be equal to the average of the three preceding years.
On the basis of this information, the MOST accurate of the following statements is that the number of investigations conducted in

    A. 2007 is larger than the number anticipated for 2010
    B. 2008 is smaller than the number anticipated for 2010
    C. 2009 is equal to the number conducted in 2007
    D. 2009 is larger than the number anticipated for 2010

40. *The office manager thought it advisable to MOLLIFY his subordinate.*
    The word *mollify* as used in this sentence means MOST NEARLY

    A. reprimand   B. caution   C. calm   D. question

41. *The bureau chief adopted a DILATORY policy.* The word *dilatory* as used in this sentence means MOST NEARLY

    A. tending to cause delay   B. acceptable to all affected
    C. severe but fair   D. prepared with great care

42. *He complained about the PAUCITY of requests.* The word *paucity* as used in this sentence means MOST NEARLY

    A. great variety   B. unreasonableness
    C. unexpected increase   D. scarcity

43. To say that an event is *imminent* means MOST NEARLY that it is

    A. near at hand   B. unpredictable
    C. favorable or happy   D. very significant

44. *The general manager delivered a LAUDATORY speech.*
    The word *laudatory* as used in this sentence means MOST NEARLY

    A. clear and emphatic   B. lengthy
    C. introductory   D. expressing praise

45. *We all knew of his AVERSION for performing statistical work.*
    The word *aversion* as used in this sentence means MOST NEARLY

    A. training   B. dislike
    C. incentive   D. lack of preparation

46. *The engineer was CIRCUMSPECT in making his recommendations.* The word *circumspect* as used in this sentence means MOST NEARLY

    A. hostile   B. outspoken   C. biased   D. cautious

47. To say that certain clerical operations were *obviated* means MOST NEARLY that these operations were

    A. extremely distasteful   B. easily understood
    C. made unnecessary   D. very complicated

48. *The interviewer was impressed with the client's DEMEANOR.* The word *demeanor* as used in this sentence means MOST NEARLY

    A. outward manner   B. plan of action
    C. fluent speech   D. extensive knowledge

49. To say that the information was *gratuitous* means MOST NEARLY that it was

    A. given freely   B. deeply appreciated
    C. brief   D. valuable

50. *The supervisor was unaware of this EXIGENCY.*
    The word *exigency* as used in this sentence means MOST NEARLY

    A. unexplained absence   B. costly delay
    C. pressing need   D. final action

51. *She considered the supervisor's action to be ARBITRARY.* The word *arbitrary* as used in this sentence means MOST NEARLY

    A. inconsistent   B. justifiable
    C. appeasing   D. dictatorial

52. *His report on the activities of the agency was VERBOSE.*
The word *verbose* as used in this sentence means MOST NEARLY

    A. vivid   B. wordy   C. vague   D. oral

Questions 53-61.

DIRECTIONS: Questions 53 through 61 are to be answered SOLELY on the basis of the following information.

Assume that the following rules for computing service ratings are to be used experimentally in determining the service ratings of seven permanent employees. (Note that these rules are hypothetical and are NOT to be confused with the existing method of computing service ratings for employees.) The personnel record of each of these seven employees is given in Table II. You are to determine the answer to each of the questions on the basis of the rules given below for computing service ratings and the data contained in the personnel records of these seven employees.

All computations should be made as of the close of the rating period ending March 31, 2007.

RULES FOR COMPUTING SERVICE RATINGS

Service Rating
The service rating of each permanent competitive class employee shall be computed by adding the following three scores: (1) a basic score, (2) the employee's seniority score, and (3) the employee's efficiency score.

Seniority Score
An employee's seniority score shall be computed by crediting him with 1/2% per year for each year of service starting with the date of the employee's entrance as a permanent employee into the competitive class, up to a maximum of 15 years (7 1/2%). A residual fractional period of eight months or more shall be considered as a full year and credited with 1/2%. A residual fraction of from four to, but not including, eight months shall be considered as a half-year and credited with 1/4%. A residual fraction of less than four months shall receive no credit in the seniority score. For example, a person who entered the competitive class as a permanent employee on August 1, 1999 would, as of March 31, 2002, be credited with a seniority score of 1 1/2% for his two years and 8 months of service.

Efficiency Score
An employee's efficiency score shall be computed by adding the annual efficiency ratings received by him during his service in his PRESENT position. (Where there are negative efficiency ratings, such ratings shall be subtracted from the sum of the positive efficiency ratings.) An employee's annual efficiency rating shall be based on the grade he receives from his supervisor for his work performance during the annual efficiency rating period.

Basic Score

A basic score of 70% shall be given to each employee upon permanent appointment to a competitive class position.

An employee shall receive a grade of "A" for performing work of the highest quality and shall be credited with an efficiency rating of plus (+) 3%, An employee shall receive a grade of "F" for performing work of the lowest quality and shall receive an efficiency rating of minus (-) 2%. Table I, entitled "Basis for Determining Annual Efficiency Ratings," lists the six grades of work performance with their equivalent annual efficiency ratings. Table I also lists the efficiency ratings to be assigned for service in a position for less than a year during the annual efficiency rating period. The annual efficiency rating period shall run from April 1 to March 31, inclusive.

TABLE I
BASIS FOE DETERMINING ANNUAL EFFICIENCY RATINGS

Quality of Work Performed	Grade Assigned A	Annual Efficiency Rating for Service in a Position for:		
		8 months to a full year	At least 4 months but less than 8 months	Less than 4 months
Highest Quality	A	+ 3%	+1½%	0%
Good Quality	B	+ 2%	+ 1%	0%
Standard Quality	C	+ 1%	+½%	0%
Substandard Quality	D	0%	0%	0%
Poor Quality	E	-1%	-½%	0%
Lowest Quality	F	-2%	-1%	0%

Appointment or Promotion during an Efficiency Rating Period

An employee who has been appointed or promoted during an efficiency rating period shall receive for that period an efficiency rating only for work performed by him during the portion of the period that he served in the position to which he was appointed or promoted. His efficiency rating for the period shall be determined in accordance with Table I.

Sample Computation of Service Rating

John Smith entered the competitive class as a permanent employee on December 1, 2002 and was promoted to his present position as a Clerk, Grade 3 on November 1, 2005. As a Clerk, Grade 3, he received a grade of "B" for work performed during the five-month period extending from November 1, 2005 to March 31, 2006 and a grade of "C" for work performed during the full annual period extending from April 1, 2006 to March 32, 2007.

On the basis of the Rules for Computing Service Ratings, John Smith should be credited with:

70 % basic score
2 1/4% seniority score - for 4 years and 4 months of service (from 12-1-02 to 3-31-07)
2 % efficiency score - for 5 months of "B" service and a full year of "C" service
74 1/4%

TABLE II
PERSONNEL RECORD OF SEVEN PERMANENT COMPETITIVE CLASS EMPLOYEES

Employee	Present Position	Date of Appointment or Promotion to Present Position	Date of Entry as Permanent Employee in Competitive Class
Allen	Clerk, Gr. 5	6-1-03	7-1-90
Brown	Clerk, Gr. 4	1-1-05	7-1-97
Cole	Clerk, Gr. 3	9-1-03	11-1-00
Fox	Clerk, Gr. 3	10-1-03	9-1-98
Green	Clerk, Gr. 2	12-1-01	12-1-01
Hunt	Clerk, Gr. 2	7-1-02	7-1-02
Kane	Steno, Gr. 3	11-16-04	3-1-01

Grades Received Annually for Work Performed in Present Position

Employee	4-1-01 to 3-31-02	4-1-02 to 3-31-03	4-1-03 to 3-31-04	4-1-04 to 3-31-05	4-1-05 to 3-31-06	4-1-06 to 3-31-07
Allen			C*	C	B	C
Brown				C*	C	B
Cole			A*	B	C	C
Fox			C*	C	D	C
Green	C*	D	C	D	C	C
Hunt		C*	C	E	C	C
Kane				B*	B	C

Explanatory Notes:
* Served in present position for less than a full year during this rating period. (Note date of appointment, or promotion, to present period.)

All seven employees have served continuously as permanent employees since their entry into the competitive class.

Questions 53 through 61 refer to the employees listed in Table II. You are to answer these questions SOLELY on the basis of the preceding Rules for Computing Service Ratings and on the information concerning these seven employees given in Table II. You are reminded that all computations are to be made as of the close of the rating period ending March 31, 2007. Candidates may find it helpful to arrange their computations on their scratch paper in an orderly manner since the computations for one question may also be utilized in answering another question.

53. The seniority score of Allen is

    A. 74%   B. 8 1/2%   C. 8%   D. 8 1/4%

54. The seniority score of Fox exceeds that of Cole by

    A. 1 1/2%   B. 2%   C. 1%   D. 3/4 1/4

55. The seniority score of Brown is

    A. equal to Hunt's
    B. twice Hunt's
    C. more than Hunt's by 1 1/2%
    D. less than Hunt's by 1/2%

56. Green's efficiency score is

    A. twice that of Kane
    B. equal to that of Kane
    C. less than Kane's by 1/2%
    D. less than Kane's by 1%

57. Of the following employees, the one who has the LOWEST efficiency score is

    A. Brown   B. Fox   C. Hunt   D. Kane

58. A comparison of Hunt's efficiency score with his seniority score reveals that his efficiency score is

    A. less than his seniority score by 1/2%
    B. less than his seniority score by 3/4%
    C. equal to his seniority score
    D. greater than his seniority score by 1/2%

59. Fox's service rating is

    A. 72 1/2%   B. 74%   C. 76 1/2%   D. 76 3/4%

60. Brown's service rating is

    A. less than 78%
    B. 78%
    C. 78 1/4%
    D. more than 78 1/4%

61. Cole's service rating exceeds Kane's by

    A. less than 2%
    B. 2%
    C. 2 1/4%
    D. more than 2 1/4%

Questions 62-71.

DIRECTIONS: Each of the sentences numbered 62 to 71 may be classified under one of the following four options:
  (A) faulty; contains an error in grammar only
  (B) faulty; contains an error in spelling only
  (C) faulty; contains an error in grammar and an error in spelling
  (D) correct; contains no error in grammar or in spelling

Examine each sentence carefully to determine under which of the above four options it is best classified. Then, in the correspondingly numbered space at the right, write the letter preceding the option which is the BEST of the four listed above.

62. A recognized principle of good management is that an assignment should be given to whomever is best qualified to carry it out. 62._____

63. He considered it a privilege to be allowed to review and summarize the technical reports issued annually by your agency. 63._____

64. Because the warehouse was in an inaccessable location, deliveries of electric fixtures from the warehouse were made only in large lots. 64._____

65. Having requisitioned the office supplies, Miss Brown returned to her desk and resumed the computation of petty cash disbursements. 65._____

66. One of the advantages of this chemical solution is that records treated with it are not inflammable. 66._____

67. The complaint of this employee, in addition to the complaints of the other employees, were submitted to the grievance committee. 67._____

68. A study of the duties and responsibilities of each of the various categories of employees was conducted by an unprejudiced classification analyst. 68._____

69. Ties of friendship with this subordinate compels him to withold the censure that the subordinate deserves. 69._____

70. Neither of the agencies are affected by the decision to institute a program for rehabilitating physically handicaped men and women. 70._____

71. The chairman stated that the argument between you and he was creating an intolerable situation. 71._____

Questions 72-75.

DIRECTIONS: Each of Questions 72 through 75 consists of a statement containing five words in capital letters. One of these capitalized words is not in keeping with the meaning which the statement is evidently intended to convey. The five words in capital letters in each statement are reprinted after the statement. In the correspondingly numbered space at the right, write the letter preceding the one of the five words which does MOST to spoil the true meaning of the statement.

72. The alert employee will find, EVEN in the best managed offices, violations of some of the rules of good office management. However, further study will reveal that the correction of such violations is by ALL means a SIMPLE matter, BUT requires research, time, patience, and often a high degree of MANAGERIAL ability. 72._____

   A. Even   B. All   C. Simple   D. But   E. Managerial

73. The information clerk in any organization must DELEGATE tact, courtesy, and good judgment in DEALING with callers, many of whom, on the other hand, DISREGARD business ETIQUETTE in their CONTACT with the information clerk. 73._____

   A. Delegate   B. Dealing   C. Disregard
   D. Etiquette   E. Contact

74. When the supervisor gives advancement or other rewards only to SUBORDINATES who have REQUESTED them, or shows a sincere INTEREST in the welfare of his staff, he is building FAVORABLE ATTITUDES.

    A. Subordinates   B. Requested   C. Interest
    D. Favorable   E. Attitudes

75. An appointee to the City's civil service must be a bona fide resident of the City for at least three years immediately prior to his APPOINTMENT. An appointee who served in the Armed Forces retains as his legal address that place where he resided prior to his ENTRY into the MILITARY service, PROVIDED he has taken definite action to establish a new RESIDENCE.

    A. Appointment   B. Entry   C. Military
    D. Provided   E. Residence

KEY (CORRECT ANSWERS)

1. D	16. D	31. B	46. D	61. A
2. B	17. C	32. D	47. C	62. A
3. B	18. B	33. C	48. A	63. D
4. A	19. C	34. A	49. A	64. B
5. C	20. D	35. D	50. C	65. D
6. A	21. D	36. B	51. D	66. B
7. C	22. C	37. A	52. B	67. A
8. B	23. A	38. B	53. A	68. D
9. A	24. B	39. C	54. C	69. C
10. D	25. A	40. C	55. B	70. C
11. B	26. B	41. A	56. C	71. A
12. C	27. B	42. D	57. B	72. B
13. A	28. D	43. A	58. D	73. A
14. B	29. A	44. D	59. D	74. B
15. D	30. C	45. B	60. B	75. D

EXAMINATION SECTION
TEST 1

DIRECTIONS: Each question or incomplete statement is followed by several suggested answers or completions. Select the one that BEST answers the question or completes the statement. *PRINT THE LETTER OF THE CORRECT ANSWER IN THE SPACE AT THE RIGHT.*

1. From time to time, your subordinates are assigned to other units to do reception work and other duties. You receive a note from Mr. Jones, the head of one of these other units, stating that the work of Miss Smith, one of your subordinates, was unsatisfactory when she worked for him, and asking you not to assign her to him again. Although Miss Smith has worked in your unit for a long time, this is the first time that anyone has complained about her work.
   The one of the following actions that you should take FIRST in this situation is to ask
   A. the heads of the other units for whom Miss Smith has worked whether or not her work has been satisfactory
   B. Mr. Jones in what way Miss Smith's work has been unsatisfactory
   C. Miss Smith to explain in what way her work for Mr. Jones was unsatisfactory
   D. Mr. Jones which of your subordinates he would prefer to have assigned to him

1.____

2. Suppose that you are the supervisor of a small unit in a city agency. You have given one of your subordinates, Mr. Smith, an assignment which must be completed by the end of the day. Because he is unfamiliar with the assignment, Mr. Smith will be unable to complete it on time. Your other subordinates are too busy to help Mr. Smith, but you have the time to help him complete the assignment.
   For you to help Mr. Smith complete the assignment would be
   A. *desirable*; because a supervisor is expected to be familiar with his subordinates' work
   B. *undesirable*; because Mr. Smith will come to depend on you to help him do his work
   C. *desirable*; because Mr. Smith is likely to appreciate your help and give you his cooperation when you need it
   D. *undesirable*; because a supervisor should not perform the same type of work as his subordinates do

2.____

3. For a supervisor to listen to the personal problems which his subordinates bring to him is GENERALLY
   A. *desirable*; it is likely that the supervisor has broader experience in solving personal problems than do his subordinates
   B. *undesirable*; the supervisor may be unable to solve such problems

3.____

C. *desirable*; the supervisor can better understand his subordinates' behavior on the job
D. *undesirable*; permitting a subordinate to talk about his personal problems may only make them seem worse

4. A generally accepted concept of management is that the authority given to a person should be commensurate with his
   A. responsibility
   B. ability
   C. seniority
   D. dependability

4._____

5. It has been said that the best supervisor is the one who gives the fewest orders. The one of the following supervisor practices that would be MOT likely to increase the number of orders that a supervisor must give to get out the work is to
   A. set general goals for his subordinates and give them the authority for reaching the goals
   B. train subordinates to make decisions for themselves
   C. establish routines for his subordinates' jobs
   D. introduce frequent changes in the work methods his subordinates are using

5._____

6. The one of the following supervisory practices that would be MOST likely to give subordinates a feeling of satisfaction in their work is to
   A. establish work goals that take a long time to achieve
   B. show the subordinates how their work goals are related to the goals of the agency
   C. set work goals higher than the subordinates can achieve
   D. refrain from telling the subordinates that they are failing to meet their work goals

6._____

7. You are about to design a system for measuring the quantity of work produced by your subordinates.
   The one of the following which is the FIRST step that you should take in designing this system is to
   A. establish the units of work measurement to be used in the system
   B. determine the actual advantages and disadvantages of the system
   C. determine the abilities of each of your subordinates
   D. ascertain the types of work done in the unit

7._____

8. One of your subordinates tells you that he is dissatisfied with his work assignment and that he wishes to discuss the matter with you.   The employee is obviously very angry and upset.
   Of the following, the course of action that you should take FIRST in this situation is to
   A. postpone discussion of the employee's complaint, explaining to him that the matter can be settled more satisfactorily if it is discussed calmly
   B. have the employee describe his complaint, correcting him whenever he makes what seems to be an erroneous charge against you

8._____

C. permit the employee to present his complaint in full, withholding your comments until he has finished describing his complaint
D. promise the employee that you will review all the work assignments in the unit to determine whether or not any changes should be made

9. Assume that you are the supervisor of a unit in a city agency. One of your subordinates has violated an important rule of the agency. For such a violation, you are required to impose discipline in the form of a reprimand given in private.
Of the following, the MOST important reason for disciplining the employee for violating the rule is to
   A. obtain his compliance with the rule
   B. punish him for his action in an impartial manner
   C. establish your authority to administer discipline
   D. impress upon all the employees in the unit the need for observing the rule

10. You are the newly appointed supervisor of a small unit in a city agency. One of your subordinates, Mr. Smith, a competent employee, has resented your appointment as his supervisor and has not been as cooperative toward you as you have wanted him to be. One day, Mr. Smith fails to observe an important rule of the agency. You are required to reprimand any employee who fails to observe the rule.
The one of the following courses of action you should take in this situation is to
   A. attempt to overcome Mr. Smith's resentment by explaining to him that although you should reprimand him, you will not do so
   B. reprimand Mr. Smith after pointing out to him that he failed to observe the rule
   C. tell Mr. Smith that if he becomes more cooperative, you will overlook his failure to observe the rule
   D. tell Mr. Smith that although you did not originate the rule, nevertheless you are required to reprimand him

11. Suppose that a clerk who has injured himself on the job because of his carelessness informs his supervisor of the accident. The supervisor has been newly appointed to his job and is anxious to keep accidents at a minimum. The action taken by the supervisor is to criticize the subordinate for his carelessness and to tell him that he is holding him responsible for the accident.
Of the following, it would be MOST reasonable to conclude that, as a result of the supervisor's action, his subordinates may
   A. tend to withhold information from him about future accidents
   B. be critical of him, in turn, if he himself is injured on the job
   C. expect him to supervise them more closely in the future
   D. attempt to correct hazardous job conditions without his knowledge

12. The one of the following which is GENERALLY the basic reason for using standard procedures in an agency is to
   A. provide sequences of steps for handling recurring activities
   B. facilitate periodic review of standard practices

C. train new employees in the agency's policies and objectives
D. serve as a basis for formulating agency policies

13. Assume that the operations of a certain unit in an agency enable the supervisor to allow each of his subordinates wide discretion in selecting the kind and amount of work he chooses to do. However, in evaluating the work of his subordinates, the supervisor places more emphasis on some area of work than on others. Factors such as number of applications processed and number of letters written are given great weight in evaluation, while factors such as number of papers filed and number of forms checked are given little weight. Hence, a subordinate who processes a large number of applications would receive a high evaluation even if he checked very few forms.
The supervisor's method of evaluation would MOST likely result in a(n)
   A. increase in the amount of time spent on processing each application
   B. backlog of papers waiting to be filed
   C. improvement in the quality of letters written
   D. decline in output in all areas of work

14. Some management authorities propose that work assignments be made by assigning a varied set of tasks to a group of employees and then allowing the group to decide for itself how to organize the work to be done. This method of assigning work is called *job enlargement*.
The one of the following which is considered to be the CHIEF advantage of job enlargement is that it
   A. encourages employees to specialize in the work they are assigned to do
   B. reduces the amount of control that employees have over their work
   C. increases the employees' job satisfaction
   D. reduces the number of skills that each employee is required to learn

15. In conducting a meeting to pass along information to his subordinates, a supervisor may talk to his subordinates without giving them the opportunity to interrupt him. This method is called one-way communication. On the other hand, the supervisor may talk to his subordinates and give them the opportunity to ask questions or make comments while he is speaking. This method is called two-way communication.
It would be MORE desirable for the supervisor to use two-way communication rather than one-way communication at a meeting when his primary purpose is to
   A. avoid, during the meeting, open criticism of any mistakes he may make
   B. conduct the meeting in an orderly fashion
   C. pass along information quickly
   D. transmit information which must be clearly understood

16. Assume that you are the leader of a training conference on supervisory techniques and problems. One of the participants in the conference proposes what you consider to be an unsatisfactory technique for handling the problem under discussion.

The one of the following courses of action which you should take in this situation is to
- A. explain to the participants why the proposed technique is unsatisfactory
- B. stimulate the other participants to discuss the appropriateness of the proposed technique
- C. proceed immediately to another problem without discussing the proposed technique
- D. end further discussion of the problem but explain to the participant in private, after the conference is over, why he proposed technique is unsatisfactory

17. In measuring the work of his subordinates, the supervisor of a unit performing routine filing began by observing his subordinates at work. If a subordinate seemed to be busy, then the supervisor concluded that the subordinate was producing a great deal of work. On the other hand, the supervisor concluded that a subordinate was not producing much work if he did not seem to be busy. The supervisor's work measurement method was faulted CHIEFLY because
    - A. it did not use a standard against which a subordinate's work could be measured
    - B. the type of work performed by his subordinates did not lend itself to accurate measurement
    - C. his subordinates may not have worked at their normal rates if they were aware that their work was being observed
    - D. the supervisor may not have observed a subordinate's work for a long enough period of time

17.____

18. Assume that a system of statistical reports designed to provide information about employee work performance is put into effect in a unit of a city agency. There is some evidence that the employees of this unit are working below their capacities. The information obtained from the system is to be used by management to improve employee work and performance and to evaluate such performance. The employees whose work is to be recorded by the reports resent them. Nevertheless, the employees' work performance improves substantially after the reporting system is put into effect, and before management has put the information to use.
The one of the following which is the MOST accurate conclusion to be drawn from this situation is that
    - A. a statistical reporting system may fail to provide the information it is designed to provide
    - B. low employee morale may have been the cause of the employees' former level of work performance
    - C. a statistical reporting system designed only to provide information about problems may also help to solve the problems
    - D. willing employee cooperation is essential to the success of a system of statistical reports

18.____

19. In setting the work standard for a certain task, a unit supervisor took the total output of all the employees in the unit and divided it by the number of employees. He thus established the average output as the work standard for the task.
The method that the supervisor used to establish the work standard is GENERALLY considered to be
    A. *proper,* since the method takes into account the output of the outstanding, as well as of the less productive, employees
    B. *improper,* since the average output may not be what could reasonably be expected of a competent, satisfactory employee
    C. *proper,* since the standard is based on the actual output of the employees who are to be evaluated
    D. *improper,* since all the employees in the unit may be successful in meeting the work standard

19.____

20. There are disadvantages as well as advantages in using statistical controls to measure specific aspects of subordinates' jobs.
The one of the following which can LEAST be considered to be an advantage of statistical controls to a supervisor is that such controls may
    A. reduce the need for close, detailed supervision
    B. give the supervisor information that he needs for making decisions
    C. stimulate subordinates whose work is measured by statistical controls to improve their performance
    D. encourage subordinates to emphasize aspects being measured rather than their jobs as a whole

20.____

21. Mr. Stone, who has been recently placed in charge of a clerical unit staffed with ten employees, plans to institute several radical changes in the procedures of his unit.
Of the following actions he may take before adopting any of the revisions, the MOST desirable one is for Mr. Stone to
    A. distribute to each staff member a memorandum describing the revised procedures and requesting the staff's cooperation in giving the revised procedures a fair trial
    B. issue to each staff member a memorandum describing the proposed changes and inviting him to submit his written criticism of these proposed changes
    C. issue to each staff member a memorandum describing the proposed changes and notifying him of the time and date of a staff conference to be held on the merits
    D. of the proposed changes discuss the proposed changes with each staff member independently and obtain his opinion of the proposed changes

21.____

22. An assignment completed by Frank King is returned to him by his unit supervisor for certain changes. Frank King objects to making these changes.
Of the following, the MOST appropriate action for the unit supervisor to take FIRST is to
    A. permit Frank King to present his arguments against making these changes

22.____

7 (#1)

    B. inform Frank King that he is free to take the matter up with a higher authority
    C. reprimand Frank King for objecting and assign another employee to make these changes
    D. state briefly that his decision is final and indicate by his manner that further discussion would be useless

23. Of the following, it is LEAST essential for a supervisor, in assigning work to a subordinate, to issue written instructions when the
    A. supervisor will be on hand to check the work
    B. instructions are to be passed on to other employees
    C. assignment involves many details
    D. subordinate is to be held strictly accountable for the work performed

23.____

24. Assume that you have been placed in charge of a unit where the quality of the work performed is poor. You plan to discuss the matter of improving the quality of the wok at a staff meeting of the unit.
Of the following courses of action which you might take at this meeting, the BEST one is to
    A. describe a few cases of exceptionally poor work performance; then have the employees performing this work explain why their work was done poorly
    B. inform the staff that you will be criticized by your own superior if the quality of the unit's work does not improve; then discuss, in general terms, the problem of improving the quality of the work
    C. discuss the problem of improving the quality of the unit's work; then call upon each employee by name for his suggestions for improving the work he performs
    D. present the problem to the staff; then indicate and discuss specific methods for improving the quality of the work

24.____

25. Suppose that certain office responsibilities require you to be frequently absent from the unit you supervise. You have, therefore, decided to designate one of your staff members to act as unit head in your absence.
Of the following factors, the one which is MOST important in selecting the employee best fitted for this assignment is his
    A. manner and personal appearance
    B. estimated ability to perform work of a supervisory nature
    C. ability to perform his present duties
    D. relative seniority in the service

25.____

KEY (CORRECT ANSWERS)

1.	B	11.	A
2.	C	12.	A
3.	C	13.	B
4.	A	14.	C
5.	D	15.	D
6.	B	16.	B
7.	D	17.	A
8.	C	18.	C
9.	A	19.	B
10.	B	20.	D

21.	C
22.	A
23.	A
24.	D
25.	B

TEST 2

DIRECTIONS: Each question or incomplete statement is followed by several suggested answers or completions. Select the one that BEST answers the question or completes the statement. *PRINT THE LETTER OF THE CORRECT ANSWER IN THE SPACE AT THE RIGHT.*

1. Assume that your supervisor has placed you in complete charge of an important project and that several clerks have been assigned to assist you. You have been given authority to establish any new procedures or revise existing procedures in order to complete the project as soon as possible. Just before you begin work on the project, one of the clerks suggests a change in the procedure which you realize at once would result in completion of the project in about half the time you expected to spend on it.
   Of the following, the MOST effective course of action for you to take is to
   A. adopt the suggestion immediately to expedite the completion of the project
   B. discuss the suggestion with your superior to obtain his consent to the change
   C. point out to the clerk that an adequate procedure has already been established, but that his suggestion may be used in future projects of this type
   D. encourage the other clerks to make further suggestions

2. A supervisor of a unit may safely delegate certain of his functions to his subordinates.
   Of the following, the function which can MOST safely be delegated is the
   A. settlement of employee grievances
   B. planning and scheduling of the production of the unit
   C. improvement of production methods of the unit
   D. maintenance of records of the work output of the unit

3. Some organizations now question the effectiveness of extreme job specialization. It is felt that in some instances it may be more advantageous to enlarge the scope of individual jobs, thus providing the employee with a greater variety of tasks.
   Of the following, the one which is LEAST likely to be a result of enlarging the scope of jobs is a(n)
   A. increase in the employee's job responsibilities
   B. decrease in the number of job titles in the organization
   C. increase in the number of tasks performed by an employee
   D. decrease in employee flexibility

4. A manual that is essentially designed to present detailed procedures and policies is not necessarily a good training medium, nor is a manual designed for high-level administrators likely to be satisfactory for use at lower levels.
   The MOST valid implication of this quotation is that
   A. a manual, to be effective, should be flexible enough to apply to any working level in an organization

B. the uses to which a manual will be put and the people who will use it should be carefully determined before it is prepared
C. the more detailed procedures a manual contains, the more effective it will be for the use of administrators
D. the degree of difficulty encountered in the preparation of a manual varies with the purpose for which it is designed and the people for whom it is written

5. In assigning a complicated task to a group of subordinates, Mr. Jones, a unit supervisor, neither indicates the specific steps to be followed in performing the assignment nor designates the subordinate to be responsible for seeing that the task is done on time.
This supervisor's method of assigning the task is MOST likely to result in
   A. the loss of skills previously acquired by his subordinates
   B. assumption of authority by the most capable subordinates
   C. friction and misunderstanding among subordinates with consequent delays in work
   D. greater individual effort and self-reliance on the part of his subordinates

6. Assume that the head of your agency has appointed you to a committee that has been assigned the task of reviewing the clerical procedures used in a large bureau of the agency and of recommending appropriate changes in the procedures where necessary.
Of the following, the FIRST step that should be taken by the committee in carrying out its assignment is to
   A. survey the most efficient procedures used in comparable agencies
   B. study the organization of the bureau and the work it is required to do
   C. evaluate the possible effects of proposed revisions in the procedures
   D. determine the effectiveness of existing procedures

7. A recently developed practice in administration favors reducing the number of levels of authority in an organization, increasing the number of subordinates reporting to a superior, and also increasing the authority delegated to the subordinates.
This practice would MOST likely result in a(n)
   A. increase in the span of control exercised by superiors
   B. increase in detailed information that flows to a superior from each subordinate
   C. decrease in the responsibility exercised by the subordinates
   D. decrease in the number of functions performed by the subordinates

8. As an organization grows larger, the amount of personal contact between the top administrative officials and the rank and file employees diminishes. Consequently, management comes to rely more heavily upon written reports and records for securing information and exercising control.
The MOST valid implication of this quotation is that, as an organization grows larger,
   A. evaluation of the work of rank and file employees becomes more objective because of greater reliance upon written reports and records

B. relations between first-line supervisors and their subordinates grow more impersonal
C. top administrative officials depend upon less direct methods for controlling the work of their subordinates
D. it becomes more difficult for top administrative officials to maintain high morale among rank and file employees

9. A supervisor whose unit has a good production record is usually found to be more occupied with the functions associated with leadership than with the performance of the same functions as his subordinates.
The MOST valid implication of this quotation is that
   A. a supervisor whose unit has a good production record usually is not as competent in performing routine tasks as are his subordinates
   B. ability to lead and competence in performing the day-to-day tasks of his subordinates are the requirements of a successful supervisor
   C. a supervisor who spends more time on planning and organizing the work of his unit than on performing the routine tasks of his subordinates will find that a his unit's production record will be good
   D. a supervisor whose unit has a good production record usually places less emphasis on performing the day-to-day tasks of his subordinates than on planning the work of his unit

10. To delegate work is one of the main functions of the supervisor. In delegating work, the supervisor should remember that even though an assignment is delegated to a subordinate, the supervisor ultimately is responsible for seeing that the work is done.
The MOST valid implication of this quotation for a supervisor is that he should
   A. delegate as few difficult tasks as possible so as to minimize the consequences of inadequate performance by his subordinates
   B. delegate to his subordinates those tasks which he considers difficult or time-consuming
   C. check the progress of delegated assignments periodically to make certain that the work is being done properly
   D. assign work to a subordinate without holding him directly accountable for carrying it out

11. A supervisor should select and develop an understudy to take charge of the unit in the supervisor's absence and to assist the supervisor whenever necessary.
Of the following, the technique that would be LEAST effective in developing an understudy is for the supervisor to
   A. permit him to exercise complete supervision over certain parts of the work
   B. assign him to work in which there is little likelihood of his making mistakes, so as to increase his self-confidence
   C. accustom him to making reports on the progress of work he is supervising
   D. give him responsibility gradually so that he will have time to absorb each new responsibility

12. A procedure manual of an agency is potentially more usable than are files of individual messages or bulletins, but usability and usefulness are not routine by-products of the manual form.
The MOST valid implication of this is that
   A. the purpose of a manual should not be confined to an explanation of routine procedures
   B. a manual may prove to be unsuitable for some of its anticipated uses
   C. individual messages or bulletins are more likely to be of use than are manuals
   D. a manual suffers from certain limitations that are not found in individual messages or bulletins

12.____

13. As the supervisor of a unit in an agency, you have just been instructed to put into effect a new procedure which you know will be disliked by your subordinates.
Of the following, the MOST important reason for calling a meeting of your staff before putting the new procedure into effect is to
   A. help you to determine which workers will be reluctant to cooperate in carrying out the new procedure
   B. allow you to announce that the new procedure must be put into effect despite any objections which might be raised
   C. enable you to explain that you don't approve of the new procedure and to give the reasons why it must nevertheless be put into effect
   D. permit you to discuss the purpose of the new procedure and to present the reasons for its adoption

13.____

14. Assume that you are a training conference leader and that you have just begun a series of conferences on supervisory techniques for new supervisors. Each conference is scheduled to last for three hours. A thorough discussion of all the material planned for the first session, which you had estimated would last until 4 P.M., is completed by 3:30 P.M.
For you to summarize the points that have been made and close the meeting would be
   A. *advisable*; the participants will lose interest in the conference if it is permitted to continue merely to occupy the remaining time
   B. *inadvisable*; the participants should be asked if there are any other topics that they would like to discuss
   C. *advisable*; the participants in a training conference should not be kept from their regular work for long periods of time
   D. *inadvisable*; material scheduled for discussion at future sessions should be used for the remainder of this session

14.____

15. In any agency, the top administrative officials are concerned largely with the work of overall creative planning with respect to the anticipated progress of the agency. The first-line supervisors, on the other hand, are concerned largely with the control of current action for the execution of current jobs.
On the basis of this quotation, a first-line supervisor would be CHIEFLY responsible for

15.____

A. increasing or decreasing the responsibilities of his unit to reflect changes in the policies of the agency
B. modifying the work assignments of his present staff to handle a seasonal variation in the activities of the unit
C. revising the procedure that is used for transmitting instructions from the head of the agency to the unit heads
D. raising and lowering the production goals of his unit as often as necessary to adjust them to the abilities of his subordinates

16. The control of clerical work in an agency appears impossible if the clerical work is regarded merely as a series of duties unrelated to the functions of the agency. However, this control becomes feasible when it is realized that clerical work links and coordinates the functions of the agency.
On the basis of this quotation, the MOST accurate of the following statements is that the
    A. complexity of clerical work may not be fully understood by those assigned to control it
    B. clerical work can be readily controlled if it is coordinated by other work of the agency
    C. number of clerical tasks may be reduced by regarding coordination as the function of clerical work
    D. purposes of clerical work must be understood to make possible its proper control

17. Assume that as supervisor of a unit you are to prepare a vacation schedule for the employees in your unit.
Of the following, the factor which is LEAST important for you to consider in setting up this schedule is
    A. the vacation preferences of each employee in the unit
    B. the anticipated workload in the unit during the vacation period
    C. how well each employee has performed his work
    D. how essential a specific employee's services will be during the vacation period

18. In order to promote efficiency and economy in an agency, it is advisable for the management systematize and standardize procedures and relationships insofar as this can be done; however, excessive routinizing which does not permit individual contributions or achievements should be avoided.
On the basis of this quotation, it is MOST accurate to state that
    A. systematized procedures should be designed mainly to encourage individual achievements
    B. standardized procedures should allow for individual accomplishments
    C. systematization of procedures may not be possible in organizations which have a large variety of functions
    D. individual employees of an organization must fully accept standardized procedures if the procedures are to be effective

16.____

17.____

18.____

19. Trained employees work most efficiently and with a minimum expenditure of time and energy. Suitable equipment and definite, well-developed procedures are effective only when employees know how to use the equipment and procedures.
This quotation means MOST NEARLY that
   A. employees can be trained most efficiently when suitable equipment and definite procedures are used
   B. training of employees is a costly but worthwhile investment
   C. suitable equipment and definite procedures are of greatest value when employees have been properly traced to use them
   D. the cost of suitable equipment and definite procedures is negligible when the saving in time and energy that they bring is considered

19.____

20. Assume that your supervisor has asked you to present to him comprehensive, periodic reports on the progress that your unit is making in meeting its work goals.
For you to give your superior oral reports rather than written ones is
   A. *desirable*; it will be easier for him to transmit your oral reports to his superiors
   B. *undesirable*; the oral reports will provide no permanent record to which he may refer
   C. *undesirable*; there will be less opportunity for you to discuss the oral reports with him than the written ones
   D. *desirable*; the oral reports will require little time and effort to prepare

20.____

21. Assume that an employee under your supervision complains to you that your evaluation of his work is too low.
The MOST appropriate action for you to take FIRST is to
   A. explain how you arrived at the evaluation of his work
   B. encourage him to improve the quality of his work by pointing out specifically how he can do so
   C. suggest that he appeal to an impartial higher authority if he disagrees with your evaluation
   D. point out to him specific instances in which his work has been unsatisfactory

21.____

22. The nature of the experience and education that are made a prerequisite to employment determines in large degree the training job to be done after employment begins.
On the basis of this quotation, it is MOST accurate to state that
   A. the more comprehensive the experience and education required for employment, the more extensive the training that is usually given after appointment
   B. the training that is given to employees depends upon the experience and education required of them before appointment
   C. employees who possess the experience and education required for employment should need little additional training after appointment
   D. the nature of the work that employees are expected to perform determines the training that they will need

22.____

23. Assume that you are preparing a report evaluating the work of a clerk who was transferred to your unit from another unit in the agency about a year ago.
Of the following, the method that would probably be MOST helpful to you in making this evaluation is to
    A. consult the evaluations this employee received from his former supervisors
    B. observe this employee at his work for a week shortly before you prepare the report
    C. examine the employee's production records and compare them with the standards set for the position
    D. obtain tactfully from his fellow employees their frank opinions of his work

23.____

24. Of the following, the CHIEF value of a flow of work chart to the management of an organization is its usefulness in
    A. locating the causes of delay in carrying out an operation
    B. training new employees in the performance of their duties
    C. determining the effectiveness of the employees in the organization
    D. determining the accuracy of its organization chart

24.____

25. Assume that a procedure for handling certain office forms has just been extensively revised. As supervisor of a small unit, you are to instruct your subordinates in the use of the new procedure, which is rather complicated.
Of the following, it would be LEAST helpful to your subordinates for you to
    A. compare the revised procedure with the one it has replaced
    B. state that you believe the revised procedure to be better than the one it has replaced
    C. tell them that they will probably find it difficult to learn the new procedure
    D. give only a general outline of the revised procedure at first and then follow with more detailed instructions

25.____

KEY (CORRECT ANSWERS)

1.	A		11.	B
2.	D		12.	B
3.	D		13.	D
4.	B		14.	A
5.	C		15.	B
6.	B		16.	B
7.	A		17.	C
8.	C		18.	B
9.	D		19.	C
10.	C		20.	B

21. A
22. B
23. C
24. A
25. C

TEST 3

DIRECTIONS: Each question or incomplete statement is followed by several suggested answers or completions. Select the one that BEST answers the question or completes the statement. *PRINT THE LETTER OF THE CORRECT ANSWER IN THE SPACE AT THE RIGHT.*

1. A methods improvement program might be called a war against habit. The MOST accurate implication of this statement is that
    A. routine handling of routine office assignments should be discouraged
    B. standardization of office procedures may encourage employees to form inefficient work habits
    C. employees tend to continue the use of existing procedures, even when such procedures are inefficient
    D. procedures should be changed consistently to prevent them from becoming habits

    1.____

2. An office supervisor may give either a written or an oral order to his subordinates when making an assignment.
    Of the following, it would be MOST appropriate for a supervisor to issue an order in writing when
    A. a large number of two-page reports must be stapled together before the end of the day
    B. the assignment is to be completed within two hours after it is issued to his subordinates
    C. his subordinates have completed an identical assignment the day before
    D. several entries must be made on a form at varying intervals of time by different clerks

    2.____

3. A supervisor should always remember that the instruction or training of new employees is most effective if it is given when and where it is needed.
    On the basis of this quotation, it is MOST appropriate to conclude that
    A. the new employee should be trained to handle any aspect of his work at the time he starts his job
    B. the new employee should be given the training essential to get him started and additional training when he requires it
    C. an employee who has received excessive training will be just as ineffective as one who has received inadequate training
    D. a new employee is trained most effectively by his own supervisor

    3.____

4. A supervisor may make assignments to his subordinates in the form of a command, a request, or a call for volunteers.
    It is LEAST desirable for a supervisor to make an assignment in the form of a command when
    A. a serious emergency has risen
    B. an employee objects to carrying out an assignment
    C. the assignment must be completed immediately
    D. the assignment is an unpleasant one

    4.____

5. For an office supervisor to confer periodically with his subordinates in order to anticipate job problems which are likely to arise is desirable MAINLY because
   A. there will be fewer problems for which hasty decisions will have to be made
   B. some problems which are anticipated may not arise
   C. his subordinates will learn to refer the problems arising in the unit to him
   D. constant anticipation of future problems tends to raise additional problems

6. As the supervisor of a staff of clerical employees performing various types of work, you are responsible for the accuracy and efficiency with which their work is performed.
   Of the following actions you may take to insure the accuracy of their work, the MOST practical one is for you to
   A. review each operation completed by a staff member before permitting the employee to proceed to the next operation
   B. keep a record of every error made by an employee and use this record to determine whether a careless employee should be transferred or discharged
   C. assign work in such a way that every operation is performed independently by two employees
   D. determine what errors are likely to occur and set up safeguards to prevent the occurrence of these errors

7. One of your subordinates has violated a staff regulation by failing to inform you that he will be absent on a certain day.
   Of the following, the MOST appropriate action for you to take FIRST is to
   A. discuss this matter with your immediate superior
   B. find out the reason for his failure to obey this staff regulation
   C. determine what disciplinary action other supervisors have taken in similar cases
   D. take no action if his absence did not interfere with the work of the unit; reprimand him if it did

8. A newly appointed clerk is assigned to a unit of an agency at a time when the supervisor of the unit is very busy and has little time to devote to instructing the new employee in the work he is to perform.
   Of the following, the MOST appropriate method of training this employee is for the supervisor to
   A. instruct the new employee to observe several experienced clerks at work and question them regarding any aspect of the work he does not understand
   B. delegate the job of training this employee to an employee in the unit who is qualified to instruct him
   C. assign the new employee a simple task and inform him that more complex and varied duties will be given him when the supervisor is less busy
   D. have the employee spend his time reading the agency's annual reports and the laws, rules, and regulations governing its work

9. The channels of communication between the management of a bureau and its employees not only should be kept open and working, but they should also be two-way channels.
Of the following, the MOST effective method for a supervisor to use to carry out this recommendation is to
   A. arrange periodic staff meetings and individual conferences to discuss problems and procedures with his subordinates
   B. change subordinates' assignments regularly so that they will be able to see how their work is related to the objectives of the bureau
   C. issue regular instructions, both written and oral, which clearly show each subordinate's assignments
   D. encourage his subordinates to discuss personal problems with him

9.____

10. Work measurement is an essential control tool to an office supervisor.
Of the following, the LEAST important reason for using work measurement as a control tool is that work measurement
   A. may indicate training needs of his subordinates
   B. simplifies the procedures used by the supervisor's subordinates in carrying out their assignments
   C. can indicate whether the supervisor is employing more subordinates than he really needs
   D. is a basis for determining which of the supervisor's subordinates are his most efficient

10.____

11. Internal management reporting in agencies is becoming more statistical in nature. Statistics have thus become a major tool in management supervision in agencies.
Before deciding to adopt statistical reporting as a management tool, the management of an agency should FIRST determine whether the
   A. employees of the agency understand the need for, and the use of, statistics in reporting
   B. supervisory staff in the agency is capable of putting reports into statistical form
   C. major activities of the agency can be reported statistically
   D. present achievements of the agency can be compared statistically with those of previous years

11.____

12. When assigning work, which of the following criteria would be BEST for a supervisor to use?
   A. Allow each employee to select the tasks he or she does best
   B. Assign all unimportant work to the slower employees
   C. Assign the more tiring tasks to the newer employees
   D. Assign tasks based on the abilities of employees

12.____

13. You have been supervising ten people for sixteen months. During that time, your employees have never reported any problems to you.
It is LIKELY that
   A. you are doing such a good job there is no room for improvement

13.____

B. since your staff is small, the chances of problems arising are smaller than in a larger unit
C. for some reason your staff is reluctant to discuss problems with you
D. your employees are very competent and are handling all of the problems well by themselves

14. Your supervisor informs you that three of your fifteen employees have complained to her about your inconsistent methods of supervision.
You should
    A. offer to attend a supervisory training program
    B. first ask her if it is proper for her to allow these employees to go over your head
    C. ask her what specific acts have been considered inconsistent
    D. explain that you have purposely been inconsistent because of the needs of these three employees

14.____

15. On short notice, a supervisor must ask her staff to work overtime.
Of the following, it would be BEST to
    A. explain they would be doing her a personal favor which she would appreciate a great deal
    B. explain why it is necessary
    C. reassure them that they can take the time off in the near future
    D. remind them that working overtime occasionally is part of the job requirement

15.____

16. One of your employees has begun reporting to work late on the average of twice a week.
You should
    A. send a memo to everyone in your unit, stressing that lateness cannot be tolerated
    B. privately discuss the matter with the employee to determine if there are any unusual circumstances causing the behavior
    C. bring the issue up at the next staff meeting, without singling out any employee
    D. ask one of your employees to discuss the matter with the individual

16.____

17. One of your employees submitted an application for acceptance into a career development workshop two months ago and has heard nothing. The individual tells you that when one of her co-workers submitted an application, he received a reply a week later.
Which is the BEST response for you to make?
    A. This is obviously a case of discrimination. I'll bring it to the Affirmative Action officer immediately.
    B. Next time you submit a request for something of this nature, let me know and I will write a cover letter that will carry more weight.
    C. Perhaps it was an oversight. Why don't you call the organization and ask why you've heard nothing?
    D. it looks like you won't be accepted this year. Be sure to try again next year.

17.____

18. In order to meet deadlines, a supervisor should
    A. schedule the work and keep informed of its progress
    B. delegate work
    C. hire temporary personnel
    D. know the capabilities of his or her most reliable employees

19. Your supervisor has given instructions to your employees in your absence that differ from those you had given them.
    You should
    A. have your employees follow your instructions
    B. have your employees follow your supervisor's instructions
    C. discuss the matter with your supervisor
    D. discuss the matter with your employees and find out which method they think is best

20. You have found it necessary to return an assignment completed by one of your employees so that several changes can be made. The employee objects to making these changes.
    The MOST appropriate action for you to take FIRST is to
    A. inform the employee that he or she is free to object to your supervisor
    B. ask if the employee has carefully read your proposed changes
    C. calmly state that your decision is final, and further discussion will most likely be useless
    D. allow the employee to present his or her objections against making the changes

21. Among the problems that confront a new supervisor in relation to her or his employees, the one which requires the MOST unusual degree of skill and diplomacy is
    A. changing established ideas
    B. calling attention to mistakes
    C. gaining the respect of employees
    D. training new employees

22. Of the following, the BEST indication of high morale in a supervisor's unit would be the
    A. unit never has to work overtime
    B. supervisor often enjoys staying late to plan work for the following day
    C. unit gives expensive birthday presents to each other
    D. employees are willing to give first priority to attaining group objectives, subordinating personal desires they may have

23. In the satisfactory handling of an employee's complaint which is fancied rather than real, the complaint should be considered
    A. not very important since it has no basis in fact
    B. as important as a grievance grounded in fact
    C. an attempt by the employee to create trouble
    D. an indication of a psychological problem on the part of the employee

24. You are attempting to teach a new employee in your unit how to change a typewriter ribbon. The employee is having a great deal of difficulty changing the ribbon, even though you have always found it simple to do.
Before you spend more time instructing the individual, you should
   A. ask if the employee working nearest would take responsibility for changing the ribbon in the future
   B. tell the employee that you never found this difficult and ask what he or she finds difficult about it
   C. review each of the steps you have already explained and determine whether the individual understands them
   D. tell the employee that you will continue after lunch because you are getting irritable

25. One of your workers has relatives who raise chickens. One day, you mention in casual conversation that you bought some eggs of poor quality at the grocery store. The following Monday, the worker places a box of fresh eggs on your desk. You thank him and offer to pay, but he refuses. On several occasions thereafter, he brings in additional eggs but still refuses to take payment. He is obviously proud of these products and seems to take great pleasure in sharing them with you. However, you begin to hear rumors that the other workers believe that you and the worker are very friendly and that he is receiving special privileges from you.
You should
   A. explain the situation to the worker, pointing out that he is being hurt by the conditions because of the feelings of others
   B. ignore the situation since the worker is merely being friendly and is actually receiving no favors in return
   C. supervise this worker more carefully than the others to insure that he will not take advantage of the situation
   D. refuse all gifts from the worker thereafter without further explanation

KEY (CORRECT ANSWERS)

1. C
2. D
3. B
4. D
5. A

6. D
7. B
8. B
9. A
10. B

11. C
12. D
13. C
14. C
15. B

16. B
17. C
18. A
19. C
20. D

21. A
22. D
23. B
24. C
25. A

TEST 4

DIRECTIONS: Each question or incomplete statement is followed by several suggested answers or completions. Select the one that BEST answers the question or completes the statement. *PRINT THE LETTER OF THE CORRECT ANSWER IN THE SPACE AT THE RIGHT.*

1. Lax supervision has been blamed largely on the unwillingness of supervisors to supervise their employees.
   The CHIEF reason for this unwillingness to supervise is based MAINLY on the supervisors'
   A. failure to accept modern concepts of proper supervision
   B. doubt of their ability to keep pace with modern techniques and developments in supervision
   C. fear of complaints from employees and the supervisors' wish to avoid unpleasantness
   D. inability to adhere to the same high standards of performance which are required of employees

1.____

2. The appraisal of employees and their performance is an integral part of the supervisor's job. There is wide agreement that several basic principles must be taken into account by supervisors involved in the appraisal process in order to perform this function correctly.
   The one of the statements below that LEAST represents a basic principle of the appraisal process is:
   A. Appraisals should be based more on performance of definite tasks than on personality considerations.
   B. Appraisal of long-range potential should rely heavily on subjective judgment of that potential.
   C. Appraisal involves the use of value judgments by the supervisor and does, therefore, require reference to pre-established standards.
   D. Appraisal should aim at emphasizing employees' strengths rather than weaknesses.

2.____

3. Although accuracy and speed are both important in the performance of work, accuracy should be considered more important MAINLY because
   A. most supervisors insist on accurate work
   B. much time is lost in correcting errors
   C. a rapid rate of work cannot be maintained for any length of time
   D. speedy workers are often inaccurate

3.____

4. If an employee has done a complicated task well, his or her supervisor should
   A. tell the employee that he or she has done a good job
   B. call a staff meeting to see if anyone has suggestions for improving future performance of the task
   C. avoid commending the employee as performing competently is what they are paid to do
   D. confide in the employee that he or she is the best worker in your unit

4.____

2 (#4)

5. You are a newly appointed supervisor in a large office. It had been the practice in that office for the employees to take an unauthorized coffee break at 10:00 A.M. You have been successful in stopping this practice, and for one week no one had gone out for coffee at 10:00 A.M. One day, a stenographer comes over to you at 10:15 A.M., appearing to be ill. She states that she doesn't feel well and that she would like to go out for a cup of tea. She asks your permission to leave the office for a few minutes.
You should
   A. telephone and have a cup of tea delivered to her
   B. permit her to go out
   C. refuse her permission, explaining that you don't wish to set a bad example
   D. tell her she can leave for an early lunch

5.____

6. One of the employees you supervise has just put up a small poster in her work area that two of your eight employees find obscene and distasteful. While you don't like the poster either, it doesn't upset you. The two employees already have complained to you about the poster.
Of the following, you should
   A. have the two employees talk to the individual and explain why they are offended
   B. privately explain to the individual that her poster is causing some problems and seek her cooperation in removing it
   C. do nothing as the employee has the right to express her feelings
   D. compromise and allow her to display the poster half of the time

6.____

7. One of the most effective ways to build a sense of employee pride, teamwork, and motivation is for the supervisor to seek advice, suggestions, and information from employees concerning ways in which work should be solved. Many experiments in group decision-making have indicated that work groups can help the supervisor in improving decision-making. Where employees feel that they are really part of a team and that they have a significant influence on the decisions that are made, they are more likely to accept the decisions and to seek new solutions to future difficult problems.
According to the above passage, a supervisor should
   A. almost always follow the advice of his or her employees in handling difficult problems
   B. always seek advice from employees when handling difficult problems
   C. choices A and D, but not B
   D. look to employees for assistance in decision-making

7.____

8. You have just had a private discussion with the employee with the poster in Question 6 above. You have explained that her poster is causing some problems, and have asked for her cooperation in removing it. She has politely refused to do so, saying, "looking at it cheers her up, and she's been depressed lately."
You should
   A. wait a day or two to see if the incident blows over before deciding whether to take any further action

8.____

B. call in the two disgruntled employees within the hour and let them know they'll have to live with the poster as you are not going to act as a censor in the office
C. check agency policies to see if it is legal to have posters down as it is interfering with the work of the unit

9. An employee reprimanded for poor performance tells her supervisor that her recent behavior has been due to a serious family problem. The supervisor suggests several programs which may be able to help her.
The action of the supervisor was
   A. *inappropriate*; the supervisor should not involve herself in the personal affairs of her subordinates
   B. *appropriate*; personal problems frequently affect job performance
   C. *inappropriate*; the employee may consider the supervisor responsible for the subsequent action of the social agencies
   D. *appropriate*; the discussion with the supervisor will in itself tend to solve the problem

10. Your supervisor informs you that the employee turnover rate in your office is well above the norm and must be reduced.
Which one of the following initial steps would be LEAST appropriate in attempting to overcome this problem?
   A. Decide to be more lenient about the performance standards and about employee requests for time off, so that your office will gain a reputation as a good place to work.
   B. Discuss the problem with a few of your employees whose judgment you trust to see if they can provide insight into the underlying causes of the problem.
   C. Review the records of employees who have left during the past year to see if they can shed some light on the underlying causes of the problem.
   D. Carefully review your training procedures to see if they can be improved

11. The management principle that each employee should be under the direct control of one immediate supervisor at any one time is known as the principle of
   A. chain of command   B. span of control
   C. unity of command   D. homogeneous assignment

12. The employees of a unit have been wasteful in the use of office supplies.
Of the following, the MOST desirable action for the supervisor to take to reduce this waste is to
   A. determine the average quantity of supplies used daily by each employee
   B. find out which employees have been most wasteful and reprimand those employees
   C. discuss this matter at a conference with the staff, pointing out the necessity for, and methods of, eliminating waste
   D. issue supplies for an assignment at the time the assignment is made and limit the quantity to the amount needed for that assignment only

13. You supervise nineteen employees in a unit which is located directly across from the commissioner's office. One of your new employees has a habit of *showing off* whenever the commissioner is nearby. You have just heard other employees laughing about this behavior among themselves. You like the new employee and would like the employee to be accepted by the others.
Of the following, you should
    A. discuss the situation with two of the older employees and seek their cooperation in being a little more tolerant
    B. talk with the new employee and gently explain the situation
    C. discuss the situation with your most trusted employees and ask them to talk to the others
    D. do nothing

14. One of your employees comes to you and complains of sexual harassment by your supervisor. The employee has frequently complained about minor issues in the six months she's been there. You have known your supervisor for thirteen years and respect him a great deal. You have known your supervisor for thirteen years and respect him a great deal.
Of the following, you should
    A. firmly let the employee know what a serious allegation she is bringing against your supervisor
    B. let the employee know you will take her concerns seriously
    C. call your supervisor and give him a chance to prepare a defense
    D. inform the employee that she had better have concrete proof for a charge of this nature

15. The one of the following which is usually the POOREST reason for transferring an employee is to
    A. grant a doctor's request that the employee work nearer to his or her home
    B. take care of changes in workload
    C. relieve the monotony of work assignments

16. You find that you have unjustly reprimanded one of your subordinates.
You should
    A. ignore the matter, but be more careful in the future
    B. readily admit your mistake to the employee
    C. admit your mistake at your next staff meeting so that your employees will know how fair you are
    D. admit your mistake, but blame the misunderstanding on your supervisor

17. An experienced, self-confident employee carelessly omitted an essential operation on a job assigned to her. As a result, the completion of an important urgent report was delayed for several hours. A few days later, a relatively inexperienced, sensitive co-worker made a similar careless mistake with similar negative results. The supervisor of the two employees was more gentle in reprimanding the latter than the former employee.

The supervisor's action in administering reprimands of unequal severity to these two subordinates was
  A. *not appropriate*, because fairness requires that subordinates responsible for like mistakes receive reprimands of like severity
  B. *appropriate*, because supervisors should consider the temperament of subordinates when reprimanding them
  C. *appropriate*, because subordinates who accept greater responsibilities must likewise accept the consequent greater penalties for their mistakes
  D. *not appropriate*, because more experienced employees benefit less, in general, from reprimands than less experienced employees

18. You have just overheard a tense discussion in the cafeteria between two of your best employees. One of them has owed the other $40 for several months and has not paid it back or even mentioned the debt. The employees do not realize that you have heard them.
    During that week, you should
      A. not discuss the matter with either of them
      B. discuss the matter with both of them, as the conflict may adversely affect their job performance
      C. discuss the matter with the one who has not paid back the money
      D. put a clever but meaningful cartoon up on your wall about the importance of paying back debts to friends

19. You have been supervising twenty employees for three months. You suspect that one of your employees, who has worked in the unit longer than anyone else, has perfected the art of looking busy. You wish to find out how much work she is really accomplishing.
    Of the following, it would be LEAST appropriate to
      A. have a frank discussion with the employee about her performance
      B. set specific time limits on when you would like to get work back from her
      C. try to observe her more carefully while she is working
      D. be more careful when monitoring her work output

20. The supervisor of a central files bureau which has fifty employees customarily spends a considerable portion of time in spot-checking the files, reviewing material being transferred from active to inactive files, and similar activities. From the viewpoint of the department management, the MOST pertinent evaluation which can be made on the basis of this information is that the
      A. supervisor is conscientious and hardworking
      B. bureau may need additional staff
      C. supervisor has not made a sufficient delegation of authority and responsibility
      D. bureau needs an in-service training course as the work of its employees requires an abnormal amount of review

21. You have just been appointed as supervisor of ten employees. The supervisor you are replacing demanded that her subordinate accept their assignments without question. She refused to allow them to exercise initiative in carrying out assignments and maintained a constant check on their work performance.

The MOST appropriate policy for you to adopt would be to
- A. gradually remove the controls you consider too strict and provide opportunities for your staff to participate in formulating work plans and procedures
- B. continue her rigid policies, as the employees are used to this
- C. discontinue all strict controls immediately and give the employees complete freedom in carrying out their assignments
- D. ask your employees what method of supervision they would prefer

22. In any agency, the top administrative officials are concerned largely with the work of overall creative planning with respect to the anticipated progress of the agency. The first-line supervisors, on the other hand, are concerned largely with the control of current action for the execution of current jobs.
On the basis of this quotation, a first-line supervisor would be CHIEFLY responsible for
    - A. increasing or decreasing the responsibilities of his or her unit to reflect changes in the policies of the agency
    - B. modifying the work assignments of his or her present staff to handle a seasonal variation in the activities of the unit
    - C. revising the procedure that is used for transmitting instructions from the head of the agency to the unit heads
    - D. raising and lowering the production goals of his or her unit as often as necessary to adjust them to the abilities of employees

22.____

23. As a supervisor, you may find it necessary to consult with your superior before taking action on some matters.
Of the following, the action for which it is MOST important that you obtain the prior approval of your superior is one that involves
    - A. assuming additional functions for your unit
    - B. rotating assignments among your staff members
    - C. initiating regular meetings of your staff
    - D. assigning certain members of your staff to work overtime on an emergency job

23.____

24. Suppose that a clerk who is employed in a unit under your supervision performs his work quickly but carelessly. He is about to be transferred to another unit in your department. The chief of this other unit asks you for your opinion of this employee's work habits. The chief of this other unit asks you for your opinion of this employee's work habits.
Of the following, the MOST appropriate reply for you to make is to
    - A. point out this employee's good qualities only since he may correct his bad qualities after his transfer is effected
    - B. say nothing good or bad about this employee, thus permitting him to start his new assignment with a clean slate
    - C. inform the unit chief that this clerk performed his work speedily but was careless
    - D. emphasize his employee's good points and minimize his bad points

24.____

25. Of the following, the action that is likely to contribute MOST to the prestige of a supervisor is for him to
    A. expect al his subordinates to perform with equal efficiency any tasks assigned to them
    B. observe the same rules of conduct that he expects his subordinates to observe
    C. seek their advice on his personal problems and offer them his advice on their personal problems
    D. be always frank and outspoken to his subordinates in pointing out their faults

KEY (CORRECT ANSWERS)

1.	C	11.	C
2.	B	12.	C
3.	B	13.	D
4.	A	14.	B
5.	B	15.	D
6.	B	16.	B
7.	D	17.	B
8.	A	18.	A
9.	B	19.	A
10.	A	20.	C

21.	A
22.	B
23.	A
24.	C
25.	C

EXAMINATION SECTION
TEST 1

DIRECTIONS: Each question or incomplete statement is followed by several suggested answers or completions. Select the one that BEST answers the question or completes the statement. *PRINT THE LETTER OF THE CORRECT ANSWER IN THE SPACE AT THE RIGHT.*

1. A supervisor notices that one of his more competent subordinates has recently been showing less interest in his work. The work performed by this employee has also fallen off and he seems to want to do no more than the minimum acceptable amount of work. When his supervisor questions the subordinate about his decreased interest and his mediocre work performance, the subordinate replies: *Sure, I've lost interest in my work. I don' see any reason why I should do more than I have to. When I do a good job, nobody notices it. But, let me fall down on one minor job and the whole place knows about it! So why should I put myself out on this job?*
   If the subordinate's contentions are true, it would be correct to assume that the
   A. subordinate has not received adequate training
   B. subordinate's workload should be decreased
   C. supervisor must share responsibility for this employee's reaction
   D. supervisor has not been properly enforcing work standards

   1.____

2. How many subordinates should report directly to each supervisor? While there is agreement that there are limits to the number of subordinates that a manager can supervise well, this limit is determined by a number of important factors. Which of the following factors is MOST likely to increase the number of subordinates that can be effectively supervised by one supervisor in a particular unit?
   A. The unit has a great variety of activities.
   B. A staff assistant handles the supervisor's routine duties.
   C. The unit has a relatively inexperienced staff.
   D. The office layout is being rearranged to make room for more employees.

   2.____

3. Mary Smith, an Administrative Assistant, heads the Inspection Records Unit of Department Y. She is a dedicated supervisor who not only strives to maintain an efficient operation, but she also tries to improve the competence of each individual member of her staff. She keeps these considerations in mind when assigning work to her staff. Her bureau chief asks her to compile some data based on information contained in her records. She feels that any member of her staff should be able to do this job.
   The one of the following members of her staff who would probably be given LEAST consideration for this assignment is
   A. Jane Abel, a capable Supervising Clerk with considerable experience in the unit
   B. Kenneth Brown, a Senior Clerk recently transferred to the unit who has not had an opportunity to demonstrate his capabilities

   3.____

C. Laura Chance, a Clerk who spends full time on a single routine assignment
D. Michael Dunn, a Clerk who works on several minor jobs but still has the lightest workload

4. There are very few aspects of a supervisor's job that do not involve communication, either in writing or orally.
   Which of the following statements regarding oral and written orders is NOT correct?
   A. Oral orders usually permit more immediate feedback than do written orders.
   B. Written orders, rather than oral orders, should generally be given when the subordinate will be held strictly accountable.
   C. Oral orders are usually preferable when the order contains lengthy detailed instructions.
   D. Written orders, rather than oral orders, should usually be given to a subordinate who is slow to understand or is forgetful.

5. Assume that you are the head of a large clerical unit in Department R. Your department's personnel office has appointed a Clerk, Roberta Rowe, to fill a vacancy in your unit. Before bringing this appointee to your office, the personnel office has given Roberta the standard orientation on salary, fringe benefits, working conditions, attendance, and the department's personnel rules. In addition, he has supplied her with literature covering these areas.
   Of the following, the action that you should take FIRST after Roberta has been brought to your office is to
   A. give her an opportunity to read the literature furnished by the personnel office so that she can ask you questions about it
   B. escort her to the desk she will use and assign her to work with an experienced employee who will act as her trainer
   C. explain the duties and responsibilities of her job and its relationship with the jobs being performed by the other employees of the unit
   D. summon the employee who is currently doing the work that will be performed by Roberta and have him explain and demonstrate how to perform the required tasks

6. Your superior informs you that the employee turnover rate in your office is well above the norm and must be reduced.
   Which one of the following initial steps would be LEAST appropriate in attempting to overcome this problem?
   A. Decide to be more lenient about performance standards and about employee requests for time off, so that your office will gain a reputation as an easy place to work
   B. Discuss the problem with a few of your key people whose judgment you trust to see if they can shed some light on the underlying causes of the problem

C. Review the records of employees who have left during the past year to see if there is a pattern that will help you understand the problem
D. Carefully review your training procedures to see whether they can be improved

7. In issuing instructions to a subordinate on a job assignment, the supervisor should ordinarily explain why the assignment is being made.
Omission of such an explanation is BEST justified when the
   A. subordinate is restricted in the amount of discretion he can exercise in carrying out the assignment
   B. assignment is one that will be unpopular with the subordinate
   C. subordinate understands the reason as a result of previous similar assignments
   D. assignment is given to an employee who is in need of further training

7._____

8. When a supervisor allows sufficient time for training and makes an appropriate effort in the training of his subordinates, his CHIEF goal is to
   A. increase the dependence of one subordinate upon another in their everyday work activities
   B. spend more time with his subordinates in order to become more involved in their work
   C. increase the capability and independence of his subordinates in carrying out their work
   D. increase his frequency of contact with his subordinates in order to better evaluate their performance

8._____

9. In preparing an evaluation of a subordinate's performance, which one of the following items is usually irrelevant?
   A. Remarks about tardiness or absenteeism
   B. Mention of any unusual contributions or accomplishments
   C. A summary of the employee's previous job experience
   D. An assessment of the employee's attitude toward the job

9._____

10. The ability to delegate responsibility while maintaining adequate controls is one key to a supervisor's success.
Which one of the following methods of control would minimize the amount of responsibility assumed by the subordinate?
   A. Asking for a monthly status report in writing
   B. Asking to receive copies of important correspondence so that you can be aware of potential problems
   C. Scheduling periodic project status conferences with your subordinate
   D. Requiring that your subordinate confer with you before making decisions on a project

10._____

11. You wish to assign an important project to a subordinate who you think has good potential.
Which one of the following approaches would be MOST effective in successfully completing the project while developing the subordinate's abilities?
    A. Describe the project to the subordinate in general terms and emphasize that it must be completed as quickly as possible
    B. Outline the project in detail to the subordinate and emphasize that its successful completion could lead to career advancement
    C. Develop a detailed project outline and timetable, discuss the details and timing with him and assign the subordinate to carry out the plan on his own
    D. Discuss the project objectives and suggested approaches with the subordinate, and ask the subordinate to develop a detailed project outline and timetable of your approval

12. Research studies reveal that an important difference between high-production and low-production supervisors lies not in their interest in eliminating mistakes, but in their manner of handling mistakes.
High-production supervisors are MOST likely to look upon mistakes as primarily
    A. an opportunity to provide training
    B. a byproduct of subordinate negligence
    C. an opportunity to fix blame in a situation
    D. a result of their own incompetence

13. Supervisors should try to establish what has been called *positive discipline*, an atmosphere in which subordinates willingly abide by rules which they consider fair.
When a supervisor notices a subordinate violating an important rule, his FIRST course of action should be to
    A. stop the subordinate and tell him what he is doing wrong
    B. wait a day or two before approaching the employee involved
    C. call a meeting of all subordinates to discuss the rule
    D. forget the matter in the hope that it will not happen again

14. The working climate is the feeling, degree of freedom, the tone and the mood of the working environment.
Which of the following contributes MOST to determining the working climate in a unit or group?
    A. The rules set for rest periods
    B. The example set by the supervisor
    C. The rules set for morning check-in
    D. The wages paid to the employee

5 (#1)

15. John Polk is a bright, ingenious clerk with a lot of initiative. He has made many good suggestions to his supervisor in the Training Division of Department T, where he is employed. However, last week one of his bright ideas literally *blew up*. In setting up some electronic equipment in the training classroom, he cross some wires resulting in a damaged tape recorder and a classroom so filled with smoke that the training class had to be held in another room. When Mr. Brown, his supervisor, learned of this occurrence, he immediately summoned John to his private office. There Mr. Brown spent five minutes bawling John out, calling him an overzealous, overgrown kid, and send him back to his job without letting John speak once.
Of the following, the action of Mr. Brown that MOST deserves approval is that he
   A. took disciplinary action immediately without regard for past performance
   B. kept the disciplinary interview to a brief period
   C. concentrated his criticism on the root cause of the occurrence
   D. held the disciplinary interview in his private office

15.____

16. Typically, when the technique of *supervision by results* is practiced, higher management sets down, either implicitly or explicitly, certain performance standards or goals that the subordinate is expected to meet. So long as these standards are met, management interferes very little.
The MOST likely result of the use of this technique is that it will
   A. lead to ambiguity in terms of goals
   B. be successful only to the extent that close direct supervision is practiced
   C. make it possible to evaluate both employee and supervisory effectiveness
   D. allow for complete autonomy on the subordinate's part

16.____

17. Assume that you, an Administrative Assistant, are the supervisor of a large clerical unit performing routine clerical operations. One of your clerks consistently produces much less work than other members of our staff performing similar tasks.
Of the following, the action you should take FIRST is to
   A. ask the clerk if he wants to be transferred to another unit
   B. reprimand the clerk for his poor performance and warn him that further disciplinary action will be taken if his work does not improve
   C. quietly ask the clerk's co-workers whether they know why his performance is poor
   D. discuss this matter with the clerk to work out plans for improving his performance

17.____

18. When making written evaluations and reviews of the performance of subordinates, it is usually ADVISABLE to
   A. avoid informing the employee of the evaluation if it is critical because it may create hard feelings
   B. avoid informing the employee of the evaluation whether critical or favorable because it is tension-producing

18.____

C. permit the employee to see the evaluation but not to discuss it with him because the supervisor cannot be certain where the discussion might lead
D. discuss the evaluation openly with the employee because it helps the employee understand what is expected of him

19. There are a number of well-known and respected human relations principles that successful supervisors have been using for years in building good relationships with their employees.
Which of the following does NOT illustrate such a principle?
A. Give clear and complete instructions
B. Let each person know how he is getting along
C. Keep an open-door policy
D. Make all relationships personal ones

19.____

20. Assume that it is your responsibility as an Administrative Assistant to maintain certain personnel records that are continually being updated. You have three senior clerks assigned specifically to this task. Recently, you have noticed that the volume of work has increased substantially, and the processing of personnel records by the clerks is backlogged. Your supervisor is now receiving complaints due to the processing delay.
Of the following, the BEST course of action for you to take FIRST is to
A. have a meeting with the clerks, advise them of the problem, and ask that they do their work faster; then confirm your meeting in writing for the record
B. request that an additional position be authorized for your unit
C. review the procedures being used for processing the work, and try to determine if you can improve the flow of work
D. get the system moving faster by spending some of your own time processing the backlog

20.____

21. Assume that you are in charge of a payroll unit consisting of four clerks. It is Friday, November 14. You have just arrived in the office after a conference. Your staff is preparing a payroll that must be forwarded the following Monday. Which of the following new items on your desk should you attend to FIRST?
A. A telephone message regarding very important information needed for the statistical summary of salaries paid for the month of November
B. A memorandum regarding a new procedure that should be followed in preparing the payroll
C. A telephone message from an employee who is threatening to endorse his paycheck *Under Protest* because he is dissatisfied with the amount
D. A memorandum from your supervisor reminding you to submit the probationary period report on a new employee

21.____

22. You are an Administrative Assistant in charge of a unit that orders and issues supplies. On a particular day you are faced with the following four situations. Which one should you take care of FIRST?

22.____

A. One of your employees who is in the process of taking the quarterly inventory of supplies has telephoned and asked that you return his call as soon as possible
B. A representative of a company that is noted for producing excellent office supplies will soon arrive with samples for you to distribute to the various offices in your agency
C. A large order of supplies which was delivered this morning has been checked and counted and a deliveryman is waiting for you to sign the receipt
D. A clerk from the purchase division asks you to search for a bill you failed to send to them which is urgently needed in order for them to complete a report due this morning

23. As an Administrative Assistant, assume that it is necessary for you to give an unpleasant assignment to one of your subordinates. You expect this employee to raise some objections to this assignment.
The MOST appropriate of the following actions for you to take FIRST is to issue the assignment
    A. orally, with the further statement that you will not listen to any complaints
    B. in writing, to forestall any complaints by the employee
    C. orally, permitting the employee to express his feelings
    D. in writing, with a note that any comments should be submitted in writing

24. Assume that you are an Administrative Assistant supervising the Duplicating and Reproduction Unit of Department B. One of your responsibilities is to prepare a daily schedule showing when and on which of your unit's four duplicating machine jobs are to be run off.
Of the following, the factor that should be given LEAST consideration in preparing the schedule is the
    A. priority of each of the jobs to be run off
    B. production speed of the different machines that will be used
    C. staff available to operate the machines
    D. date on which the job order was received

25. Cycling is an arrangement where papers are processed throughout a period according to an orderly plan rather than as a group all at one time. This technique has been used for a long time by public utilities in their cycle billing.
Of the following practices, the one that BEST illustrates this technique is that in which
    A. paychecks for per annum employees are issued bi-weekly and those for per diem employees are issued weekly
    B. field inspectors report in person to their offices one day a week, on Fridays, when they do all their paperwork and also pick up their paychecks
    C. the dates for issuing relief checks to clients vary depending on the last digit of the clients' social security numbers
    D. the last day for filing and paying income taxes is the same for Federal, State, and City income taxes

26. The employees in your division have recently been given an excellent up-to-date office manual, but you find that a good number of employees are not following the procedures outlined in it.
Which one of the following would be MOST likely to ensure that employees begin using the manual effectively?
    A. Require each employee to keep a copy of the manual in plain sight on his desk
    B. Issue warnings periodically to those employees who deviate most from procedures prescribed in the manual
    C. Tell an employee to check his manual when he does not follow the proper procedures
    D. Suggest to the employees that the manual be studied thoroughly

27. The one of the following factors which should be considered FIRST in the design of office forms is the
    A. information to be included in the form
    B. sequence of the information
    C. purpose of the form
    D. persons who will be using the form

28. Window envelopes are being used to an increasing extent by government and private industry.
The one of the following that is NOT an advantage of window envelopes is that they
    A. cut down on addressing costs
    B. eliminate the need to attach envelopes to letters being sent forward for signature by a superior
    C. are less costly to buy than regular envelopes

29. Your bureau head asks you to prepare the office layouts for several of his units being moved to a higher floor in your office building.
Of the following possibilities, the one that you should AVOID in preparing the layouts is to
    A. place the desks of the first-line supervisors near those of the staffs they supervise
    B. place the desks of employees whose work is most closely related near one another
    C. arrange the desks so that employees do not face one another
    D. locate desks with many outside visitors farthest from the office entrance

30. Which one of the following conditions would be LEAST important in considering a change of the layout in a particular office?
    A. Installation of a new office machine
    B. Assignment of five additional employees to your office
    C. Poor flow of work
    D. Employees' personal preferences of desk location

9 (#1)

31. Suppose Mr. Bloom, an Administrative Assistant, is dictating a letter to a stenographer. His dictation begins with the name of the addressee and continues to the body of the letter. However, Mr. Bloom does not dictate the address of the recipient of the letter. He expects the stenographer to locate it. The use of this practice by Mr. Bloom is
    A. *acceptable*, especially if he gives the stenographer the letter to which he is responding
    B. *acceptable*, especially if the letter is lengthy and detailed
    C. *unacceptable*, because it is not part of a stenographer's duties to search for information
    D. *unacceptable*, because he should not rely on the accuracy of the stenographer

31.____

32. Assume that there are no rules, directives or instructions concerning the filing of materials in your office or the retention of such files. A system is now being followed of placing in inactive files any materials that are more than one year old.
    Of the following, the MOST appropriate thing to do with material that has been in an inactive file in your office for more than one year is to
    A. inspect the contents of the files to decide how to dispose of them
    B. transfer the material to a remote location, where it can be obtained if necessary
    C. keep the material intact for a minimum of another three years
    D. destroy the material which has not been needed for at least a year

32.____

33. Suppose you, an Administrative Assistant, have just returned to your desk after engaging in an all-morning conference. Joe Burns, a Clerk, informs you that Clara McClough, an administrator in another agency, telephoned during the morning and that, although she requested to speak with you, he was able to give her the desired information.
    Of the following, the MOST appropriate action for you to take in regard to Mr. Burns' action is to
    A. thank him for assisting Ms. McClough in your absence
    B. explain to him the proper telephone practice to use in the future
    C. reprimand him for not properly channeling Ms. McClough's call
    D. issue a memo to all clerical employees regarding proper telephone practices

33.____

34. When interviewing subordinates with problems, supervisors frequently find that asking direct questions of the employee results only in evasive responses. The supervisor may, therefore, resort to the non-directive interview technique. In this technique, the supervisor avoids pointed questions; he leads the employee to continue talking freely uninfluenced by the supervisor's preconceived notions. This technique often enables the employee to bring his problem into sharp focus and to reach a solution to his problem. Suppose that you are a supervisor interviewing a subordinate about his recent poor attendance record.

34.____

On calling his attention to his excessive lateness record, he replies: *I just don't seem to be able to get up in the morning. Frankly, I've lost interest in this job. don't care about it. When I get up in the morning, I have to skip breakfast and I'm still late. I don't care about this job.*
If you are using the non-directive technique in this interview, the MOST appropriate of the following responses for you to make is
  A. You don't care about this job?
  B. Don't you think you are letting your department down?
  C. Are you having trouble at home?
  D. Don't you realize your actions are childish?

35. An employee in a work group made the following comment to a co-worker: 35.____
It's great to be a lowly employee instead of an Administrative Assistant because you can work without thinking. The Administrative Assistant is getting paid to plan, schedule, and think. Let him see to it that you have a productive day.
Which one of the following statements about his quotation BEST reflects an understanding of good personnel management techniques and the role of the supervising Administrative Assistant?
  A. The employee is wrong in attitude and in his perception of the role of the Administrative Assistant.
  B. The employee is correct in attitude but is wrong in his perception of the role of the Administrative Assistant.
  C. The employee is correct in attitude and in his perception of the role of the Administrative Assistant.
  D. The employee is wrong in attitude but is right in his perception of the role of the Administrative Assistant.

KEY (CORRECT ANSWERS)

1.	C	11.	D	21.	B	31.	A
2.	B	12.	A	22.	C	32.	A/B
3.	A	13.	A	23.	C	33.	A
4.	C	14.	B	24.	D	34.	A
5.	C	15.	D	25.	C	35.	D
6.	A	16.	C/D	26.	C		
7.	C	17.	D	27.	C		
8.	C	18.	D	28.	C		
9.	C	19.	D	29.	D		
10.	D	20.	C	30.	D		

TEST 2

DIRECTIONS: Each question or incomplete statement is followed by several suggested answers or completions. Select the one that BEST answers the question or completes the statement. *PRINT THE LETTER OF THE CORRECT ANSWER IN THE SPACE AT THE RIGHT.*

Questions 1-5.

DIRECTIONS: Questions 1 through 5 are to be answered SOLELY on the basis of the following passage.

    General supervision, in contrast to close supervision, involves a high degree of delegation of authority and requires some indirect means to ensure that employee behavior conforms to management needs. Not everyone works well under general supervision; however, general supervision works best where subordinates desire responsibility. General supervision also works well where individuals in work groups have strong feelings about the quality of the finished work products. Strong identification with management goals is another trait of persons who work well under general supervision. There are substantial differences in the amount of responsibility people are willing to accept on the job. One person lay flourish under supervision that another might find extremely restrictive.
    Psychological research provides evidence that the nature of a person's personality affects his attitude toward supervision. There are some employees with a low need for achievement and high fear of failure who shy away from challenges and responsibilities. Many seek self-expression off the job and ask only to be allowed to daydream on it. There are others who have become so accustomed to the authoritarian approach in their culture, family and previous work experience that they regard general supervision as no supervision at all. They abuse the privileges it bestows on them and refuse to accept the responsibilities it demands.
    Different groups develop different attitudes toward work. Most college graduates, for example, expect a great deal of responsibility and freedom. People with limited education, on the other hand, often have trouble accepting the concept that people should make decisions for themselves, particularly decisions concerning work. Therefore, the extent to which general supervision will be effective varies greatly with the subordinates involved.

1. According to the above passage, which one of the following is a NECESSARY part of management policy regarding general supervision?
    A. Most employees should formulate their own work goals.
    B. Deserving employees should be rewarded periodically.
    C. Some controls on employee work patterns should be established.
    D. Responsibility among employees should generally be equalized.

2. It can be inferred from the above passage that an employee who avoids responsibilities and challenges is MOST likely to
    A. gain independence under general supervision
    B. work better under close supervision than under general supervision
    C. abuse the liberal guidelines of general supervision
    D. become more restricted and cautious under general supervision

3. Based on the above passage, employees who succeed under general supervision are MOST likely to
   A. have a strong identification with people and their problems
   B. accept work obligations without fear
   C. seek self-expression off the job
   D. value the intellectual aspects of life

3.____

4. Of the following, the BEST title for the passage is
   A. Benefits and Disadvantages of General Supervision
   B. Production Levels of Employees Under General Supervision
   C. Employee Attitudes Toward Work and the Work Environment
   D. Employee Background and Personality as a Factor in Utilizing General Supervision

4.____

5. It can be inferred from the above passage that the one of the following employees who is MOST likely to work best under general supervision is one who
   A. is a part-time graduate student
   B. was raised by very strict parents
   C. has little confidence
   D. has been closely supervised in past jobs

5.____

Questions 6-10.

DIRECTIONS: Questions 6 through 10 are to be answered SOLELY on the basis of the following passage.

The concept of *program management* was first developed in order to handle some of the complex projects undertaken by the U.S. Department of Defense in the 1950's. Program management is an administrative system combining planning and control techniques to guide and coordinate all the activities which contribute to one overall program or project. It has been used by the federal government to manage space exploration and other programs involving many contributing organizations. It is also used by state and local governments and by some large firms to provide administrative integration of work from a number of sources, be they individuals, departments or outside companies.

One of the specific administrative techniques for program management is Program Evaluation Review Technique (PERT). PERT begins with the assembling of a list of all the activities needed to accomplish an overall task. The next step consists of arranging these activities in a sequential network showing both how much time each activity will take and which activities must be completed before others can begin. The time required for each activity is estimated by simple statistical techniques by the persons who will be responsible for the work, and the time required to complete the entire string of activities along each sequential path through the network is then calculated. There may be dozens or hundreds of these paths, so the calculation is usually done by computer. The longest path is then labeled the *critical path* because no matter how quickly events not on this path are completed, the events long the longest path must be finished before the project can be terminated. The overall starting and completion dates are then pinpointed, and target dates are established for each task. Actual progress can later be checked by comparison to the network plan.

6. Judging from the information in the above passage, which one of the following projects is MOST suitable for handling by a program management technique?
    A. Review and improvement of the filing system used by a city office
    B. Computerization of accounting data already on file in an office
    C. Planning and construction of an urban renewal project
    D. Announcing a change in city tax regulations to thousands of business firms

7. The above passage indicates that program management methods are now in wide use by various kinds of organizations.
Which one of the following organizations would you LEAST expect to make much use of such methods today?
    A. An automobile manufacturer
    B. A company in the aerospace business
    C. The government of a large city
    D. A library reference department

8. In making use of the PERT technique, the FIRST step is to determine
    A. every activity that must take place in order to complete the project
    B. a target date for completion of the project
    C. the estimated time required to complete each activity which is related to the whole
    D. which activities will make up the longest path on the chart

9. Who estimates the time required to complete a particular activity in a PERT program?
    A. The people responsible for the particular activity
    B. The statistician assigned to the program
    C. The organization that has commissioned the project
    D. The operator who programs the computer

10. Which one of the following titles BEST describes the contents of the passage?
    A. The Need For Computers in Today's Projects
    B. One Technique For Program Management
    C. Local Governments Can Now Use Space-Age Techniques
    D. Why Planning Is Necessary For Complex Projects

11. An Administrative Assistant has been criticized for the low productivity in the group which he supervises.
Which of the following BEST reflects an understanding of supervisory responsibilities in the area of productivity?
An Administrative Assistant should be held responsible for his own
    A. individual productivity and the productivity of the group he supervises, because he is in a position where he maintains or increases production through others
    B. personal productivity only, because the supervisor is not likely to have any effect on the productivity of subordinates

C. individual productivity but only for a drop in the productivity of the group he supervises, since subordinates will receive credit for increased productivity individually
D. personal productivity only, because this is how he would be evaluated if he were not a supervisor

12. A supervisor has held a meeting in his office with an employee about the employee's grievance. The grievance concerned the sharp way in which the supervisor reprimanded the employee for an error the employee made in the performance of a task assigned to him. The problem was not resolved.
Which one of the following statements about this meeting BEST reflects an understanding of good supervisory techniques?
    A. It is awkward for a supervisor to handle a grievance involving himself. The supervisor should not have held the meeting.
    B. It would have been better is the supervisor had held the meeting at the employee's workplace, even though there would have been frequent distractions, because the employee would have been more relaxed.
    C. The resolution of a problem is not the only sign of a successful meeting. The achievement of communication was worthwhile.
    D. The supervisor should have been forceful. There is nothing wrong with raising your voice to an employee every once in a while.

13. John Hayden, the owner of a single-family house, complains that he submitted an application for reduction of assessment that obviously was not acted upon before his final assessment notice was sent to him. The timely receipt of the application has been verified in a departmental log book.
As the supervisor of the clerical unit through which this application was processed and where this delay occurred, you should be LEAST concerned with
    A. what happened
    B. who is responsible
    C. why it happened
    D. what can be learned from it

14. The one of the following that applies MOST appropriate to the role of the first-line supervisor is that usually he is
    A. called upon to help determine agency policy
    B. involved in long-range agency planning
    C. responsible for determining some aspects of basic organization structure
    D. a participant in developing procedures and methods

15. Sally Jones, an Administrative Assistant, gives clear and precise instructions to Robert Warren, a Senior Clerk. In these instructions, Ms. Jones clearly delegates authority to Mr. Warren to undertake a well-defined task.
In this situation, Ms. Jones should expect Mr. Warren to
    A. come to her to check out details as he progresses with the task
    B. come to her only with exceptional problems
    C. ask her permission if he wishes to use his delegated authority
    D. use his authority to redefine the task and its related activities

16. Planning involves establishing departmental goals and programs and determining ways of reaching them.
    The MAIN advantage of such planning is that
    A. there will be no need for adjustments once a plan is put into operation
    B. it ensures that everyone is working on schedule
    C. it provides the framework for an effective operation
    D. unexpected work problems are easily overcome

17. As a result of reorganization, the jobs in a large clerical unit were broken down into highly specialized tasks. Each specialized task was then assigned to a particular employee to perform.
    This action will probably lead to an increase in
    A. flexibility
    B. job satisfaction
    C. need for coordination
    D. employee initiative

18. Your office carries on a large volume of correspondence concerned with the purchase of supplies and equipment for city offices. You use form letters to deal with many common situations.
    In which one of the following situations would use of a form letter be LEAST appropriate?
    A. Informing suppliers of a change in city regulations concerning purchase contracts
    B. Telling a new supplier the standard procedures to be followed in billing
    C. Acknowledging receipt of a complaint and saying that the complaint will be investigated
    D. Answering a city councilman's request for additional information on a particular regulation affecting suppliers

19. Assume that you are an Administrative Assistant heading a large clerical unit. Because of the great demands being made on your time, you have designated Tom Smith, a Supervising Clerk, to be your assistant and to assume some of your duties.
    Of the following duties performed by you, the MOST appropriate one to assign to Tom Smith is to
    A. conduct the on-the-job training of new employees
    B. prepare the performance appraisal reports on your staff members
    C. represent your unit in dealings with the heads of other units
    D. handle matters that require exception to general policy

20. In establishing rules for his subordinates, a superior should be PRIMARILY concerned with
    A. creating sufficient flexibility to allow for exceptions
    B. making employees aware of the reasons for the rules and the penalties for infractions
    C. establishing the strength of his own position in relation to his subordinates
    D. having his subordinates know that such rules will be imposed in a personal manner

21. The practice of conducting staff training sessions on a periodic basis is generally considered
    A. *poor*; it takes employees away from their work assignments
    B. *poor*; all staff training should be done on an individual basis
    C. *good*; it permits the regular introduction of new methods and techniques
    D. *good*; it ensures a high employee productivity rate

21.____

22. Suppose, as an Administrative Assistant, you have just announced at a staff meeting with your subordinates that a radical reorganization of work will take place next week. Your subordinates at the meeting appear to be excited, tense, and worried.
    Of the following, the BEST action for you to take at that time is to
    A. schedule private conferences with each subordinate to obtain his reaction to the meeting
    B. close the meeting and tell your subordinates to return immediately to their work assignments
    C. give your subordinates some time to ask questions and discuss your announcement
    D. insist that your subordinates do not discuss your announcement among themselves or with other members of the agency

22.____

23. Suppose that as an Administrative Assistant you were recently placed in charge of the Duplicating and Stock Unit of Department Y. From your observation of the operations of your unit during your first week as its head, you get the impression that there are inefficiencies in its operations causing low productivity.
    To obtain an increase in its productivity, the FIRST of the following actions you should take is to
    A. seek the advice of your immediate superior on how he would tackle this problem
    B. develop plans to correct any unsatisfactory conditions arising from other than manpower deficiencies
    C. identify the problems causing low productivity
    D. discuss your productivity problem with other unit heads to find out how they handled similar problems

23.____

24. Assume that you are an Administrative Assistant recently placed in charge of a large clerical unit. At a meeting, the head of another unit tells you: *My practice is to give a worker more than he can finish. In that way you can be sure that you are getting the most out of him.*
    For you to accept this practice would be
    A. *advisable*, since your actions would be consistent with those practiced in your agency
    B. *inadvisable*, since such a practice is apt to create frustration and lower staff morals
    C. *advisable* since a high goal stimulates people to strive to attain it
    D. *inadvisable*, since management may, in turn, set too high a productivity goal for the unit

24.____

7 (#2)

25. Suppose that you are the supervisor of a unit in which there is an increasing amount of friction among several of your staff members. One of the reasons for this friction is that the work of some of these staff members cannot be completed until other staff members complete related work.
Of the following, the MOST appropriate action for you to take is to
   A. summon these employees to a meeting to discuss the responsibilities each has and to devise better methods of coordination
   B. have a private talk with each employee involved and make each understand that there must be more cooperation among the employees
   C. arrange for interviews with each of the employees involved to determine what his problems are
   D. shift the assignments of these employees so that each will be doing a job different from his current one

25.____

26. An office supervisor has a number of responsibilities with regard to his subordinates.
Which one of the following functions should NOT be regarded as a basic responsibility of the office supervisor?
   A. Telling employees how to solve personal problems that may be interfering with their work
   B. Training new employees to do the work assigned to them
   C. Evaluating employees' performance periodically and discussing the evaluation with each employee
   D. Bringing employee grievances to the attention of higher-level administrators and seeking satisfactory resolutions

26.____

27. One of your most productive subordinates frequently demonstrates a poor attitude toward his job. He seems unsure of himself, and he annoys his co-workers because he is continually belittling himself and the work that he is doing.
In trying to help him overcome this problem, which of the following approaches is LEAST likely to be effective?
   A. Compliment him on his work and assign him some additional responsibilities, telling him that he is being given these responsibilities because of his demonstrated ability
   B. Discuss with him the problem of his attitude, and warn him that you will have to report it on his next performance evaluation
   C. Assign him a particularly important and difficult project, stressing your confidence in his ability to complete it successfully
   D. Discuss with him the problem of his attitude, and ask him for suggestions as to how you can help him overcome it

27.____

28. You come to realize that a personality conflict between you and one of your subordinates is adversely affecting his performance.
Which one of the following would be the MOST appropriate FIRST step to take?
   A. Report the problem to your superior and request assistance. His experience may be helpful in resolving this problem.

28.____

107

B. Discuss the situation with several of the subordinate's co-workers to see if they can suggest any remedy
C. Suggest to the subordinate that he get professional counseling or therapy
D. Discuss the situation candidly with the subordinate, with the objective of resolving the problem between yourselves

29. Assume that you are an Administrative Assistant supervising the Payroll Records Section in Department G. Your section has been requested to prepare and submit to the department's budget officer a detailed report giving a breakdown of labor costs under various departmental programs and sub-programs. You have assigned this task to a Supervising Clerk, giving him full authority for seeing that this job is performed satisfactorily. You have given him a written statement of the job to be done and explained the purpose and use of this report.
The next step that you should take in connection with this delegated task is to
    A. assist the Supervising Clerk in the step-by-step performance of the job
    B. assure the Supervising Clerk that you will be understanding of mistakes if made at the beginning
    C. require him to receive your approval for interim reports submitted at key points before he can proceed further with his task
    D. give him a target date for the completion of this report

30. Assume that you are an Administrative Assistant heading a unit staffed with six clerical employees. One Clerk, John Snell, is a probationary employee appointed four months ago. During the first three months, John learned his job quickly, performed his work accurately and diligently, and was cooperative and enthusiastic in his attitude. However, during the past few weeks his enthusiasm seems dampened, he is beginning to make mistakes and at times appears bored.
Of the following, the MOST appropriate action for you to take is to
    A. check with John's co-workers to find out whether they can explain John's change in attitude and work habits
    B. wait a few more weeks before taking any action, so that John will have an opportunity to make the needed changes on his own initiative
    C. talk to John about the change in his work performance and his decreased enthusiasm
    D. change John's assignment since this may be the basic cause of John's change in attitude and performance

31. The supervisor of a clerical unit, on returning from a meeting, finds that one of his subordinates is performing work not assigned by him. The subordinate explains that the group supervisor had come into the office while the unit supervisor was out and directed the employee to work on an urgent assignment. This is the first time the group supervisor had bypassed the unit supervisor.
Of the following, the MOST appropriate action for the unit supervisor to take is to

9 (#2)

- A. explain to the group supervisor that bypassing the unit supervisor is an undesirable practice
- B. have the subordinate stop work on the assignment until the entire matter can be clarified with the group supervisor
- C. raise the matter of bypassing a supervisor at the next staff conference held by the group supervisor
- D. forget about the incident

32. Assume that you are an Administrative Assistant in charge of the Mail and Records Unit of Department K. On returning from a meeting, you notice that Jane Smith is not at her regular work location. You learn that another employee, Ruth Reed, had become faint, and that Jane took Ruth outdoors for some fresh air. It is a long-standing rule in your unit that no employee is to leave the building during office hours except on official business or with the unit head's approval. Only a few weeks ago, John Duncan was reprimanded by you for going out at 10:00 A.M. for a cup of coffee.
With respect to Jane Smith's violation of this rule, the MOST appropriate of the following actions for you to take is to
    - A. issue a reprimand to Jane Smith, with an explanation that all employees must be treated in exactly the same way
    - B. tell Jane that you should reprimand her, but you will not do so in this instance
    - C. overlook this rule violation in view of the extenuating circumstances
    - D. issue the reprimand with no further explanation, treating her in the same manner that you treated John Duncan

32.____

33. Assume that you are an Administrative Assistant recently assigned as supervisor of Department X's Mail and Special Services Unit. In addition to processing your department's mail, your clerical employees are often sent on errands in the city. You have learned that, while on such official errands, these clerks sometimes take care of their own personal matters or those of their co-workers. The previous supervisor had tolerated this practice even though it violated a departmental personnel rule.
The MOST appropriate of the following actions for you to take is to
    - A. continue to tolerate this practice so long as it does not interfere with the work of your unit
    - B. take no action until you have proof that an employee has violated this rule; then give a mild reprimand
    - C. wait until an employee has committed a gross violation of this rule; then bring him up on charges
    - D. discuss this rule with your staff and caution them that its violation might necessitate disciplinary action

33.____

34. Supervisor who exercise "close supervision" over their subordinate usually check up on their employees frequently, give them frequent instructions and, in general, limit their freedom to do their work in their own way. Those who exercise "general supervision" usually set forth the objectives of a job, tell their subordinates what they want accomplished, fix the limits within which the subordinates can work and let the employees (if they are capable) decide how the job is to be done.
Which one of the following conditions would contribute LEAST to the success of the general supervision approach in an organization?
    A. Employees in the unit welcome increased responsibilities
    B. Work assignments in the unit are often challenging
    C. Work procedures must conform with those of other units
    D. Staff members support the objectives of the unit

35. Assume that you are an Administrative Assistant assigned as supervisor of the Clerical Services Unit of a large agency's Labor Relations Division. A member of your staff comes to you with a criticism of a policy followed by the Labor Relations Division. You also have similar views regarding this policy.
Of the following, the MOST appropriate action for you to take in response to his criticism is to
    A. agree with him, but tell him that nothing can be done about it at your level
    B. suggest to him that it is not wise for him to express criticism of policy
    C. tell the employee that he should direct his criticism to the head of your agency if he wants quick action
    D. ask the employee if he has suggestions for revising the policy

KEY (CORRECT ANSWERS)

1.	C	11.	A	21.	C	31.	D
2.	B	12.	C	22.	C	32.	C
3.	B	13.	B	23.	C	33.	D
4.	D	14.	D	24.	B	34.	C
5.	A	15.	B	25.	A	35.	D
6.	C	16.	C	26.	A		
7.	D	17.	C	27.	B		
8.	A	18.	D	28.	D		
9.	A	19.	A	29.	D		
10.	B	20.	B	30.	C		

TEST 3

DIRECTIONS: Each question or incomplete statement is followed by several suggested answers or completions. Select the one that BEST answers the question or completes the statement. *PRINT THE LETTER OF THE CORRECT ANSWER IN THE SPACE AT THE RIGHT.*

1. At the request of your bureau head, you have designed a simple visitor's referral form. The form will be cut from 8½" x 11" stock.
   Which of the following should be the dimensions of the form if you want to be sure that there is no waste of paper?
   A. 2¾" x 4¼"   B. 3¼" x 4¾"   C. 3¾" x 4¾"   D. 4½" x 5½"

   1.____

2. An office contains six file cabinets, each containing three drawers. One of your responsibilities as a new Administrative Assistant is to see that there is sufficient filing space. At the present time, 1/4 of the file space contains forms, 2/9 contains personnel records, 1/3 contains reports, and 1/7 of the remaining space contains budget records.
   If each drawer may contain more than one type of record, how much drawer space is now empty?
   A. 0 drawers   B. ¹³/₁₄ of a drawer
   C. 3 drawers   D. 3½ drawers

   2.____

3. Assume that there were 21 working days in March. The five clerks in your unit had the following number of absences in March:
   Clerk H: 2 absences
   Clerk J: 1 absence
   Clerk K: 6 absences
   Clerk L: 0 absences
   Clerk M: 10 absences
   To the nearest day, what was the AVERAGE attendance in March for the five clerks in your unit?
   A. 4   B. 17   C. 18   D. 21

   3.____

Questions 4-12.

DIRECTIONS: Questions 4 through 12 each consist of a sentence which may or may not be an example of good English usage. Consider grammar, punctuation, spelling, capitalization, verbosity, awkwardness, etc. Examine each sentence, and then choose the CORRECT statement about it from the four choices below it. If the English usage in the sentence is better as given than with any of the changes suggested in options B, C, or D, choose option A.

4. The stenographers who are secretaries to commissioners have more varied duties than the stenographic pool.
   A. This is an example of effective writing.
   B. In this sentence there would be a comma after *commissioners* in order to break up the sentence into clauses.
   C. In this sentence, the words *stenographers in* should be inserted after the word "than".
   D. In this sentence, the word *commissioners* is misspelled.

4._____

5. A person who becomes an administrative assistant will be called upon to provide leadership, to insure proper quantity and quality of production, and many administrative chores must be performed.
   A. This sentence is an example of effective writing.
   B. The sentence should be divided into three separate sentences, each describing a duty.
   C. The words *many administrative chores must be performed* should be changed to *to perform many administrative chores*.
   D. The words *to provide leadership* should be changed to *to be a leader*.

5._____

6. A complete report has been submitted by our branch office, giving details about this transaction.
   A. This sentence is an example of effective writing.
   B. The phrase *giving details about this transaction* should be placed between the words *report* and *has*.
   C. A semi-colon should replace the comma after the word *office* to indicate independent clauses.
   D. A colon should replace the comma after the word *office* since the second clause provides further explanation.

6._____

7. The report was delayed because of the fact that the writer lost his rough draft two days before the deadline.
   A. This sentence is an example of effective writing.
   B. In this sentence the words *of the fact that* are unnecessary and should be deleted.
   C. In this sentence the words *because of the fact that* should be shortened to *due to*.
   D. In this sentence the word *before* should be replaced by *prior to*.

7._____

8. Included in this offer are a six months' guarantee, a complete set of instructions, and one free inspection of the equipment.
   A. This sentence is an example of effective writing.
   B. The word *is* should be substituted for the word *are*.
   C. The word *months* should have been spelled *month's*.
   D. The word *months* should be spelled *months*.

8._____

9. Certain employees come to the attention of their employers. Especially those with poor work records and excessive absences.
   A. This sentence is an example of effective writing.
   B. The period after the word *employers* should be changed to a comma, and the first letter of the word *Especially* should be changed to a small *e*.
   C. The period after the word *employers* should be changed to a semicolon, and the first letter of the word *Especially* should be changed to a small *e*.
   D. The period after the word *employers* should be changed to a colon.

10. The applicant had decided to decline the appointment by the time he was called for the interview.
    A. This sentence is an example of effective writing.
    B. In this sentence the word *had* should be deleted.
    C. In this sentence the phrase *was called* should be replaced by *had been called*.
    D. In this sentence the phrase *had decided to decline* should be replaced by *declined*.

11. There are two elevaters, each accommodating ten people
    A. This sentence is correct.
    B. In this sentence the word *elevaters* should be spelled *elevators*.
    C. In this sentence the word *each* should be replaced by the word *both*.
    D. In this sentence the word *accommodating* should be spelled *accomodating*.

12. With the aid of a special device, it was possible to alter the letterhead on the department's stationary.
    A. This sentence is correct.
    B. The word *aid* should be spelled *aide*.
    C. The word *device* should be spelled *devise*.
    D. The word *stationary* should be spelled *stationery*.

13. Examine the following sentence and then choose from the options below the correct word to be inserted in the blank space.
    Everybody in both offices _____ involved in the project.
    A. are   B. feel   C. is

Questions 14-18.

DIRECTIONS: Questions 14 through 18 are to be answered SOLELY on the basis of the information in the following passage.

A new way of looking at job performance promises to be a major advance in measuring and increasing a person's true effectiveness in business. The fact that individuals differ enormously in their judgment of when a piece of work is actually finished is significant. It is believed that more than half of all people in the business world are defective in the *sense of closure*, that is they do not know the proper time to throw the switch that turns off their effort in one direction and diverts it to a new job. Only a minority of workers at any level have the required judgment and the feeling of responsibility to work on a job to the point of maximum effectiveness. The vast majority let go of each task far short of the completion point.

Very often, a defective sense of closure exists in an entire staff. When that occurs, it usually stems from a long-standing laxness on the part of higher management. A low degree of responsibility has been accepted and it has come to e standard. Combating this requires implementation of a few basic policies. Firstly, it is important to make each responsibility completely clear and to set certain guideposts as to what constitutes complete performance. Secondly, excuses for delays and failures should not be dealt with too sympathetically, but interest should be shown in the encountered obstacles. Lastly, a checklist should be used periodically to determine whether new levels of expectancy and new closure values have been set.

14. According to the above passage, a *majority of* people in the business world
    A. do not complete their work on time
    B. cannot properly determine when a particular job is completed
    C. make lame excuses for not completing a job on time
    D. can adequately judge their own effectiveness at work

15. It can be *inferred* from the above passage that when a poor sense of closure is observed among all the employees in a unit, the responsibility for raising the performance level belongs to
    A. non-supervisory employees   B. the staff as a whole
    C. management   D. first-line supervisors

16. It is *implied* by the above passage that, by the establishment of work guideposts, employees may develop a
    A. better understanding of expected performances
    B. greater interest in their work relationships
    C. defective sense of closure
    D. lower level of performance

17. It can be *inferred* from the above passage that an individual's idea of whether a job is finished is MOST closely associated with his
    A. loyalty to management
    B. desire to overcome obstacles
    C. ability to recognize his own defects
    D. sense of responsibility

18. Of the following, the BEST heading for the above passage is
    A. Management's Role in a Large Bureaucracy
    B. Knowing When a Job is Finished
    C. The Checklist, a Supervisor's Tool For Effectiveness
    D. Supervisory Techniques

Questions 19-25.

DIRECTIONS: Answer Questions 19 through 25 assuming that you are in charge of public information for an office which issues report and answers questions from other offices and from the public on changes in land use. The charts below represent comparative land use in four neighborhood. The area of each neighborhood is expressed in city blocks. Assume that all city blocks are the same size.

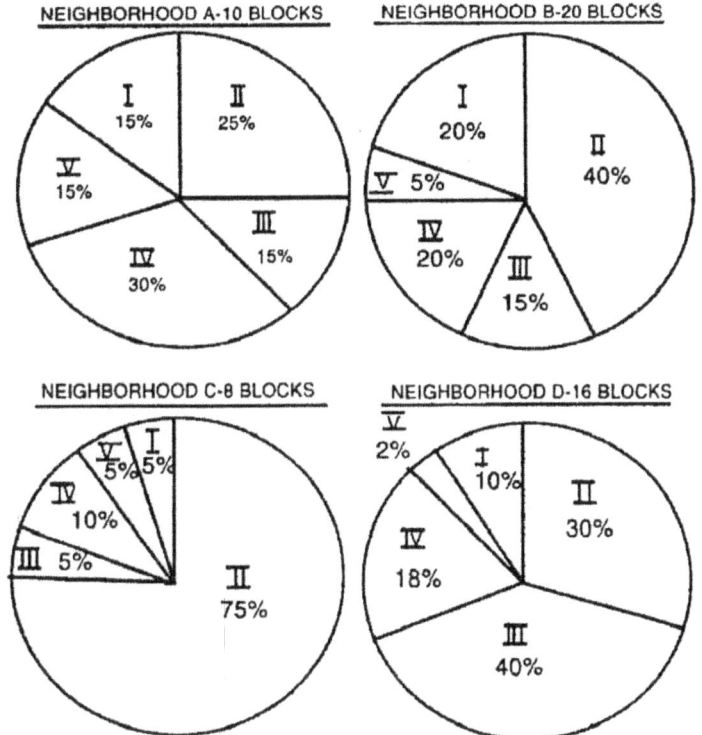

KEY: I – One- and two-family houses
      II – Apartment buildings
      III – Office buildings
      IV – Retail stores
      V - Factories and warehouses

19. In how many of these neighborhoods does residential use (categories I and II together) account for *more than 50%* of the land use?
    A. 1   B. 2   C. 3   D. 4

20. How many of the neighborhoods have an area of land occupied by apartment buildings which is GREATER than the area of land occupied by apartment buildings in Neighborhood C?
    A. None   B. 1   C. 2   D. 3

21. Which neighborhood has the LARGEST land area occupied by factories and warehouses?
    A. A   B. B   C. C   D. D

22. In which neighborhood is the LARGEST percentage of the land devoted to *both* office buildings and retail stores?
    A. A   B. B   C. C   D. D

23. What is the difference, to the nearest city block, between the amount of land devoted to one- and two-family houses in Neighborhood A and the amount devoted to similar use in Neighborhood C?
    A. 1 block   B. 2 blocks   C. 5 blocks   D. 10 blocks

24. Which one of the following types of buildings occupies the same amount of land area in Neighborhood B as the amount of land area occupied by retail stores in Neighborhood A?
    A. Apartment buildings   B. Office buildings
    C. Retail stores   D. Factories and warehouses

25. Based on the information in the charts, which one of the following statements must be TRUE?
    A. Factories and warehouses are gradually disappearing from all the neighborhoods except Neighborhood A.
    B. Neighborhood B has more land area occupied by retail stores than any of the other neighborhoods.
    C. There are more apartment dwellers living in Neighborhood C than in any of the other neighborhoods.
    D. All four of these neighborhoods are predominantly residential.

KEY (CORRECT ANSWERS)

1.	A	11.	B
2.	C	12.	D
3.	B	13.	C
4.	C	14.	B
5.	C	15.	C
6.	B	16.	A
7.	B	17.	D
8.	A	18.	B
9.	B	19.	B
10.	A	20.	B

21.	A
22.	D
23.	A
24.	B
25.	B

EXAMINATION SECTION
TEST 1

DIRECTIONS: Each question or incomplete statement is followed by several suggested answers or completions. Select the one that BEST answers the question or completes the statement. *PRINT THE LETTER OF THE CORRECT ANSWER IN THE SPACE AT THE RIGHT.*

1. Suppose that one of the forms you fill out daily requires some information which you know is unnecessary.
   Which is the BEST action to take?
   A. Refuse to supply the information you think is unnecessary.
   B. Continue to fill out the form as required, even though the information is unnecessary.
   C. Suggest to your supervisor that the form be revised to reflect useful information.
   D. Suggest that fewer copies of the form be required.

   1.____

2. Of the following, the MOST likely reason for recommending that your department establish a standard form for recording certain information would be that this information
   A. will be produced at some disciplinary hearing
   B. concerns a secret or confidential record about an unusual incident at the garage
   C. contains a detailed explanation of a complex procedure
   D. must be taken from a large number of people on a regular basis

   2.____

3. If the four steps listed below for processing records were given in logical sequence, the one that would be the THIRD step is
   A. coding the records, using a chart or classification system
   B. inspecting the records to make sure they have been released for filing
   C. preparing cross-reference sheets or cards
   D. skimming the records to determine filing captions

   3.____

4. Which of the following BEST describes "office work simplification"?
   A. An attempt to increase the rate of production by speeding up the movements of employees
   B. Eliminating wasteful steps in order to increase efficiency
   C. Making jobs as easy as possible for employees so they will not be overworked
   D. Eliminating all difficult tasks from an office and leaving only simple ones

   4.____

5. The use of the same method of recordkeeping and reporting by all sections is
   A. *desirable*, mainly because it saves time in section operations
   B. *undesirable*, mainly because it kills the initiative of the individual section foreman
   C. *desirable*, mainly because it will be easier for the superior to evaluate and compare section operations
   D. *undesirable*, mainly because operations vary from section to section and uniform recordkeeping and reporting is not appropriate

6. The GREATEST benefit the section officer will have from keeping complete and accurate records of section operations is that
   A. he will find it easier to run his section efficiently
   B. he will need less equipment
   C. he will need less manpower
   D. the section will run smoothly when he is out

7. You have prepared a report to your superior and are ready to send it forward. But on reading it, you think some parts are not clearly expressed and the superior may have difficulty getting your point.
   Of the following, it would be BEST for you to
   A. give the report to one of your men to read, and, if he has no trouble understanding it, send it through
   B. forward the report and call the superior the next day to ask if it was all right
   C. forward the report as is; higher echelons should be able to understand any report prepared by a section officer
   D. do the report over, re-writing the sections you are doubtful of

8. Of the following, a flow chart is BEST described as a chart which shows
   A. the places through which work moves in the course of the job process
   B. which employees perform specific functions leading to the completion of a job
   C. the schedules for production and how they eliminate waiting time between jobs
   D. how work units are affected by the actions of related work units

9. A superior decided to hold a problem-solving conference with his entire staff and distributed an announcement and agenda one week before the meeting. Of the following, the BEST reason for providing each participate with an agenda is that
   A. participants will feel that something will be accomplished
   B. participants may prepare for the conference
   C. controversy will be reduced
   D. the top man should state the expected conclusions

3 (#1)

10. The one of the following activities which is generally the LEAST proper function of a centralized procedures section is
    A. issuing new and revised procedural instructions
    B. coordinating forms revision and procedural changes
    C. accepting or rejecting authorized procedural changes
    D. controlling standard numbering systems for procedural releases

10.____

11. Assume that it is the policy of an operating unit to act on all requests received within five working days. Several operations are involved in acting on these requests. Each operation is performed by a separate sub-unit. The staff of the unit is reasonable adequate to handle this workload.
    If only one of the following can be done, the MOST effective procedure for maintaining adherence to the unit's five-day processing policy is to
    A. maintain a central "tickler" file in each sub-unit for the requests received daily in that sub-unit
    B. prepare a "tickler" card for each request and follow it up five days later to determine whether action has been taken
    C. rely on standards of production for each operation as an incentive to the employees of each sub-unit to meet the schedule
    D. schedule the operations on a timetable basis so that the request will be forwarded from one sub-unit to another within specified time limits

11.____

12. When one or two simple changes are needed in a memo to another unit or in a letter to a citizen, a unit head follows the practice of making such simple changes neatly in ink.
    This practice is GENERALLY
    A. *poor*, chiefly because it reflects unfavorably on the originating unit's ability to make a decision
    B. *good*, chiefly because the department's public image is likely to be improved when people see it as trying to save money and speed up its processes
    C. *poor*, chiefly because a letter or document prepared in final form represents an investment of department time and effort and should go out only as a perfect finished product
    D. *good*, chiefly because the document may be important, and sending it back for retyping may delay it too long to achieve its purpose

12.____

13. Suppose that one of the office machines in your unit is badly in need of replacement.
    Of the following, the MOST important reason for postponing immediate purchase of a new machine would be that
    A. a later model of the machine is expected on the market in a few months
    B. the new machine is more expensive than the old machine
    C. the operator of the present machine will have to be instructed by the manufacturer in the operation of the new machine
    D. the employee operating the old machine is not complaining

13.____

14. To avoid cutting off parts of letters when using an automatic letter opener, it is BEST to
    A. arrange all of the letters so that the addresses are right side up
    B. hold the envelopes up to the light to make sure their contents have not settled to the side that is to be opened
    C. strike the envelopes against a table or desktop several times so that the contents of all the envelopes settle to one side
    D. check the enclosures periodically to make sure that the machine has not been cutting into them

14._____

15. Of the following, the BEST reason for setting up a partitioned work area for the typists in our office is that
    A. an uninterrupted flow of work among the typists will be possible
    B. complaints about ventilation and lighting will be reduced
    C. the first-line supervisor will have more direct control over the typists
    D. the noise of the typewriters will be less disturbing to other workers

15._____

16. From the viewpoint of use of a typewriter to fill in a form, the MOST important design factor to consider is
    A. standard spacing   B. box headings
    C. serial numbering   D. vertical guide lines

16._____

17. Requests to repair office equipment which appears to be unsafe should be given priority MAINLY because, if repairs are delayed,
    A. there may be injuries to staff
    B. there may be further deterioration of the equipment
    C. work flow may be interrupted
    D. the cost of repair may increase

17._____

18. A clerk is asked to complete two assignments – transcribe a handwritten business letter and create a spreadsheet. Which two computer programs would the clerk use?
    A. Microsoft Word and Microsoft Excel
    B. Microsoft Word and Microsoft PowerPoint
    C. Google Docs and Google Chrome
    D. Adobe Reader and Microsoft PowerPoint

18._____

19. Generally, the actual floor space occupied by a standard letter-size office file cabinet, when closed, is MOST NEARLY
    A. ½ square foot   B. 3 square feet
    C. 7 square feet   D. 11 square feet

19._____

20. Suppose a clerk under your supervision accidentally opens a personal letter while handling office mail.
    Under such circumstances, you should tell the clerk to put the letter back into the envelope and
    A. take the letter to the person to whom it belongs and make sure he understands that the clerk did not read it
    B. try to seal the envelope so it won't appear to have been opened

20._____

C. write on the envelope "Sorry – opened by mistake," and put his initials on it
D. write on the envelope "Sorry – opened by mistake," but not put his initials on it

21. Standard forms frequently call for entries on them to be printed.
The MAIN reason for this practice is that printing, as compared to writing, is GENERALLY
    A. more compact
    B. more legal
    C. more legible
    D. easier to do

22. After a stenographer types a letter which has been dictated, the finished letter should be carefully read for errors.
If he dictator follows the procedure of carefully reading each transcribed letter, a stenographer, under your supervision, should, unless you instruct her otherwise
    A. not take time to proofread transcribed letters
    B. continue to carefully proofread transcribed letters
    C. review transcribed letters for meaning rather than for errors in typing or transcription
    D. review transcribed letters for errors in typing rather than for errors in transcription

23. In transcribing a letter, the secretary notes that the dictator said, "The series of conferences are planned to be relevant to today's problems." In such a case, the secretary should
    A. type the sentence as it appears in the notes
    B. check with the dictator to see whether he would prefer a different grammatical construction
    C. change the noun so that it is correct
    D. revise the sentence as much as necessary to make it read better

24. Of the following, the BEST procedure for your staff to follow in transcribing several letters that were dictated is to
    A. transcribe first the letters that are most difficult so that they can return immediately to the dictator with any questions
    B. read through the notes for each letter to be sure they have all the information needed before preparing the transcript
    C. transcribe first those letters that are shortest and simplest in order to get them out of the way
    D. read all the notes aloud to a co-worker to see whether they sound right

25. In typing long letters, which of the following is generally considered the LEAST desirable practice?
    A. Numbering the second and succeeding pages of the letter
    B. Typing a single line of a new paragraph as the last line of a page
    C. Dividing a word at the end of a line of typing
    D. Typing the name of the recipient of the letter on the second and succeeding pages

KEY (CORRECT ANSWERS)

1. C
2. D
3. D
4. B
5. C

6. A
7. D
8. A
9. B
10. C

11. D
12. B
13. A
14. C
15. D

16. A
17. A
18. A
19. B
20. C

21. C
22. B
23. B
24. B
25. B

TEST 2

DIRECTIONS: Each question or incomplete statement is followed by several suggested answers or completions. Select the one that BEST answers the question or completes the statement. *PRINT THE LETTER OF THE CORRECT ANSWER IN THE SPACE AT THE RIGHT.*

1. The use of a microfilm system for information storage and retrieval would make the MOST sense in an office where
    A. a great number of documents must be kept available for permanent reference
    B. documents are ordinarily kept on file for less than six months
    C. filing is a minor and unimportant part of the office work
    D. most of the records on file are working forms on which additional entries are frequently made

    1.____

2. Of the following concepts, the one which CANNOT be represented suitably by a pie chart is
    A. percent shares
    B. shares in absolute units
    C. time trends
    D. successive totals over time, with their shares

    2.____

3. A pictogram is ESSENTIALLY another version of a(n) _____ chart.
    A. plain bar   B. component bar
    C. pie   D. area

    3.____

4. A time series for a certain cost is presented in a graph. It is drawn so that the vertical (cost) axis starts at a point well above zero. This is a legitimate method of presentation for some purposes, but it may have the effect of
    A. hiding fixed components of the cost
    B. exaggerating changes which, in actual amounts, may be insignificant
    C. minimizing variable components of the cost
    D. impairing correlation analysis

    4.____

5. Certain budgetary data may be represented by bar, area, or volume charts. Which one of the following BEST expressed the most appropriate order of usefulness?
    A. Descends from bar to volume and area charts, the last two being about the same
    B. Descends from volume to area, to bar charts
    C. Depends on the nature of the data presented
    D. Descends from bar to area to volume charts

    5.____

6. One weekend, you develop a painful infection in one hand. You know that your typing speed will be much slower than normal and the likelihood of your making mistakes will be increased.
   Of the following, the BEST course of action for you to take in this situation is to
   A. report to work as scheduled and do your typing assignments as best you can without complaining
   B. report to work as scheduled and ask your co-workers to divide your typing assignments until your hand heals
   C. report to work as scheduled and ask your supervisor for non-typing assignments until your hand heals
   D. call in sick and remain on medical leave until your hand is completely healed so that you can perform your normal duties

6._____

7. When filling out a departmental form during an interview concerning a citizen complaint, an interviewer should know the purpose of each question that he asks the citizen. For such information to be supplied by your department is
   A. *advisable*, because the interviewer may lose interest in the job if he is not fully informed about the questions he has to ask
   B. *inadvisable*, because the interviewer may reveal the true purpose of the questions to the citizens
   C. *advisable*, because the interviewer might otherwise record superficial or inadequate answers if he does not fully understand the questions
   D. *inadvisable*, because the information obtained through the form may be of little importance to the interviewer

7._____

8. The one of the following which is the BEST reason for placing the date and time of receipt on incoming mail is that this procedure
   A. aids the filing of correspondence in alphabetical order
   B. fixes responsibility for promptness in answering correspondence
   C. indicates that the mail has been checked for the presence of a return address
   D. makes it easier to distribute the main in sequence

8._____

9. Which one of the following is the FIRST step that you should take when filing a document by subject?
   A. Arrange related documents by date with the latest date in front
   B. Check whether the document has been released for filing
   C. Cross-reference the document if necessary
   D. Determine the category under which the document will be filed

9._____

10. The one of the following which is NOT generally employed to keep track of frequently used material requiring future attention is a
    A. card tickler file   B. dated follow-up folder
    C. periodic transferal of records   D. signal folder

10._____

11. Which one of the following is NOT a useful filing practice?
    A. Filing active records in the most accessible parts of the file cabinet
    B. Filing a file drawer to capacity in order to save space
    C. Gluing small documents to standard-size paper before filing
    D. Using different colored labels for various filing categories

12. The one of the following cases in which you would NOT place a special notation in the left margin of a letter that you have typed is when
    A. one of the copies is intended for someone other than the addressee of the letter
    B. you enclose a flyer with the letter
    C. you sign your superior's name to the letter, at his or her request
    D. the letter refers to something being sent under separate cover

13. Suppose that you accidentally cut a letter or enclosure as you are opening an envelope with a paper knife. The one of the following that you should do FIRST is to
    A. determine whether the document is important
    B. clip or staple the pieces together and process as usual
    C. mend the cut document with transparent tape
    D. notify the sender that the communication was damaged and request another copy

14. It is generally advisable to leave at least six inches of working space in a file drawer. This procedure is MOST useful in
    A. decreasing the number of filing errors
    B. facilitating the sorting of documents and folders
    C. maintaining a regular program of removing inactive records
    D. preventing folders and papers from being torn

15. Of the following, the MOST important reason to sort large volumes of documents before filing is that sorting
    A. decreases the need for cross-referencing
    B. eliminates the need to keep the filing up-to-date
    C. prevents overcrowding of the file drawers
    D. saves time and energy in filing

16. When typing a preliminary draft of a report, the one of the following which you should generally NOT do is to
    A. erase typing errors and deletions rather than "X"ing them out
    B. leave plenty of room at the top, bottom, and sides of each page
    C. make only the number of copies that you are asked to make
    D. type double or triple space

17. When printing a 500-page office manual, the most efficient method is to use which of the following office machines?
    A. Inkjet printer
    B. Copy machine
    C. Word processor
    D. All-in-one scanner/fax/copier

17._____

18. When typing name or titles on a roll of folder labels, the one of the following which it is MOST important to do is to type the caption
    A. as it appears son the papers to be placed in the folder
    B. in capital letters
    C. in exact indexing or filing order
    D. so that it appears near the bottom of the folder tab when the label is attached

18._____

19. The MOST important reason for having color cartridges on hand for an office copier even though most prints are black and white is because
    A. color ink is used for all copies
    B. some copiers or printers will not print black and white if any of the color cartridges are empty
    C. black ink is cheaper when purchasing along with color cartridges
    D. lack of color ink can cause copier malfunctions

19._____

20. All of the following pertain to the formatting of word-processing documents EXCEPT
    A. headers and footers
    B. rows and columns
    C. indents and page breaks
    D. alignment and justified type

20._____

KEY (CORRECT ANSWERS)

1.	A	11.	B
2.	C	12.	C
3.	A	13.	C
4.	B	14.	D
5.	D	15.	D
6.	C	16.	A
7.	C	17.	B
8.	B	18.	C
9.	B	19.	B
10.	C	20.	B

RECORD KEEPING
EXAMINATION SECTION
TEST 1

DIRECTIONS: Each question or incomplete statement is followed by several suggested answers or completions. Select the one that BEST answers the question or completes the statement. *PRINT THE LETTER OF THE CORRECT ANSWER IN THE SPACE AT THE RIGHT.*

Questions 1-15.

DIRECTIONS: Questions 1 through 15 are to be answered on the basis of the following list of company names below. Arrange a file alphabetically, word-by-word, disregarding punctuation, conjunctions, and apostrophes. Then answer the questions.

    A Bee C Reading Materials
    ABCO Parts
    A Better Course for Test Preparation
    AAA Auto Parts Co.
    A-Z Auto Parts, Inc.
    Aabar Books
    Abbey, Joanne
    Boman-Sylvan Law Firm
    BMW Autowerks
    C Q Service Company
    Chappell-Murray, Inc.
    E&E Life Insurance
    Emcrisco
    Gigi Arts
    Gordon, Jon & Associates
    SOS Plumbing
    Schmidt, J.B. Co.

1. Which of these files should appear FIRST?
   A. ABCO Parts
   B. A Bee C Reading Materials
   C. A Better Course for Test Preparation
   D. AAA Auto Parts Co.

2. Which of these files should appear SECOND?
   A. A-Z Auto Parts, Inc.
   B. A Bee C Reading Materials
   C. A Better Course for Test Preparation
   D. AAA Auto Parts Co.

3. Which of these files should appear THIRD?
   A. ABCO Parts
   B. A Bee C Reading Materials
   C. Aabar Books
   D. AAA Auto Parts Co.

4. Which of these files should appear FOURTH?
   A. Aabar Books
   B. ABCO Parts
   C. Abbey, Joanne
   D. AAA Auto Parts Co.

5. Which of these files should appear LAST?
   A. Gordon, Jon & Associates
   B. Gigi Arts
   C. Schmidt, J.B. Co.
   D. SOS Plumbing

6. Which of these files should appear between A-Z Auto Parts, Inc. and Abbey, Joanne?
   A. A Bee C Reading Materials
   B. AAA Auto Parts Co.
   C. ABCO Parts
   D. A Better Course for Test Preparation

7. Which of these files should appear between ABCO Parts and Aabar Books?
   A. A Bee C Reading Materials
   B. Abbey, Joanne
   C. Aabar Books
   D. A-Z Auto Parts

8. Which of these files should appear between Abbey, Joanne and Boman-Sylvan Law Firm?
   A. A Better Course for Test Preparation
   B. BMW Autowerks
   C. Chappell-Murray, Inc.
   D. Aabar Books

9. Which of these files should appear between Abbey, Joanne and C Q Service?
   A. A-Z Auto Parts, Inc.
   B. BMW Autowerks
   C. Choices A and B
   D. Chappell-Murray, Inc.

10. Which of these files should appear between C Q Service Company and Emcrisco?
    A. Chappell-Murray, Inc.
    B. E&E Life Insurance
    C. Gigi Arts
    D. Choices A and B

11. Which of these files should NOT appear between C Q Service Company and E&E Life Insurance?
    A. Gordon, Jon & Associates
    B. Emcrisco
    C. Gigi Arts
    D. All of the above

12. Which of these files should appear between Chappell-Murray, Inc. and Gigi Arts?   12.____
    A. C Q Service Inc., E&E Life Insurance, and Emcrisco
    B. Emcrisco, E&E Life Insurance, and Gordon, Jon & Associates
    C. E&E Life Insurance, and Emcrisco
    D. Emcrisco and Gordon, Jon & Associates

13. Which of these files should appear between Gordon, Jon & Associates and SOS Plumbing?   13.____
    A. Gigi Arts
    B. Schmidt, J.B. Co.
    C. Choices A and B
    D. None of the above

14. Each of the choices lists the four files in their proper alphabetical order EXCEPT   14.____
    A. E&E Life Insurance; Gigi Arts; Gordon, Jon & Associates; SOS Plumbing
    B. E&E Life Insurance; Emcrisco; Gigi Arts; SOS Plumbing
    C. Emcrisco; Gordon, Jon & Associates; SOS Plumbing; Schmidt, J.B. Co.
    D. Emcrisco; Gigi Arts; Gordon, Jon & Associates; SOS Plumbing

15. Which of the choices lists the four files in their proper alphabetical order?   15.____
    A. Gigi Arts; Gordon, Jon & Associates; SOS Plumbing; Schmidt, J.B. Co.
    B. Gordon, Jon & Associates; Gigi Arts; Schmidt, J.B. Co.; SOS Plumbing
    C. Gordon, Jon & Associates; Gigi Arts; SOS Plumbing; Schmidt, J.B. Co.
    D. Gigi Arts; Gordon, Jon & Associates; Schmidt, J.B. Co.; SOS Plumbing

16. The alphabetical filing order of two businesses with identical names is determined by the   16.____
    A. length of time each business has been operating
    B. addresses of the businesses
    C. last name of the company president
    D. no one of the above

17. In an alphabetical filing system, if a business name includes a number, it should be   17.____
    A. disregarded
    B. considered a number and placed at the end of an alphabetical section
    C. treated as though it were written in words and alphabetized accordingly
    D. considered a number and placed at the beginning of an alphabetical section

18. If a business name includes a contraction (such as *don't* or *it's*), how should that word be treated in an alphabetical system?   18.____
    A. Divide the word into its separate parts and treat it as two words
    B. Ignore the letters that come after the apostrophe
    C. Ignore the word that contains the contraction
    D. Ignore the apostrophe and consider all letters in the contraction

19. In what order should the parts of an address be considered when using an alphabetical filing system?   19._____
    A. City or town; state; street name; house or building number
    B. State; city or town; street name; house or building number
    C. House or building number; street name; city or town; state
    D. Street name; city or town; state

20. A business record should be cross-referenced when a(n)   20._____
    A. organization is known by an abbreviated name
    B. business has a name change because of a sale, incorporation, or other reason
    C. business is known by a *coined* or common name which differs from a dictionary spelling
    D. all of the above

21. A geographical filing system is MOST effective when   21._____
    A. location is more important than name
    B. many names or titles sound alike
    C. dealing with companies who have offices all over the world
    D. filing personal and business files

Questions 22-25.

DIRECTIONS: Questions 22 through 25 are to be answered on the basis of the list of items below, which are to be filed geographically. Organize the items geographically and then answer the questions.

I. University Press at Berkeley, U.S.
II. Maria Sanchez, Mexico City, Mexico
III. Great Expectations Ltd. in London, England
IV. Justice League, Cape Town, South Africa, Africa
V. Crown Pearls Ltd. in London, England
VI. Joseph Prasad in London, England

22. Which of the following arrangements of the items is composed according to the policy of: *Continent, Country, City, Firm or Individual Name*?   22._____
    A. V, III, IV, VI, II, I   B. IV, V, III, VI, II, I
    C. I, IV, V, III, VI, II   D. IV, V, III, VI, I, II

23. Which of the following files is arranged according to the policy of: *Continent, Country, City, Firm or Individual Name*?   23._____
    A. South Africa; Africa; Cape Town; Justice League
    B. Mexico; Mexico City; Maria Sanchez
    C. North America; United States; Berkeley; University Press
    D. England; Europe; London; Prasad, Joseph

5 (#1)

24. Which of the following arrangements of the items is composed according to the policy of: *Country, City, Firm or Individual Name*? 24._____
    A. V, VI, III, II, IV, I
    B. I, V, VI, III, II, IV
    C. VI, V, III, II, IV, I
    D. V, III, VI, II, IV, I

25. Which of the following files is arranged according to a policy of: *Country, City, Firm or Individual Name*? 25._____
    A. England; London; Crown Pearls Ltd.
    B. North America; United States; Berkeley; University Press
    C. Africa; Cape Town; Justice League
    D. Mexico City; Mexico; Maria Sanchez

26. Under which of the following circumstances would a phonetic filing system be MOST effective? 26._____
    A. When the person in charge of filing can't spell very well
    B. With large files with names that sound alike
    C. With large files with names that are spelled alike
    D. All of the above

Questions 27-29.

DIRECTIONS: Questions 27 through 29 are to be answered on the basis of the following list of numerical files.

   I.   391-023-100
   II. 361-132-170
   III. 385-732-200
   IV. 381-432-150
   V.   391-632-387
   VI. 361-423-303
   VII. 391-123-271

27. Which of the following arrangements of the files follows a consecutive-digit system? 27._____
    A. II, III, IV, I   B. I, V, VII, III   C. II, IV, III, I   D. III, I, V, VII

28. Which of the following arrangements follows a terminal-digit system? 28._____
    A. I, VII, II, IV, III
    B. II, I, IV, V, VII
    C. VII, VI, V, IV, III
    D. I, IV, II, III, VII

29. Which of the following lists follows a middle-digit system? 29._____
    A. I, VII, II, VI, IV, V, III
    B. I, II, VII, IV, VI, V, III
    C. VII, II, I, III, V, VI, IV
    D. VII, I, II, IV, VI, V, III

Questions 30-31.

DIRECTIONS: Questions 30 and 31 are to be answered on the basis of the following information.

  I. Reconfirm Laura Bates appointment with James Caldecort on December 12 at 9:30 A.M.
  II. Laurence Kinder contact Julia Lucas on August 3 and set up a meeting for week of September 23 at 4 P.M.
  III. John Lutz contact Larry Waverly on August 3 and set up appointment for September 23 at 9:30 A.M.
  IV. Call for tickets for Gerry Stanton August 21 for New Jersey on September 23, flight 143 at 4:43 P.M.

30. A chronological file for the above information would be 30._____
  A. IV, III, II, I B. III, II, IV, I C. IV, II, III, I D. III, I, II, IV

31. Using the above information, a chronological file for the date September 23 would be 31._____
  A. II, III, IV B. III, I, IV C. III, II, IV D. IV, III, II

Questions 32-34.

DIRECTIONS: Questions 32 through 34 are to be answered on the basis of the following information.

  I. Call Roger Epstein, Ashoke Naipaul, Jon Anderson, and Sara Washingon on April 19 at 1:00 P.M. to set up meeting with Alika D'Ornay for June 6 in New York.
  II. Call Martin Ames before noon on April 19 to confirm afternoon meeting with Bob Greenwood on April 20th.
  III. Set up meeting room at noon for 2:30 P.M. meeting on April 19th.
  IV. Ashley Stanton contact Bob Greenwood at 9:00 A.M. on April 20 and set up meeting for June 6 at 8:30 A.M.
  V. Carol Guiland contact Shelby Van Ness during afternoon of April 20 and set up meeting for June 6 at 10:00 A.M.
  VI. Call airline and reserve tickets on June 6 for Roger Epstein trip to Denver on July 8.
  VII. Meeting at 2:30 P.M. on April 19th.

32. A chronological file for all of the above information would be 32._____
  A. II, I, III, VII, V, IV, VI B. III, VII, II, I, IV, V, VI
  C. III, VII, I, II, V, IV, VI D. II, III, I, VII, IV, V, VI

33. A chronological file for the date of April 19th would be 33._____
  A. II, III, VII, I B. II, III, I, VII C. VII, I, III, II D. III, VII, I, II

34. Add the following information to the file, and then create a chronological file for April 20th: VIII. April 20: 3:00 P.M. meeting between Bob Greenwood and Martin Ames.
 A. IV, V, VIII   B. IV, VIII, V   C. VIII, V, IV   D. V, IV, VIII

35. The PRIMARY advantage of computer records over a manual system is
 A. speed of retrieval
 B. accuracy
 C. cost
 D. potential file loss

KEY (CORRECT ANSWERS)

1. B	11. D	21. A	31. C
2. C	12. C	22. B	32. D
3. D	13. B	23. C	33. B
4. A	14. C	24. D	34. A
5. D	15. D	25. A	35. A
6. C	16. B	26. B	
7. B	17. C	27. C	
8. B	18. D	28. D	
9. C	19. A	29. A	
10. D	20. D	30. B	

PREPARING WRITTEN MATERIALS
EXAMINATION SECTION
TEST 1

DIRECTIONS: Each question contains a sentence. Read each sentence carefully to decide whether it is correct. Then, in the space at the right, mark your answer:
- A. If the sentence is incorrect because of bad grammar or sentence structure;
- B. If the sentence is incorrect because of bad punctuation
- C. If the sentence is incorrect because of bad capitalization
- D. If the sentence is correct.

Each incorrect sentence has only one type of error. Consider a sentence correct if it has no errors, although there may be other correct ways of saying the same thing.

SAMPLE QUESTION I: One of our clerks were promoted yesterday.

The subject of this sentence is *one*, so the verb should be *was promoted* instead of *were promoted*. Since the sentence is incorrect because of bad grammar, the answer to Sample Question I is A.

SAMPLE QUESTION II: Between you and me, I would prefer not going there.

Since this sentence is correct, the answer to Sample Question II is D.

1. The National alliance of Businessmen is trying to persuade private businesses to hire youth in the summertime.   1.____

2. The supervisor who is on vacation, is in charge of processing vouchers.   2.____

3. The activity of the committee at its conferences is always stimulating.   3.____

4. After checking the addresses again, the letters went to the mailroom.   4.____

5. The director, as well as the employees, are interested in sharing the dividends.   5.____

6. The experiments conducted by professor Alford were described at a recent meeting of our organization.   6.____

7. I shall be glad to discuss these matters with whoever represents the Municipal Credit Union.   7.____

8. In my opinion, neither Mr. Price nor Mr. Roth knows how to operate this office appliance.   8.____

9. The supervisor, as well as the other stenographers, were unable to transcribe Miss Johnson's shorthand notes. 9._____

10. Important functions such as, recruiting and training, are performed by our unit. 10._____

11. Realizing that many students are interested in this position, we sent announcements to all the High Schools. 11._____

12. After pointing out certain incorrect conclusions, the report was revised by Mr. Clark and submitted to Mr. Batson. 12._____

13. The employer contributed two hundred dollars; the employees, one hundred dollars. 13._____

14. He realized that the time, when a supervisor could hire and fire, was over. 14._____

15. The complaints received by Commissioner Regan was the cause of the change in policy. 15._____

16. Any report, that is to be sent to the Federal Security Administration, must be approved and signed by Mr. Yound. 16._____

17. Of the two stenographers, Miss Rand is the more accurate. 17._____

18. Since the golf courses are crowded during the summer, more men are needed to maintain the courses in good playing condition. 18._____

19. Although he invited Mr. Frankel and I to attend a meeting of the Civil Service Assembly, we were unable to accept his invitation. 19._____

20. Only the employees who worked overtime last week may leave one hour earlier today. 20._____

21. We need someone who can speak french fluently. 21._____

22. A tall, elderly, man entered the office and asked to see Mr. Brown. 22._____

23. The clerk insisted that he had filed the correspondence in the proper cabinet. 23._____

24. "Will you assist us," he asked? 24._____

25. According to the information contained in the report, a large quantity of paper and envelopes were used by this bureau last year. 25._____

KEY (CORRECT ANSWERS)

1.	C	11.	C
2.	B	12.	A
3.	D	13.	D
4.	A	14.	B
5.	A	15.	A
6.	C	16.	B
7.	D	17.	D
8.	D	18.	C
9.	A	19.	A
10.	B	20.	D

21. C
22. B
23. D
24. B
25. A

TEST 2

DIRECTIONS: Each question consists of a sentence which may be classified appropriately under one of the following four categories:
- A. Incorrect because of faulty grammar or sentence structure.
- B. Incorrect because of faulty punctuation.
- C. Incorrect because of faulty capitalization.
- D. Correct

Examine each sentence carefully. Then, in the space at the right, print the capital letter preceding the option which is the BEST of the four suggested above. All incorrect sentences contain only one type of error. Consider a sentence correct if it contains none of the types of errors mentioned, although there may be other correct ways of expressing the same thought.

1. Mrs. Black the supervisor of the unit, has many important duties. 1.____
2. We spoke to the man whom you saw yesterday. 2.____
3. When a holiday falls on sunday, it is officially celebrated on monday. 3.____
4. Of the two reports submitted, this one is the best. 4.____
5. Each staff member, including the accountants, were invited to the meeting. 5.____
6. Give the package to whomever calls for it. 6.____
7. To plan the work is our responsibility; to carry it out is his. 7.____
8. "May I see the person in charge of this office," asked the visitor? 8.____
9. He knows that it was not us who prepared the report. 9.____
10. These problems were brought to the attention of senator Johnson. 10.____
11. The librarian classifies all books periodicals and documents. 11.____
12. Any employee who uses an adding machine realizes its importance. 12.____
13. Instead of coming to the office, the clerk should of come to the supply room. 13.____
14. He asked, "will your staff assist us?" 14.____
15. Having been posted on the bulletin board, we were certain that the announcements would be read. 15.____
16. He was not informed, that he would have to work overtime. 16.____
17. The wind blew several paper off of his desk. 17.____

18. Charles Dole, who is a member of the committee, was asked to confer with commissioner Wilson. 18.____

19. Miss Bell will issue a copy to whomever asks for one. 19.____

20. Most employees, and he is no exception do not like to work overtime. 20.____

21. This is the man whom you interviewed last week. 21.____

22. Of the two cities visited, White Plains is the cleanest. 22.____

23. Although he was willing to work on other holidays, he refused to work on Labor day. 23.____

24. If an employee wishes to attend the conference, he should fill out the necessary forms. 24.____

25. The division chief reports that an engineer and an inspector is needed for this special survey. 25.____

KEY (CORRECT ANSWERS)

1.	B		11.	B
2.	D		12.	D
3.	C		13.	A
4.	A		14.	C
5.	A		15.	A
6.	A		16.	B
7.	D		17.	A
8.	B		18.	C
9.	A		19.	A
10.	C		20.	B

21. D
22. A
23. C
24. D
25. A

TEST 3

DIRECTIONS: Each question consists of a sentence which may be classified appropriately under one of the following four categories:
- A. Incorrect because of faulty grammar or sentence structure.
- B. Incorrect because of faulty punctuation.
- C. Incorrect because of faulty capitalization.
- D. Correct

Examine each sentence carefully. Then, in the space at the right, print the capital letter preceding the option which is the BEST of the four suggested above. All incorrect sentences contain only one type of error. Consider a sentence correct if it contains none of the types of errors mentioned, although there may be other correct ways of expressing the same thought.

1. We have learned that there was more than twelve people present at the meeting.   1.____

2. Every one of the employees is able to do this kind of work.   2.____

3. Neither the supervisor nor his assistant are in the office today.   3.____

4. The office manager announced that any clerk, who volunteered for the assignment, would be rewarded.   4.____

5. After looking carefully in all the files, the letter was finally found on a desk.   5.____

6. In answer to the clerk's question, the supervisor said, "this assignment must be completed today."   6.____

7. The office manager says that he can permit only you and me to go to the meeting.   7.____

8. The supervisor refused to state who he would assign to the reception unit.   8.____

9. At the last meeting, he said that he would interview us in september.   9.____

10. Mr. Jones, who is one of our most experienced employees has been placed in charge of the main office.   10.____

11. I think that this adding machine is the most useful of the two we have in our office.   11.____

12. Between you and I, our new stenographer is not as competent as our former stenographer.   12.____

13. The new assignment should be given to whoever can do the work rapidly   13.____

14. Mrs. Smith, as well as three other typists, was assigned to the new office.   14.____

2 (#3)

15. The staff assembled for the conference on time but, the main speaker arrived late.   15._____

16. The work was assigned to Miss Green and me.   16._____

17. The staff regulations state that an employee, who is frequently tardy, may receive a negative evaluation.   17._____

18. He is the kind of person who is always willing to undertake difficult assignments.   18._____

19. Mr. Wright's request cannot be granted under no conditions.   19._____

20. George Colt a new employee, was asked to deliver the report to the Domestic Relations Court.   20._____

21. The supervisor entered the room and said, "The work must be completed today."   21._____

22. The employees were given their assignments and, they were asked to begin work immediately.   22._____

23. The letter will be sent to the United States senate this week.   23._____

24. When the supervisor entered the room, he noticed that the book was laying on the desk.   24._____

25. The price of the pens were higher than the price of the pencils.   25._____

KEY (CORRECT ANSWERS)

1.	A	11.	A
2.	D	12.	A
3.	A	13.	D
4.	B	14.	D
5.	A	15.	B
6.	C	16.	D
7.	D	17.	B
8.	A	18.	D
9.	C	19.	A
10.	B	20.	B

21. D
22. B
23. C
24. A
25. A

PREPARING WRITTEN MATERIAL

PARAGRAPH REARRANGEMENT
COMMENTARY

The sentences that follow are in scrambled order. You are to rearrange them in proper order and indicate the letter choice containing the correct answer at the space at the right.

Each group of sentences in this section is actually a paragraph presented in scrambled order. Each sentence in the group has a place in that paragraph; no sentence is to be left out. You are to read each group of sentences and decide upon the best order in which to put the sentences so as to form a well-organized paragraph.

The questions in this section measure the ability to solve a problem when all the facts relevant to its solution are not given.

More specifically, certain positions of responsibility and authority require the employee to discover connection between events sometimes, apparently, unrelated. In order to do this, the employee will find it necessary to correctly infer that unspecified events have probably occurred or are likely to occur. This ability becomes especially important when action must be taken on incomplete information.

Accordingly, these questions require competitors to choose among several suggested alternatives, each of which presents a different sequential arrangement of the events. Competitors must choose the MOST logical of the suggested sequences.

In order to do so, they may be required to draw on general knowledge to infer missing concepts or events that are essential to sequencing the given events. Competitors should be careful to infer only what is essential to the sequence. The plausibility of the wrong alternatives will always require the inclusion of unlikely events or of additional chains of events which are NOT essential to sequencing the given events.

It's very important to remember that you are looking for the best of the four possible choices, and that the best choice of all may not even be one of the answers you're given to choose from.

There is no one right way to solve these problems. Many people have found it helpful to first write out the order of the sentences, as they would have arranged them, on their scrap paper before looking at the possible answers. If their optimum answer is there, this can save them some time. If it isn't, this method can still give insight into solving the problem. Others find it most helpful to just go through each of the possible choices, contrasting each as they go along. You should use whatever method feels comfortable and works for you.

While most of these types of questions are not that difficult, we've added a higher percentage of the difficult type, just to give you more practice. Usually there are only one or two questions on this section that contain such subtle distinctions that you're unable to answer confidently. And you then may find yourself stuck deciding between two possible choices, neither of which you're sure about.

EXAMINATION SECTION
TEST 1

DIRECTIONS: The sentences that follow are in scrambled order. You are to rearrange them in proper order and indicate the letter choice containing the correct answer. *PRINT THE LETTER OF THE CORRECT ANSWER IN THE SPACE AT THE RIGHT.*

1. Below are four statements labeled W, X, Y and Z.
   W. He was a strict and fanatic drillmaster.
   X. The word is always used in a derogatory sense and generally shows resentment and anger on the part of the user.
   Y. It is from the name of this Frenchman that we derive our English word, martinet.
   Z. Jean Martinet was the Inspector-General of Infantry during the reign of King Louis XIV.
   The PROPER order in which these sentences should be placed in a paragraph is:
     A. X, Z, W, Y   B. X, Z, Y, W   C. Z, W, Y, X   D. Z, Y, W, X

   1.____

2. In the following paragraph, the sentences, which are numbered, have been jumbled.
   I. Since then it has undergone changes.
   II. It was incorporated in 1955 under the laws of the State of New York.
   III. Its primary purposes, a cleaner city, has, however, remained the same.
   IV. The Citizens Committee works in cooperation with the Mayor's Inter-departmental Committee for a Clean City.
   The order in which these sentences should be arranged to form a well-organized paragraph is:
     A. II, IV, I, III   B. III, IV, I, II   C. IV, II, I, III   D. IV, III, II, I

   2.____

   3.____

Questions 3-5.

DIRECTIONS: The sentences listed below are part of a meaningful paragraph but they are not given in their proper order. You are to decide what would be the BEST order in which to put the sentences so as to form a well-organized paragraph. Each sentence has a place in the paragraph; there are no extra sentences. You are then to answer Questions 3 through 5 inclusive on the basis of your rearrangements of these scrambled sentences into a properly organized paragraph.

In 1887 some insurance companies organized an Inspection Department to advise their clients on all phases of fire prevention and protection. Probably this has been due to the smaller annual fire losses in Great Britain than in the United States. It tests various fire prevention devices and appliances and determines manufacturing hazards and their safeguards. Fire research began earlier in the United States and is more advanced than in Great Britain. Later they established a laboratory specializing in electrical, mechanical, hydraulic, and chemical fields.

149

2 (#1)

3. When the five sentences are arranged in proper order, the paragraph starts with the sentence which begins
   A. "In 1887…"
   B. "Probably this…"
   C. "It tests…"
   D. "Fire research…"
   E. "Later they…"

   3.____

4. In the last sentence listed above, "they" refers to
   A. the insurance companies
   B. the United States and Great Britain
   C. the Inspection Department
   D. clients
   E. technicians

   4.____

5. When the above paragraph is properly arranged, it ends with the words
   A. "…and protection."
   B. "…the United States."
   C. "…their safeguards."
   D. "…in Great Britain."
   E. "…chemical fields."

   5.____

KEY (CORRECT ANSWERS)

1. C
2. C
3. D
4. A
5. C

TEST 2

DIRECTIONS: In each of the questions numbered I through V, several sentences are given. For each question, choose as your answer the group of number that represents the MOST logical order of these sentences if they were arranged in paragraph form. *PRINT THE LETTER OF THE CORRECT ANSWER IN THE SPACE AT THE RIGHT.*

1. I. It is established when one shows that the landlord has prevented the tenant's enjoyment of his interest in the property leased.
    II. Constructive eviction is the result of a breach of the covenant of quiet enjoyment implied in all leases.
    III. In some parts of the United States, it is not complete until the tenant vacates within a reasonable time.
    IV. Generally, the acts must be of such serious and permanent character as to deny the tenant the enjoyment of his possessing rights.
    V. In this event, upon abandonment of the premises, the tenant's liability for that ceases.
    The CORRECT answer is:
    A. II, I, IV, III, V
    B. V, II, III, I, IV
    C. IV, III, I, II, V
    D. I, III, V, IV, II

    1.____

2. I. The powerlessness before private and public authorities that is the typical experience of the slum tenant is reminiscent of the situation of blue-collar workers all through the nineteenth century.
    II. Similarly, in recent years, this chapter of history has been reopened by anti-poverty groups which have attempted to organize slum tenants to enable them to bargain collectively with their landlords about the conditions of their tenancies.
    III. It is familiar history that many of the worker remedied their condition by joining together and presenting their demands collectively.
    IV. Like the workers, tenants are forced by the conditions of modern life into substantial dependence on these who possess great political aid and economic power.
    V. What's more, the very fact of dependence coupled with an absence of education and self-confidence makes them hesitant and unable to stand up for what they need from those in power.
    The CORRECT answer is:
    A. V, IV, I, II, III
    B. II, III, I, V, IV
    C. III, I, V, IV, II
    D. I, IV, V, III, II

    2.____

3. I. A railroad, for example, when not acting as a common carrier may contract away responsibility for its own negligence.
    II. As to a landlord, however, no decision has been found relating to the legal effect of a clause shifting the statutory duty of repair to the tenant.
    III. The courts have not passed on the validity of clauses relieving the landlord of this duty and liability.
    IV. They have, however, upheld the validity of exculpatory clauses in other types of contracts.

    3.____

151

V. Housing regulations impose a duty upon the landlord to maintain leased premises in safe condition.
VI. As another example, a bailee may limit his liability except for gross negligence, willful acts, or fraud.

The CORRECT answer is:
A. II, I, VI, IV, III, V
B. I, III, IV, V, VI, II
C. III, V, I, IV, II, VI
D. V, III, IV, I, VI, II

4. I. Since there are only samples in the building, retail or consumer sales are generally eschewed by mart occupants, and in some instances, rigid controls are maintained to limit entrance to the mart only to those persons engaged in retailing.
    II. Since World War I, in many larger cities, there has developed a new type of property, called the mart building.
    III. It can, therefore, be used by wholesalers and jobbers for the display of sample merchandise.
    IV. This type of building is most frequently a multi-storied, finished interior property which is a cross between a retail arcade and a loft building.
    V. This limitation enables the mart occupants to ship the orders from another location after the retailer or dealer makes his selection from the samples.

    The CORRECT answer is:
    A. II, IV, III, I, V
    B. IV, III, V, I, II
    C. I, III, II, IV, V
    D. I, IV, II, III, V

5. I. In general, staff-line friction reduces the distinctive contribution of staff personnel.
    II. The conflicts, however, introduce an uncontrolled element into the managerial system.
    III. On the other hand, the natural resistance of the line to staff innovations probably usefully restrains over-eager efforts to apply untested procedures on a large scale.
    IV. Under such conditions, it is difficult to know when valuable ideas are being sacrificed.
    V. The relatively weak position of staff, requiring accommodation to the line, tends to restrict their ability to engage in free, experimental innovation.

    The CORRECT answer is:
    A. IV, II, III, I, V
    B. I, V, III, II, IV
    C. V, III, I, II, IV
    D. II, I, IV, V, III

KEY (CORRECT ANSWERS)

1. A
2. D
3. D
4. A
5. B

TEST 3

DIRECTIONS: Questions 1 through 4 consist of six sentences which can be arranged in a logical sequence. For each question, select the choice which places the numbered sentences in the MOST logical sequent. *PRINT THE LETTER OF THE CORRECT ANSWER IN THE SPACE AT THE RIGHT.*

1. I. The burden of proof as to each issue is determined before trial and remains upon the same party throughout the trial.
    II. The jury is at liberty to believe one witness' testimony as against a number of contradictory witnesses.
    III. In a civil case, the party bearing the burden of proof is required to prove his contention by a fair preponderance of the evidence.
    IV. However, it must be noted that a fair preponderance of evidence does not necessarily mean a greater number of witnesses.
    V. The burden of proof is the burden which rests upon one of the parties to an action to persuade the trier of the facts, generally the jury, that a proposition he asserts is true.
    VI. If the evidence is equally balanced, or if it leaves the jury in such doubt as to be unable to decide the controversy either way, judgment must be given against the party upon whom the burden of proof rests.
    The CORRECT answer is:
    A. III, II, V, IV, I, VI
    B. I, II, VI, V, III, IV
    C. III, IV, V, I, II, VI
    D. V, I, III, VI, IV, II

    1.____

2. I. If a parent is without assets and is unemployed, he cannot be convicted of the crime of non-support of a child.
    II. The term "sufficient ability" has been held to mean sufficient financial ability.
    III. It does not matter if his unemployment is by choice or unavoidable circumstances.
    IV. If he fails to take any steps at all, he may be liable to prosecution for endangering the welfare of a child.
    V. Under the penal law, a parent is responsible for the support of his minor child only if the parent is "of sufficient ability."
    VI. An indigent parent may meet his obligation by borrowing money or by seeking aid under the provisions of the Social Welfare Law.
    The CORRECT answer is:
    A. VI, I, V, III, II, IV
    B. I, III, V, II, IV, VI
    C. V, II, I, III, VI, IV
    D. I, VI, IV, V, II, III

    2.____

3. I. Consider, for example, the case of a rabble rouser who urges a group of twenty people to go out and break the windows of a nearby factory.
    II. Therefore, the law fills the indicated gap with the crime of inciting to riot.
    III. A person is considered guilty of inciting to riot when he urges ten or more persons to engage in tumultuous and violent conduct of a kind likely to create public alarm.
    IV. However, if he has not obtained the cooperation of at least four people, he cannot be charged with unlawful assembly.

    3.____

153

2 (#3)

V. The charge of inciting to riot was added to the law to cover types of conduct which cannot be classified as either the crime of "riot" or the crime of "unlawful assembly."
VI. If he acquires the acquiescence of at least four of them, he is guilty of unlawful assembly even if the project does not materialize.

The CORRECT answer is:
A. III, V, I, VI, IV, II
B. V, I, IV, VI, II, III
C. III, IV, I, V, II, VI
D. V, I, IV, VI, III, II

4. I. If, however, the rebuttal evidence presents an issue of credibility, it is for the jury to determine whether the presumption has, in fact, been destroyed.
II. Once sufficient evidence to the contrary is introduced, the presumption disappears from the trial.
III. The effect of a presumption is to place the burden upon the adversary to come forward with evidence to rebut the presumption.
IV. When a presumption is overcome and ceases to exist in the case, the fact or facts which gave rise to the presumption still remain.
V. Whether a presumption has been overcome is ordinarily a question for the court.
VI. Such information may furnish a basis for a logical inference.

The CORRECT answer is:
A. IV, VI, II, V, I, III
B. III, II, V, I, IV, VI
C. V, III, VI, IV, II, I
D. V, IV, I, II, VI, III

KEY (CORRECT ANSWERS)

1. D
2. C
3. A
4. B

READING COMPREHENSION
UNDERSTANDING AND INTERPRETING WRITTEN MATERIAL
EXAMINATION SECTION

This exam section includes some passages and questions related to functions of the first computerized offices, which consisted of typewriters and other such manual office equipment.

TEST 1

DIRECTIONS: Each question or incomplete statement is followed by several suggested answers or completions. Select the one that BEST answers the question or completes the statement. *PRINT THE LETTER OF THE CORRECT ANSWER IN THE SPACE AT THE RIGHT.*

Questions 1-2.

DIRECTIONS: Questions 1 and 2 are to be answered SOLELY on the basis of the following passage.

The employees in a unit or division of a government agency may be referred to as a work group. Within a government agency which has existed for some time, the work groups will have evolved traditions of their own. The persons in these work groups acquire these traditions as part of the process of work adjustment within their groups. Usually, a work group in a large organization will contain *oldtimers, newcomers*, and *in-betweeners*. Like the supervisor of a group, who is not necessarily an oldtimer or the oldest member, oldtimers usually have great influence. They can recall events unknown to others and are a storehouse of information and advice about current problems in the light of past experience. They pass along the traditions of the group to the others who, in turn, become oldtimers themselves. Thus, the traditions of the group which have been honored and revered by long acceptance are continued.

1. According to the above passage, the traditions of a work group within a government agency are developed
    A. at the time the group is established
    B. over a considerable period of time
    C. in order to give recognition to oldtimers
    D. for the group before it is established

1.____

2. According to the above passage, the oldtimers within a work group
    A. are the means by which long accepted practices and customs are perpetuated
    B. would best be able to settle current problems that arise
    C. are honored because of the changes they have made in the traditions
    D. have demonstrated that they have learned to do their work well

2.____

Questions 3-4.

DIRECTIONS: Questions 3 and 4 are to be answered SOLELY on the following passage.

In public agencies, the success of a person assigned to perform first-line supervisory duties depends in large part upon the personal relations between him and his subordinate employees. The goal of supervising effort is something more than to obtain compliance with procedures established by some central office. The major objective is work accomplishment. In order for this goal to be attained, employees must want to attain it and must exercise initiative in their work. Only if employees are generally satisfied with the type of supervision which exists in an organization will they put forth their best efforts.

3. According to the above passage, in order for employees to try to do their work as well as they can, it is essential that
    A. they participate in determining their working conditions and rates of pay
    B. their supervisors support the employees' viewpoints in meetings with higher management
    C. they are content with the supervisory practices which are being used
    D. their supervisors make the changes in working procedures that the employees request

3.____

4. It can be inferred from the above passage that the goals of a unit in a public agency will not be reached unless the employees in the unit
    A. wish to reach them and are given the opportunity to make individual contributions to the work
    B. understand the relationship between the goals of the unit and goals of the agency
    C. have satisfactory personal relationships with employees of other units in the agency
    D. carefully follow the directions issued by higher authorities

4.____

Questions 5-9.

DIRECTIONS: Questions 5 through 9 are to be answered SOLELY on the basis of the following passage.

In an employee thinks he can save money, time, or material for the city or has an idea about how to do something better than it is being done, he shouldn't keep it to himself. He should send his ideas to the Employees' Suggestion Program, using the special form which is kept on hand in all departments. An employee may send in as many ideas as he wishes. To make sure that each idea is judged fairly, the name of the suggester is not made known until an award is made. The awards are certificate of merit or cash prizes ranging from $10 to $500.

5. According to the above passage, an employee who knows how to do a job in a better way should
    A. be sure it saves enough time to be worthwhile
    B. get paid the money he saves for the city
    C. keep it to himself to avoid being accused of causing a speed-up
    D. send his idea to the Employees' Suggestion Program

5.____

6. In order to send his idea to the Employees' Suggestion Program, an employee should
     A. ask the Department of Personnel for a special form
     B. get the special form in his own department
     C. mail the idea using Special Delivery
     D. send it on plain, white letter-size paper

6.____

7. An employee may send to the Employees' Suggestion Program
     A. as many ideas as he can think of
     B. no more than one idea each week
     C. no more than ten ideas in a month
     D. only one idea on each part of the job

7.____

8. The reason the name of an employee who makes a suggestion is not made known at first is to
     A. give the employee a larger award
     B. help the judges give more awards
     C. insure fairness in judging
     D. only one idea on each part of the job

8.____

9. An employee whose suggestion receives an award may be given a
     A. bonus once a year   B. certificate for $10
     C. cash prize of up to $500   D. salary increase of $500

9.____

Questions 10-12.

DIRECTIONS: Questions 10 through 12 are to be answered SOLELY on the basis of the following passage.

According to the rules of the Department of Personnel, the work of every permanent city employee is reviewed and rated by his supervisor at least once a year. The civil service rating system gives the employee and his supervisor a chance to talk about the progress made during the past year as well as about those parts of the job in which the employee needs to do better. In order to receive a pay increase each year, the employee must have a satisfactory service rating. Service ratings also count toward an employee's final mark on a promotion examination.

10. According to the above passage, a permanent city employee is rated AT LEAST once
     A. before his work is reviewed
     B. every six months
     C. yearly by his supervisor
     D. yearly by the Department of Personnel

10.____

11. According to the above passage, under the rating system the supervisor and the employee can discuss how
     A. much more work needs to be done next year
     B. the employee did his work last year
     C. the work can be made easier next year
     D. the work of the Department can be increased

11.____

12. According to the above passage, a permanent city employee will NOT receive a yearly pay increase
    A. if he received a pay increase the year before
    B. if he used his service rating for his mark on a promotion examination
    C. if his service rating is unsatisfactory
    D. unless he got some kind of a service rating

12.____

Questions 13-16.

DIRECTIONS: Questions 13 through 16 are to be answered SOLELY on the basis of the following passage.

It is an accepted fact that the rank and file employee can frequently advance worthwhile suggestions toward increasing efficiency. For this reason, an Employees' Suggestion System has been developed and put into operation. Suitable means have been provided at each departmental location for the confidential submission of suggestions. Numerous suggestions have been received thus far and, after study, about five percent of the ideas submitted are being translated into action. It is planned to set up, eventually, monetary awards for all worthwhile suggestions.

13. According to the above passage, a MAJOR reason why an Employees' Suggestion System was established is that
    A. an organized program of improvement is better than a haphazard one
    B. employees can often give good suggestions to increase efficiency
    C. once a fact is accepted, it is better to act on it than to do nothing
    D. the suggestions of rank and file employees were being neglected

13.____

14. According to the above passage, under the Employees' Suggestion System,
    A. a file of worthwhile suggestions will eventually be set up at each departmental location
    B. it is possible for employees to turn in suggestions without fellow employees knowing of it
    C. means have been provided for the regular and frequent collection of suggestions submitted
    D. provision has been made for the judging of worthwhile suggestions by an Employees' Suggestion Committee

14.____

15. According to the above passage, it is reasonable to assume that
    A. all suggestions must be turned in at a central office
    B. employees who make worthwhile suggestions will be promoted
    C. not all the prizes offered will be monetary ones
    D. prizes of money will be given for the best suggestions

15.____

16. According to the above passage, of the many suggestions made,
    A. all are first tested
    B. a small part are put into use
    C. most are very worthwhile
    D. samples are studied

16.____

Questions 17-20.

DIRECTIONS: Questions 17 through 20 are to be answered SOLELY on the basis of the following passage.

Employees may be granted leaves of absence without pay at the discretion of the Personnel Officer. Such a leave without pay shall begin on the first working day on which the employee does not report for duty and shall continue to the first day on which the employee returns to duty. The Personnel Division may vary the dates of the leave for the record so as to conform with payroll periods, but in no case shall an employee be off the payroll for a different number of calendar days than would have been the case if the actual dates mentioned above had been used. An employee who has vacation or overtime to his credit, which is available for normal use, may take time off immediately prior to beginning a leave of absence without pay, chargeable against all or part of such vacation or overtime.

17. According to the above passage, the Personnel Officer must
    A. decide if a leave of absence without pay should be granted
    B. require that a leave end on the last working day of a payroll period
    C. see to it that a leave of absence to conform with a payroll period
    D. vary the dates of a leave of absence to conform with a payroll period

18. According to the above passage, the exact dates of a leave of absence without pay may be varied provided that the
    A. calendar days an employee is off the payroll equal the actual leave granted
    B. leave conforms to an even number of payroll periods
    C. leave when granted made provision for variance to simplify payroll records
    D. Personnel Officer approves the variation

19. According to the above passage, a leave of absence without pay must extend from the
    A. first day of a calendar period to the first day the employee resumes work
    B. first day of a payroll period to the last calendar day of the leave
    C. first working day missed to the first day on which the employee resumes work
    D. last day on which an employee works through the first day he returns to work

20. According to the above passage, an employee may take extra time off just before the start of a leave of absence without pay if
    A. he charges this extra time against his leave
    B. he has a favorable balance of vacation or overtime which has been frozen
    C. the vacation or overtime that he would normally use for a leave without pay has not been charged in this way before
    D. there is time to his credit which he may use

Question 21.

DIRECTIONS: Question 21 is to be answered SOLELY on the basis of the following passage.

   In considering those things which are motivators and incentives to work, it might be just as erroneous not to give sufficient weight to money as an incentive as it is to give too much weight. It is not a problem of establishing a rank-order of importance, but one of knowing that motivation is a blend or mixture rather than a pure element. It is simple to say that cultural factors count more than financial considerations, but this leads only to the conclusion that our society is financial-oriented.

21. Based on the above passage, in our society, cultural and social motivations to work are   21.____
   A. things which cannot be avoided
   B. melded to financial incentives
   C. of less consideration than high pay
   D. not balanced equally with economic or financial considerations

Question 22.

DIRECTIONS: Question 22 is to be answered SOLELY on the basis of the following passage.

   A general principle of training and learning with respect to people is that they learn more readily if they receive *feedback*. Essential to maintaining proper motivational levels is knowledge of results which indicate level of progress. Feedback also assists the learning process by identifying mistakes. If this kind of information were not given to the learner, then improper or inappropriate job performance may be instilled.

22. Based on the above passage, which of the following is MOST accurate?   22.____
   A. Learning will not take place without feedback.
   B. In the absence of feedback, improper or inappropriate job performance will be learned.
   C. To properly motivate a learner, the learner must have his progress made known to him.
   D. Trainees should be told exactly what to do if they are to learn properly

Questions 23.

DIRECTIONS: Question 23 is to be answered SOLELY on the basis of the following passage.

   In a democracy, the obligation of public officials is twofold. They must not only do an efficient and satisfactory job of administration, but also they must persuade the public that it is an efficient and satisfactory job. It is a burden which, if properly assumed, will make democracy work and perpetuate reform government.

23. The above passage means that   23.____
   A. public officials should try to please everybody

B. public opinion is instrumental if determining the policy of public officials
C. satisfactory performance of the job of administration will eliminate opposition to its work
D. frank and open procedure in a public agency will aid in maintaining progressive government

Question 24.

DIRECTIONS: Question 24 is to be answered SOLELY on the basis of the following passage.

Upon retirement for service, a member shall receive a retirement allowance which shall consist of an annuity which shall be the actuarial equivalent of his accumulated deductions at the time of his retirement and a pension, in addition to his annuity, which shall be equal to one service-fraction of his final compensation, multiplied by the number of years of service since he last became a member credited to him, and a pension which is the actuarial equivalent of the reserve-for-increased-take-home-pay to which he may then be entitled, if any.

24. According to the above passage, a retirement allowance shall consist of a(n)   24.____
    A. annuity, plus a pension, plus an actuarial equivalent
    B. annuity, plus a pension, plus reserve-for-increased-take-home-pay, if any
    C. annuity, plus reserve-for-increased-take-home-pay, if any, plus final compensation
    D. pension, plus reserve-for-increased-take-home-pay, if any, plus accumulated deductions

Question 25.

DIRECTIONS: Question 25 is to be answered SOLELY on the basis of the following passage.

Membership in the retirement system shall cease upon the occurrence of any one of the following conditions: when the time out of service of any member who has total service of less than 25 years, shall aggregate more than 5 years; when the time out of service of any member who has total service of 25 years or more, shall aggregate more than 10 years; when any member shall have withdrawn more than 50% of his accumulated deductions; or when any member shall have withdrawn the cash benefit provided by Section B3.35.0 of the Administrative Code.

25. According to the information in the above passage, membership in the   25.____
    retirement system shall cease when an employee
    A. with 17 years of service has been on a leave of absence for 3 years
    B. withdraws 50% of his accumulated deductions
    C. with 28 years of service has been out of service for 10 years
    D. withdraws his cash benefits

KEY (CORRECT ANSWERS)

1.	B		11.	B
2.	A		12.	C
3.	C		13.	B
4.	A		14.	B
5.	D		15.	D
6.	B		16.	B
7.	A		17.	A
8.	C		18.	A
9.	B		19.	C
10.	C		20.	D

21.	B
22.	C
23.	D
24.	B
25.	D

TEST 2

DIRECTIONS: Each question or incomplete statement is followed by several suggested answers or completions. Select the one that BEST answers the question or completes the statement. *PRINT THE LETTER OF THE CORRECT ANSWER IN THE SPACE AT THE RIGHT.*

Questions 1-6.

DIRECTIONS: Questions 1 through 6 are to be answered SOLELY on the basis of the following passage.

Since almost every office has some contact with data-processed records, a stenographer should have some understanding of the basic operations of data processing. Data processing systems now handle a vast majority of all office paperwork. On coded forms and other specialized media, data are recorded before being fed into the computer for processing. The data written on the source document is converted in highly advanced ways in order to make the information accessible to the user. After data has been converted, it must be verified to guarantee absolute accuracy. In this manner, data becomes a permanent record which can be read by computers that compare, store, compute, and otherwise process data at high speeds.

One key person in a computer installation is a programmer, the man or woman who puts business and scientific problems into special symbolic languages that can be read by the computer. Jobs done by the computer range all the way from payroll operations to chemical process control, but most computer applications are directed toward management data. Most programmers employed by business come to their positions with college degrees; the rest are promoted to their positions from within the organization on the basis of demonstrated ability without regard to education.

1. Of the following, the BEST title for the above passage is
   A. The Stenographer As Data Processor
   B. The Relation of Data Input to Stenography
   C. Understanding Data Processing
   D. Permanent Office Records

2. According to the above passage, a stenographer should understand the basic operations of data processing because
   A. almost every office today has contact with data processed by computer
   B. any office worker may be asked to verify the accuracy of data
   C. most offices are involved in the production of permanent records
   D. data may be converted into computer language by specialized media

3. According to the above passage, data accuracy is reviewed during the _____ stage.
   A. processing
   B. verification
   C. programming
   D. stenographic

4. According to the above passage, computers are used MOST often to handle
   A. management data
   B. problems of higher education
   C. the control of chemical processes
   D. payroll operations

5. Computer programming is taught in many colleges and business schools. The above passage implies that programmers in industry
   A. must have professional training
   B. need professional training to advance
   C. must have at least a college education to do adequate programming tasks
   D. do not necessarily need college education to do programming work

6. According to the above passage, data to be processed by computer should be
   A. recent   B. basic   C. complete   D. verified

Questions 7-10.

DIRECTIONS: Questions 7 through 10 are to be answered SOLELY on the basis of the following passage.

There is nothing that will take the place of good sense on the part of the stenographer. You may be perfect in transcribing exactly what the dictator says and your speed may be adequate, but without an understanding of the dictator's intent as well as his words, you are likely to be a mediocre secretary.

A serious error that is made when taking dictation is putting down something that does not make sense. Most people who dictate material would rather be asked to repeat and explain than to receive transcribed material which has errors due to inattention or doubt. Many dictators request that their grammar be corrected by their secretaries, but unless specifically asked to do so, secretaries should not do it without first checking with the dictator. Secretaries should be aware that, in some cases, dictators may use incorrect grammar or slang expressions to create a particular effect.

Some people dictate commas, periods, and paragraphs, while others expect the stenographer to know when, where, and how to punctuate. A well-trained secretary should be able to indicate the proper punctuation by listening to the pauses and tones of the dictator's voice.

A stenographer who has taken dictation from the same person for a period of time should be able to understand him under most conditions. By increasing her tack, alertness, and efficiency, a secretary can become more competent.

7. According to the above passage, which of the following statements concerning the dictation of punctuation is CORRECT?
   A. Dictator may use incorrect punctuation to create a desired style.
   B. Dictator should indicate all punctuation.

C. Stenographer should know how to punctuate based on the pauses and tones of the dictator.
D. Stenographer should not type any punctuation if it has not been dictated to her.

8. According to the above passage, how should secretaries handle grammatical errors in a dictation?
Secretaries should
   A. *not correct* grammatical errors unless the dictator is aware that this is being done
   B. *correct* grammatical errors by having the dictator repeat the line with proper pauses
   C. *correct* grammatical errors if they have checked the correctness in a grammar book
   D. *correct* grammatical errors based on their own good sense

8.____

9. If a stenographer is confused about the method of spacing and indenting of a report which has just been dictated to her, she GENERALLY should
   A. do the best she can
   B. ask the dictator to explain what she should do
   C. try to improve her ability to understand dictated material
   D. accept the fact that her stenographic ability is not adequate

9.____

10. In the last line of the first paragraph, the word *mediocre* means MOST NEARLY
    A. superior   B. respected   C. disregarded   D. second-rate

10.____

Questions 11-12.

DIRECTIONS: Questions 11 and 12 are to be answered SOLELY on the basis of the following passage.

The number of legible carbon copies required to be produced determines the weight of the carbon paper to be used. When only one copy is made, heavy carbon paper is satisfactory. Most typists, however, use medium-weight carbon paper and find it serviceable for up to three or four copies. If five or more copies are to be made, it is wise to use light carbon paper. On the other hand, the finish of carbon paper to be used depends largely on the stroke of the typist and, in lesser degree, on the number of copies to be made and on whether the typewriter has pica or elite type. A soft-finish carbon paper should be used if the typist's touch is light or if a noiseless machine is used. It is desirable for the average typist to use medium-finish carbon paper for ordinary work, when only a few carbon copies are required. Elite type requires a harder carbon finish than pica type for the same number of copies.

11. According to the above passage, the lighter the carbon paper used, the
    A. softer the finish of the carbon paper will be
    B. greater the number of legible carbon copies that can be made
    C. greater the number of times the carbon paper can be used
    D. lighter the typist's touch should be

11.____

12. According to the above passage, the MOST important factor which determines whether the finish of carbon paper to be used in typing should be hard, medium, or soft is 12.____
    A. the touch of the typist
    B. the number of carbon copies required
    C. whether the type in the typewriter is pica or elite
    D. whether a machine with pica type will produce the same number of carbon copies as a machine with elite type

Questions 13-16.

DIRECTIONS: Questions 13 through 16 are to be answered SOLELY on the basis of the following passage.

   Looking back at past developments in office work, advances were made at higher speeds and at greater efficiency thanks largely to the typewriter. The typewriter was a substitute for handwriting and, in the hands of a skilled typist, not only turned out letters and other documents at least three times faster than a penman, but turned out the greater volume more uniformly and legibly. With the use of carbon paper and onionskin paper, identical copies could be made at the same time.

   The typewriter, besides its effect on the conduct of business and government, had a very important effect on the position of women. The typewriter did much to bring women into business and government, and in a short time span, women far outnumbered men as typists. Many women used the keys of the typewriter to climb the ladder to professional managerial positions.

   The typewriter, as its name implies, employs type to make an ink impression on paper. For many years, the manual typewriter was the standard machine used. Eventually, the electric typewriter became dominant, leading to innovations in and widespread use of completely automatic electronic typewriters.

   The mechanism of the office manual typewriter includes a set of keys arranged systematically in rows; a semicircular frame of type, connected to the keys by levers; the carriage, or paper carrier; a rubber roller, called a platen, against which the type strikes; and an inked ribbon which makes the impression of the type character when the key strikes it.

13. The above passage mentions a number of good features of the combination of a skilled typist and a typewriter. 13.____
    Of the following the feature which is NOT mentioned in the passage is
    A. speed   B. reliability   C. uniformity   D. legibility

14. According to the above passage, a skilled typist can 14.____
    A. turn out at least five carbon copies of typed matter
    B. type at least three times faster than a penman can write
    C. type more than 80 words in a minute
    D. readily move into a managerial position

15. According to the above passage, which of the following is NOT part of the mechanism of a manual typewriter? 15.____
    A. Carbon paper
    B. Platen
    C. Paper carrier
    D. Inked ribbon

16. According to the above passage, the typewriter helped 16.____
    A. men more than women in business
    B. women in career advancement into management
    C. men and women equally, but women have taken better advantage of it
    D. more women than men, because men generally dislike routine typing work

Questions 17-21.

DIRECTIONS: Questions 17 through 21 are to be answered SOLELY on the basis of the following passage.

The recipient gains an impression of a typewritten letter before he begins to read the message. Factors which provide for a good first impression include margins and spacing that are visually pleasing, formal parts of the letter which are correctly placed according to the style of the letter, copy which is free of obvious erasures and over-strikes, and transcript that is even and clear. The problem for the typist is that of how to produce that first, positive impression of her work.

There are several general rules which a typist can follow when she wishes to prepare a properly spaced letter on a sheet of letterhead. Ordinarily, the width of a letter should not be less than four inches nor more than six inches. The side margins should also have a desirable relation to the bottom margin and the space between the letterhead and the body of the letter. Usually the most appealing arrangement is when the side margins are even and the bottom margin is slightly wider than the side margins. In some offices, however, standard line length is used for all business letter, and the secretary then varies the spacing between the date line and the inside address according to the length of the letter.

17. The BEST title for the above passage would be 17.____
    A. Writing Office Letters
    B. Making Good First Impressions
    C. Judging Well-Typed Letters
    D. Good Placing and Spacing for Office Letters

18. According to the above passage, which of the following might be considered the way in which people very quickly judge the quality of work which has been typed? By 18.____
    A. measuring the margins to see if they are correct
    B. looking at the spacing and cleanliness of the typescript
    C. scanning the body of the letter for meaning
    D. reading the date line and address for errors

19. What, according to the above passage, would be definitely UNDESIRABLE as the average line length of a typed letter?
    A. 4"   B. 6"   C. 5"   D. 7"

20. According to the above passage, when the line length is kept standard, the secretary
    A. does not have to vary the spacing at all since this also is standard
    B. adjusts the spacing between the date line and inside address for different lengths of letters
    C. uses the longest line as a guidance for spacing between the date line and inside address
    D. varies the number of spaces between the lines

21. According to the above passage, side margins are MOST pleasing when they
    A. are even and somewhat smaller than the bottom margin
    B. are slightly wider than the bottom margin
    C. vary with the length of the letter
    D. are figured independently from the letterhead and the body of the letter

Questions 22-25.

DIRECTIONS: Questions 22 through 25 are to be answered SOLELY on the basis of the following passage.

Typed pages can reflect the simplicity of modern art in a machine age. Lightness and evenness can be achieved by proper layout and balance of typed lines and white space. Instead of solid, cramped masses of uneven, crowded typing, there should be a pleasing balance up and down as well as horizontal.

To have real balance, your page must have a center. The eyes see the center of the sheet slightly above the real center. This is the way both you and the reader see it. Try imagining a line down the center of the page that divides the paper in equal halves. On either side of your paper, white space and blocks of typing need to be similar in size and shape. Although left and right margins should be equal, top and bottom margins need not be as exact. It looks better to hold a bottom border wider than a top margin, so that your typing rests upon a cushion of white space. To add interest to the appearance of the page, try making one paragraph between one-half and two-thirds the size of an adjacent paragraph.

Thus, by taking full advantage of your typewriter, the pages that you type will not only be accurate but will also be attractive.

22. It can be inferred from the above passage that the basic importance of proper balancing on a typed page is that proper balancing
    A. makes a typed page a work of modern art
    B. provides exercise in proper positioning of a typewriter
    C. increases the amount of typed copy on the paper
    D. draws greater attention and interest to the page

23. A reader will tend to see the center of a typed page 23.____
    A. somewhat higher than the true center
    B. somewhat lower than the true center
    C. on either side of the true center
    D. about two-thirds of an inch above the true center

24. Which of the following suggestions is NOT given by the above passage? 24.____
    A. Bottom margins may be wider than top borders.
    B. Keep all paragraphs approximately the same size.
    C. Divide your page with an imaginary line down the middle.
    D. Side margins should be equalized.

25. Of the following, the BEST title for the above passage is 25.____
    A. Increasing the Accuracy of the Typed Page
    B. Determination of Margins for Typed Copy
    C. Layout and Balance of the Typed Page
    D. How to Take Full Advantage of the Typewriter

KEY (CORRECT ANSWERS)

1.	C		11.	B
2.	A		12.	A
3.	B		13.	B
4.	A		14.	B
5.	D		15.	A
6.	D		16.	B
7.	C		17.	D
8.	A		18.	B
9.	B		19.	D
10.	D		20.	B

21.	A
22.	D
23.	A
24.	B
25.	C

TEST 3

DIRECTIONS: Each question or incomplete statement is followed by several suggested answers or completions. Select the one that BEST answers the question or completes the statement. *PRINT THE LETTER OF THE CORRECT ANSWER IN THE SPACE AT THE RIGHT.*

Questions 1-5.

DIRECTIONS: Questions 1 through 5 are to be answered SOLELY on the basis of the following passage.

A written report is a communication of information from one person to another. It is an account of some matter especially investigated, however routine that matter may be. The ultimate basis of any good written report is facts, which become known through observation and verification. Good written reports may seem to be no more than general ideas and opinions. However, in such cases, the facts leading too these opinions were gathered, verified, and reported earlier, and the opinions are dependent upon these facts. Good style, proper form, and emphasis cannot make a good written report out of unreliable information and bad judgment; but on the other hand, solid investigation and brilliant thinking are not likely to become very useful until they are effectively communicated to others. If a person's work calls for written reports, then his work is often no better than his written reports.

1. Based on the information in the above passage, it can be concluded that opinions expressed in a report should be
   A. based on facts which are gathered and reported
   B. emphasized repeatedly when they result from a special investigation
   C. kept to a minimum
   D. separated from the body of the report

1._____

2. In the above passage, the one of the following which is mentioned as a way of establishing facts is
   A. authority   B. reporting
   C. communication   D. verification

2._____

3. According to the above passage, the characteristic shared by ALL written reports is that they are
   A. accounts of routine matters   B. transmissions of information
   C. reliable and logical   D. written in proper form

3._____

4. Which of the following conclusions can logically be drawn from the information given in the above passage?
   A. Brilliant thinking can make up for unreliable information in a report.
   B. One method of judging an individual's work is the quality of the written reports he is required to submit.
   C. Proper form and emphasis can make a good report out of unreliable information.
   D. Good written reports that seem to be no more than general ideas should be rewritten.

4._____

5. Which of the following suggested titles would be MOST appropriate for the above passage?
    A. Gathering and Organizing Facts
    B. Techniques of Observation
    C. Nature and Purpose of Reports
    D. Reports and Opinions: Differences and Similarities

5._____

Questions 6-8.

DIRECTIONS: Questions 6 through 8 are to be answered SOLELY on the basis of the following passage.

The most important unit of the mimeograph machine is a perforated metal drum over which is stretched a cloth ink pad. A reservoir inside the drum contains the ink which flows through the perforations and saturates the ink pad. To operate the machine, the operator first removes from the machine the protective sheet, which keeps the ink from drying while the machine is not in use. He then hooks the stencil face down on the drum, draws the stencil smoothly over the drum, and fastens the stencil at the bottom. The speed with which the drum turns determines the blackness of the copies printed. Slow turning gives heavy, black copies; fast turning gives light, clear-cut reproductions. If reproductions are run on other than porous paper, slip-sheeting is necessary to prevent smearing. Often, the printed copy fails to drop readily as it comes from the machine. This may be due to static electricity. To remedy this difficulty, the operator fastens a strip of tinsel from side to side near the impression roller so that the printed copy just touches the soft stems of the tinsel as it is ejected from the machine, thus grounding the static electricity to the frame of the machine.

6. According to the above passage,
    A. turning the drum fast produces light copies
    B. stencils should be placed face up on the drum
    C. ink pads should be changed daily
    D. slip-sheeting is necessary when porous paper is being used

6._____

7. According to the above passage, when a mimeograph machine is not in use, the
    A. ink should be drained from the drum
    B. ink pad should be removed
    C. machine should be covered with a protective sheet
    D. counter should be set at zero

7._____

8. According to the above passage, static electricity is grounded to the frame of the mimeograph machine by means of
    A. a slip-sheeting device
    B. a strip of tinsel
    C. an impression roller
    D. hooks located at the top of the drum

8._____

Questions 9-10.

DIRECTIONS: Questions 9 and 10 are to be answered SOLELY on the basis of the following passage.

The proofreading of material typed from copy is performed more accurately and more speedily when two persons perform this work as a team. The person who did not do the typing should read aloud the original copy while the person who did the typing should check the reading against the typed copy. The reader should speak very slowly and repeat the figures, using a different grouping of number when repeating the figures. For example, in reading 1967, the reader may say *one-nine-six-seven* on first reading the figure and *nineteen-sixty-seven* on repeating the figure. The reader should read all punctuation marks, taking nothing for granted. Since mistakes can occur anywhere, everything typed should be proofread. To avoid confusion, the proofreading team should use the standard proofreading marks, which are given in most dictionaries.

9. According to the above passage, the
    A. person who holds the typed copy is called the reader
    B. two members of a proofreading team should take turns in reading the typed copy aloud
    C. typed copy should be checked by the person who did the typing
    D. person who did not do the typing should read aloud from the typed copy

9.____

10. According to the above passage,
    A. it is unnecessary to read the period at the end of a sentence
    B. typographical errors should be noted on the original copy
    C. each person should develop his own set of proofreading marks
    D. figures should be read twice

10.____

Questions 11-16.

DIRECTIONS: Questions 11 through 16 are to be answered SOLELY on the basis of the following passage.

Basic to every office is the need for proper lighting. Inadequate lighting is a familiar cause of fatigue and serves to create a somewhat dismal atmosphere in the office. One requirement of proper lighting is that it be of an appropriate intensity. Intensity is measured in foot-candles. According to the Illuminating Engineering Society of New York, for casual seeing tasks such as in reception rooms, inactive file rooms, and other service areas, it is recommending that the amount of light be 30 foot-candle. For ordinary seeing tasks such as reading, work in active file rooms, and in mailrooms, the recommended lighting is 100 foot-candles. For very difficult seeing tasks such as accounting, transcribing, and business machine use, the recommended lighting is 150 foot-candles.

Lighting intensity is only one requirement. Shadows and glare are to be avoided. For example, the larger the proportion of a ceiling filled with lighting units, the more glare-free and comfortable the lighting will be. Natural lighting from window is not too dependable because on dark wintry days, windows yield little usable light, and on sunny afternoons, the glare from windows may be very distracting. Desks should not face the windows. Finally, the main lighting source ought to be overhead and to the left of the user.

11. According to the above passage, insufficient light in the office may cause 11.____
    A. glare B. tiredness C. shadows D. distraction

12. Based on the above passage, which of the following must be considered when planning lighting arrangements? The 12.____
    A. amount of natural light present
    B. amount of work to be done
    C. level of difficulty of work to be done
    D. type of activity to be carried out

13. It can be inferred from the above passage that a well-coordinated lighting scheme is LIKELY to result in 13.____
    A. greater employee productivity   B. elimination of light reflection
    C. lower lighting cost   D. more use of natural light

14. Of the following, the BEST title for the above passage is 14.____
    A. Characteristics of Light
    B. Light Measurement Devices
    C. Factors to Consider When Planning Lighting Systems
    D. comfort vs. Cost When Devising Lighting Arrangements

15. According to the above passage, a foot-candle is a measurement of the 15.____
    A. number of bulbs used
    B. strength of the light
    C. contrast between glare and shadow
    D. proportion of the ceiling filled with lighting units

16. According to the above passage, the number of foot-candles of light that would be needed to copy figures onto a payroll is _____ foot-candles. 16.____
    A. less than 30   B. 100   C. 30   D. 140

Questions 17-23.

DIRECTIONS: Questions 17 through 23 are to be answered SOLELY on the basis of the following passage.

<u>FEE SCHEDULE</u>

1. A candidate for any baccalaureate degree is not required to pay tuition fees for undergraduate courses until he exceeds 128 credits. Candidates exceeding 128 credits in undergraduate courses are charged at the rate of $100 a credit for each credit of undergraduate course work in excess of 128. Candidates for a baccalaureate degree who are taking graduate courses must pay the same fee as any other student taking graduate courses.

5 (#3)

B. Non-degree students and college graduates are charged tuition fees for courses, whether undergraduate or graduate, at the rate of $180 a credit. For such students, there is an additional charge of $150 for each class hour per week in excess of the number of course credits. For example, if a three-credit course meets five hours a week, there is an additional charge for the extra two hours. Graduate courses are shown with a (G) before the course number.

C. All students are required to pay the laboratory fees indicated after the number of credits given for that course.

D. All students must pay a $250 general fee each semester.

E. Candidates for a baccalaureate degree are charged a $150 medical insurance fee for each semester. All other students are charged a $100 medical insurance fee each semester.

17. Miss Burton is not a candidate for a degree. She registers for the following courses in the spring semester: Economics 12, 4 hours a week, 3 credits; History (G 23, 4 hours a week, 3 credits; English 1, 2 hours a week, 2 credits. The TOTAL amount in fees that Miss Burton must pay is
   A. less than $2,000
   B. at least $2,000 but less than $2,100
   C. at least $2,100 but less than $2,200
   D. $2,200 or over

17.____

18. Miss Gray is not a candidate for a degree. She registers for the following courses in the fall semester: History 3, 3 hours a week, 3 credits; English 5, 3 hours a week, 2 credits; Physics 5, 6 hours a week, 3 credits, laboratory fee $60; Mathematics 7, 4 hours a week, 3 credits. The TOTAL amount in fees that Miss Gray must pay is
   A. less than $3,150
   B. at least $3,150 but less than $3,250
   C. at least $3,250 but less than $3,350
   D. $3,350 or over

18.____

19. Mr. Wall is a candidate for the Bachelor of Arts degree and has completed 126 credits. He registers for the following courses in the spring semester, his final semester at college; French 4, 3 hours a week, 3 credits; Physics (G) 15, 6 hours a week, 3 credits, laboratory fee $80; History (G) 33, 4 hours a week, 3 credits. The TOTAL amount in fees that this candidate must pay is
   A. less than $2,100
   B. at least $2,100 but less than $2,300
   C. at least $2,300 but less than $2,500
   D. $2,500

19.____

20. Mr. Tindall, a candidate for the B.A. degree, has completed 122 credits of undergraduate courses. He registers for the following courses in his final semester: English 31, 3 hours a week, 3 credits; Philosophy 12, 4 hours a week, 4 credits; Anthropology 15, 3 hours a week, 3 credits; Economics (G) 68, 3 hours a week, 3 credits.
The TOTAL amount in fees that Mr. Tindall must pay in his final semester is
   A. less than $1,200
   B. at least $1,200 but less than $1,400
   C. at least $1,400 but less than $1,600
   D. $1,600

20.____

21. Mr. Cantrell, who was graduated from the college a year ago, registers for graduate courses in the fall semester. Each course for which he register carries the same number of credits as the number of hours a week it meets. If he pays a total of $1,530, including a $100 laboratory fee, the number of credits for which he is registered is
   A. 4   B. 5   C. 6   D. 7

21.____

22. Miss Jayson, who is not a candidate for a degree, has registered for several courses including a lecture course in History. She withdraws from the course in History for which she had paid the required course fee of $690.
The number of hours that this course is scheduled to meet is
   A. 4   B. 5   C. 2   D. 3

22.____

23. Mr. Van Arsdale, a graduate of a college in Iowa, registers for the following courses in one semester: Chemistry 35, 5 hours a week, 3 credits; Biology 14, 4 hours a week, 3 credits, laboratory fee $150; Mathematics (G) 179, 3 hours a week, 3 credits.
The TOTAL amount in fees that Mr. Van Arsdale must pay is
   A. less than $2,400
   B. at least $2,400 but less than $2,500
   C. at least $2,500 but less than $2,600
   D. at least $2,600 or over

23.____

Questions 24-25.

DIRECTIONS: Questions 24 and 25 are to be answered SOLELY on the basis of the following passage.

    A duplex envelope is an envelope composed of two sections securely fastened together so that they become one mailing piece. This type of envelope makes it possible for a first class letter to be delivered simultaneously with third or fourth class matter and yet not require payment of the much higher first class postage rate on the entire mailing. First class postage is paid only on the letter which goes in the small compartment, third or fourth class postage being paid on the contents of the larger compartment. The larger compartment generally has an ungummed flap or clasp for sealing. The first class or smaller compartment has a gummed flap for sealing. Postal regulations require that the exact amount of postage applicable to each compartment be separately attached to it.

24. On the basis of the above passage, it is MOST accurate to state that 24.____
    A. the smaller compartment is placed inside the larger compartment before mailing
    B. the two compartments may be detached and mailed separately
    C. two classes of mailing matter may be mailed as a unit at two different postage rates
    D. the more expensive postage rate is paid on the matter in the larger compartment

25. When a duplex envelope is used, the 25.____
    A. first class compartment may be sealed with a clasp
    B. correct amount of postage must be placed on each compartment
    C. compartment containing third or fourth class mail requires a gummed flap for sealing
    D. full amount of postage for both compartments may be placed on the larger compartment

KEY (CORRECT ANSWERS)

1.	A		11.	C
2.	D		12.	D
3.	B		13.	A
4.	B		14.	C
5.	C		15.	B
6.	A		16.	D
7.	C		17.	B
8.	B		18.	A
9.	C		19.	B
10.	D		20.	B

21. C
22. A
23. C
24. C
25. B

PHILOSOPHY, PRINCIPLES, PRACTICES, AND TECHNICS
OF
SUPERVISION, ADMINISTRATION, MANAGEMENT, AND ORGANIZATION

TABLE OF CONTENTS

	Page
MEANING OF SUPERVISION	1
THE OLD AND THE NEW SUPERVISION	1
THE EIGHT (8) BASIC PRINCIPLES OF THE NEW SUPERVISION	1
I. Principle of Responsibility	1
II. Principle of Authority	2
III. Principle of Self-Growth	2
IV. Principle of Individual Worth	2
V. Principle of Creative Leadership	2
VI. Principle of Success and Failure	2
VII. Principle of Science	3
VIII. Principle of Cooperation	3
WHAT IS ADMINISTRATION?	3
I. Practices Commonly Classed as "Supervisory"	3
II. Practices Commonly Classed as "Administrative"	3
III. Practices Commonly Classed as Both "Supervisory" and "Administrative"	4
RESPONSIBILITIES OF THE SUPERVISOR	4
COMPETENCIES OF THE SUPERVISOR	4
THE PROFESSIONAL SUPERVISOR-EMPLOYEE RELATIONSHIP	4
MINI-TEXT IN SUPERVISION, ADMINISTRATION, MANAGEMENT, AND ORGANIZATION	5
I. Brief Highlights	5
A. Levels of Management	6
B. What the Supervisor Must Learn	6
C. A Definition of Supervision	6
D. Elements of the Team Concept	6
E. Principles of Organization	6
F. The Four Important Parts of Every Job	7
G. Principles of Delegation	7
H. Principles of Effective Communications	7
I. Principles of Work Improvement	7
J. Areas of Job Improvement	7
K. Seven Key Points in Making Improvements	8

	L.	Corrective Techniques for Job Improvement	8
	M.	A Planning Checklist	8
	N.	Five Characteristics of Good Directions	9
	O.	Types of Directions	9
	P.	Controls	9
	Q.	Orienting the New Employee	9
	R.	Checklist for Orienting New Employees	9
	S.	Principles of Learning	10
	T.	Causes of Poor Performance	10
	U.	Four Major Steps in On-the-Job Instructions	10
	V.	Employees Want Five Things	10
	W.	Some Don'ts in Regard to Praise	11
	X.	How to Gain Your Workers' Confidence	11
	Y.	Sources of Employee Problems	11
	Z.	The Supervisor's Key to Discipline	11
	AA.	Five Important Processes of Management	12
	BB.	When the Supervisor Fails to Plan	12
	CC.	Fourteen General Principles of Management	12
	DD.	Change	12
II.	Brief Topical Summaries		13
	A.	Who/What is the Supervisor?	13
	B.	The Sociology of Work	13
	C.	Principles and Practices of Supervision	14
	D.	Dynamic Leadership	14
	E.	Processes for Solving Problems	15
	F.	Training for Results	15
	G.	Health, Safety, and Accident Prevention	16
	H.	Equal Employment Opportunity	16
	I.	Improving Communications	16
	J.	Self-Development	17
	K.	Teaching and Training	17
		1. The Teaching Process	17
		a. Preparation	17
		b. Presentation	18
		c. Summary	18
		d. Application	18
		e. Evaluation	18
		2. Teaching Methods	18
		a. Lecture	18
		b. Discussion	18
		c. Demonstration	19
		d. Performance	19
		e. Which Method to Use	19

PHILOSOPHY, PRINCIPLES, PRACTICES, AND TECHNICS OF SUPERVISION, ADMINISTRATION, MANAGEMENT, AND ORGANIZATION

MEANING OF SUPERVISION

The extension of the democratic philosophy has been accompanied by an extension in the scope of supervision. Modern leaders and supervisors no longer think of supervision in the narrow sense of being confined chiefly to visiting employees, supplying materials, or rating the staff. They regard supervision as being intimately related to all the concerned agencies of society, they speak of the supervisor's function in terms of "growth," rather than the "improvement" of employees.

This modern concept of supervision may be defined as follows: Supervision is leadership and the development of leadership within groups which are cooperatively engaged in inspection, research, training, guidance, and evaluation.

THE OLD AND THE NEW SUPERVISION

TRADITIONAL
1. Inspection
2. Focused on the employee
3. Visitation
4. Random and haphazard
5. Imposed and authoritarian
6. One person usually

MODERN
1. Study and analysis
2. Focused on aims, materials, methods, supervisors, employees, environment
3. Demonstrations, intervisitation, workshops, directed reading, bulletins, etc.
4. Definitely organized and planned (scientific)
5. Cooperative and democratic
6. Many persons involved (creative)

THE EIGHT (8) BASIC PRINCIPLES OF THE NEW SUPERVISION

I. Principle of Responsibility
   Authority to act and responsibility for acting must be joined.
   A. If you give responsibility, give authority.
   B. Define employee duties clearly.
   C. Protect employees from criticism by others.
   D. Recognize the rights as well as obligations of employees.
   E. Achieve the aims of a democratic society insofar as it is possible within the area of your work.
   F. Establish a situation favorable to training and learning.
   G. Accept ultimate responsibility for everything done in your section, unit, office, division, department.
   H. Good administration and good supervision are inseparable.

II. Principle of Authority
The success of the supervisor is measured by the extent to which the power of authority is not used.
- A. Exercise simplicity and informality in supervision
- B. Use the simplest machinery of supervision
- C. If it is good for the organization as a whole, it is probably justified.
- D. Seldom be arbitrary or authoritative.
- E. Do not base your work on the power of position or of personality.
- F. Permit and encourage the free expression of opinions.

III. Principle of Self-Growth
The success of the supervisor is measured by the extent to which, and the speed with which, he is no longer needed.
- A. Base criticism on principles, not on specifics.
- B. Point out higher activities to employees.
- C. Train for self-thinking by employees to meet new situations.
- D. Stimulate initiative, self-reliance, and individual responsibility
- E. Concentrate on stimulating the growth of employees rather than on removing defects.

IV. Principle of Individual Worth
Respect for the individual is a paramount consideration in supervision.
- A. Be human and sympathetic in dealing with employees.
- B. Don't nag about things to be done.
- C. Recognize the individual differences among employees and seek opportunities to permit best expression of each personality.

V. Principle of Creative Leadership
The best supervision is that which is not apparent to the employee.
- A. Stimulate, don't drive employees to creative action.
- B. Emphasize doing good things.
- C. Encourage employees to do what they do best.
- D. Do not be too greatly concerned with details of subject or method.
- E. Do not be concerned exclusively with immediate problems and activities.
- F. Reveal higher activities and make them both desired and maximally possible.
- G. Determine procedures in the light of each situation but see that these are derived from a sound basic philosophy.
- H. Aid, inspire, and lead so as to liberate the creative spirit latent in all good employees.

VI. Principle of Success and Failure
There are no unsuccessful employees, only unsuccessful supervisors who have failed to give proper leadership.
- A. Adapt suggestions to the capacities, attitudes, and prejudices of employees.
- B. Be gradual, be progressive, be persistent.
- C. Help the employee find the general principle; have the employee apply his own problem to the general principle.
- D. Give adequate appreciation for good work and honest effort.
- E. Anticipate employee difficulties and help to prevent them.
- F. Encourage employees to do the desirable things they will do anyway.
- G. Judge your supervision by the results it secures.

VII. Principle of Science
Successful supervision is scientific, objective, and experimental. It is based on facts, not on prejudices.
   A. Be cumulative in results.
   B. Never divorce your suggestions from the goals of training.
   C. Don't be impatient of results.
   D. Keep all matters on a professional, not a personal, level.
   E. Do not be concerned exclusively with immediate problems and activities.
   F. Use objective means of determining achievement and rating where possible.

VIII. Principle of Cooperation
Supervision is a cooperative enterprise between supervisor and employee.
   A. Begin with conditions as they are.
   B. Ask opinions of all involved when formulating policies.
   C. Organization is as good as its weakest link.
   D. Let employees help to determine policies and department programs.
   E. Be approachable and accessible—physically and mentally.
   F. Develop pleasant social relationships.

WHAT IS ADMINISTRATION

Administration is concerned with providing the environment, the material facilities, and the operational procedures that will promote the maximum growth and development of supervisors and employees. (Organization is an aspect and a concomitant of administration.)

There is no sharp line of demarcation between supervision and administration; these functions are intimately interrelated and, often, overlapping. They are complementary activities.

I. Practices Commonly Classed as "Supervisory"
   A. Conducting employees' conferences
   B. Visiting sections, units, offices, divisions, departments
   C. Arranging for demonstrations
   D. Examining plans
   E. Suggesting professional reading
   F. Interpreting bulletins
   G. Recommending in-service training courses
   H. Encouraging experimentation
   I. Appraising employee morale
   J. Providing for intervisitation

II. Practices Commonly Classified as "Administrative"
   A. Management of the office
   B. Arrangement of schedules for extra duties
   C. Assignment of rooms or areas
   D. Distribution of supplies
   E. Keeping records and reports
   F. Care of audio-visual materials
   G. Keeping inventory records
   H. Checking record cards and books

      I.   Programming special activities
      J.   Checking on the attendance and punctuality of employees

III.   Practices Commonly Classified as Both "Supervisory" and "Administrative"
      A.   Program construction
      B.   Testing or evaluating outcomes
      C.   Personnel accounting
      D.   Ordering instructional materials

RESPONSIBILITIES OF THE SUPERVISOR

A person employed in a supervisory capacity must constantly be able to improve his own efficiency and ability. He represent the employer to the employees and only continuous self-examination can make him a capable supervisor.

Leadership and training are the supervisor's responsibility. An efficient working unit is one in which the employees work with the supervisor. It is his job to bring out the best in his employees. He must always be relaxed, courteous, and calm in his association with his employees. Their feelings are important, and a harsh attitude does not develop the most efficient employees.

COMPETENCES OF THE SUPERVISOR

      I.   Complete knowledge of the duties and responsibilities of his position.
      II.   To be able to organize a job, plan ahead, and carry through.
      III.   To have self-confidence and initiative.
      IV.   To be able to handle the unexpected situation and make quick decisions.
      V.   To be able to properly train subordinates in the positions they are best suited for.
      VI.   To be able to keep good human relations among his subordinates.
      VII. To be able to keep good human relations between his subordinates and himself and to earn their respect and trust.

THE PROFESSIONAL SUPERVISOR-EMPLOYEE RELATIONSHIP

There are two kinds of efficiency: one kind is only apparent and is produced in organizations through the exercise of mere discipline; this is but a simulation of the second, or true, efficiency which springs from spontaneous cooperation. If you are a manager, no matter how great or small your responsibility, it is your job, in the final analysis, to create and develop this involuntary cooperation among the people whom you supervise. For, no matter how powerful a combination of money, machines, and materials a company may have, this is a dead and sterile thing without a team of willing, thinking, and articulate people to guide it.

The following 21 points are presented as indicative of the exemplary basic relationship that should exist between supervisor and employee:

1.   Each person wants to be liked and respected by his fellow employee and wants to be treated with consideration and respect by his superior.
2.   The most competent employee will make an error. However, in a unit where good relations exist between the supervisor and his employees, tenseness and fear do not exist. Thus, errors are not hidden or covered up, and the efficiency of a unit is not impaired.

3. Subordinates resent rules, regulations, or orders that are unreasonable or unexplained.
4. Subordinates are quick to resent unfairness, harshness, injustices, and favoritism.
5. An employee will accept responsibility if he knows that he will be complimented for a job well done, and not too harshly chastised for failure; that his supervisor will check the cause of the failure, and, if it was the supervisor's fault, he will assume the blame therefore. If it was the employee's fault, his supervisor will explain the correct method or means of handling the responsibility.
6. An employee wants to receive credit for a suggestion he has made, that is used. If a suggestion cannot be used, the employee is entitled to an explanation. The supervisor should not say "no" and close the subject.
7. Fear and worry slow up a worker's ability. Poor working environment can impair his physical and mental health. A good supervisor avoids forceful methods, threats, and arguments to get a job done.
8. A forceful supervisor is able to train his employees individually and as a team, and is able to motivate them in the proper channels.
9. A mature supervisor is able to properly evaluate his subordinates and to keep them happy and satisfied.
10. A sensitive supervisor will never patronize his subordinates.
11. A worthy supervisor will respect his employees' confidences.
12. Definite and clear-cut responsibilities should be assigned to each executive.
13. Responsibility should always be coupled with corresponding authority.
14. No change should be made in the scope or responsibilities of a position without a definite understanding to that effect on the part of all persons concerned.
15. No executive or employee, occupying a single position in the organization, should be subject to definite orders from more than one source.
16. Orders should never be given to subordinates over the head of a responsible executive. Rather than do this, the officer in question should be supplanted.
17. Criticisms of subordinates should, whoever possible, be made privately, and in no case should a subordinate be criticized in the presence of executives or employees of equal or lower rank.
18. No dispute or difference between executives or employees as to authority or responsibilities should be considered too trivial for prompt and careful adjudication.
19. Promotions, wage changes, and disciplinary action should always be approved by the executive immediately superior to the one directly responsible.
20. No executive or employee should ever be required, or expected, to be at the same time an assistant to, and critic of, another.
21. Any executive whose work is subject to regular inspection should, wherever practicable, be given the assistance and facilities necessary to enable him to maintain an independent check of the quality of his work.

MINI-TEXT IN SUPERVISION, ADMINISTRATION, MANAGEMENT, AND ORGANIZATION

I. Brief Highlights

Listed concisely and sequentially are major headings and important data in the field for quick recall and review.

A. Levels of Management
Any organization of some size has several levels of management. In terms of a ladder, the levels are:

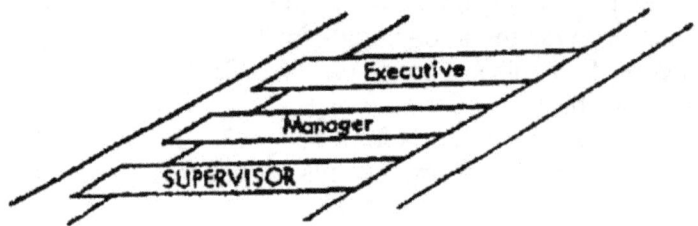

The first level is very important because it is the beginning point of management leadership.

B. What the Supervisor Must Learn
A supervisor must learn to:
1. Deal with people and their differences
2. Get the job done through people
3. Recognize the problems when they exist
4. Overcome obstacles to good performance
5. Evaluate the performance of people
6. Check his own performance in terms of accomplishment

C. A Definition of Supervisor
The term supervisor means any individual having authority, in the interests of the employer, to hire, transfer, suspend, lay-off, recall, promote, discharge, assign, reward, or discipline other employees or responsibility to direct them, or to adjust their grievances, or effectively to recommend such action, if, in connection with the foregoing, exercise of such authority is not of a merely routine or clerical nature but requires the use of independent judgment.

D. Elements of the Team Concept
What is involved in teamwork? The component parts are:
1. Members
2. A leader
3. Goals
4. Plans
5. Cooperation
6. Spirit

E. Principles of Organization
1. A team member must know what his job is.
2. Be sure that the nature and scope of a job are understood.
3. Authority and responsibility should be carefully spelled out.
4. A supervisor should be permitted to make the maximum number of decisions affecting his employees.
5. Employees should report to only one supervisor.
6. A supervisor should direct only as many employees as he can handle effectively.
7. An organization plan should be flexible.

8. Inspection and performance of work should be separate.
9. Organizational problems should receive immediate attention.
10. Assign work in line with ability and experience.

F. The Four Important Parts of Every Job
1. Inherent in every job is the *accountability* for results.
2. A second set of factors in every job is *responsibilities*.
3. Along with duties and responsibilities one must have the *authority* to act within certain limits without obtaining permission to proceed.
4. No job exists in a vacuum. The supervisor is surrounded by key *relationships*.

G. Principles of Delegation
Where work is delegated for the first time, the supervisor should think in terms of these questions:
1. Who is best qualified to do this?
2. Can an employee improve his abilities by doing this?
3. How long should an employee spend on this?
4. Are there any special problems for which he will need guidance?
5. How broad a delegation can I make?

H. Principles of Effective Communications
1. Determine the media.
2. To whom directed?
3. Identification and source authority.
4. Is communication understood?

I. Principles of Work Improvement
1. Most people usually do only the work which is assigned to them.
2. Workers are likely to fit assigned work into the time available to perform it.
3. A good workload usually stimulates output.
4. People usually do their best work when they know that results will be reviewed or inspected.
5. Employees usually feel that someone else is responsible for conditions of work, workplace layout, job methods, type of tools/equipment, and other such factors.
6. Employees are usually defensive about their job security.
7. Employees have natural resistance to change.
8. Employees can support or destroy a supervisor.
9. A supervisor usually earns the respect of his people through his personal example of diligence and efficiency.

J. Areas of Job Improvement
The areas of job improvement are quite numerous, but the most common ones which a supervisor can identify and utilize are:
1. Departmental layout
2. Flow of work
3. Workplace layout
4. Utilization of manpower
5. Work methods
6. Materials handling

7. Utilization
8. Motion economy

K. Seven Key Points in Making Improvements
1. Select the job to be improved
2. Study how it is being done now
3. Question the present method
4. Determine actions to be taken
5. Chart proposed method
6. Get approval and apply
7. Solicit worker participation

L. Corrective Techniques of Job Improvement
Specific Problems
1. Size of workload
2. Inability to meet schedules
3. Strain and fatigue
4. Improper use of men and skills
5. Waste, poor quality, unsafe conditions
6. Bottleneck conditions that hinder output
7. Poor utilization of equipment and machine
8. Efficiency and productivity of labor

General Improvement
1. Departmental layout
2. Flow of work
3. Work plan layout
4. Utilization of manpower
5. Work methods
6. Materials handling
7. Utilization of equipment
8. Motion economy

Corrective Techniques
1. Study with scale model
2. Flow chart study
3. Motion analysis
4. Comparison of units produced to standard allowance
5. Methods analysis
6. Flow chart and equipment study
7. Down time vs. running time
8. Motion analysis

M. A Planning Checklist
1. Objectives
2. Controls
3. Delegations
4. Communications
5. Resources
6. Manpower

7. Equipment
8. Supplies and materials
9. Utilization of time
10. Safety
11. Money
12. Work
13. Timing of improvements

N. Five Characteristics of Good Directions
In order to get results, directions must be:
1. Possible of accomplishment
2. Agreeable with worker interests
3. Related to mission
4. Planned and complete
5. Unmistakably clear

O. Types of Directions
1. Demands or direct orders
2. Requests
3. Suggestion or implication
4. volunteering

P. Controls
A typical listing of the overall areas in which the supervisor should establish controls might be:
1. Manpower
2. Materials
3. Quality of work
4. Quantity of work
5. Time
6. Space
7. Money
8. Methods

Q. Orienting the New Employee
1. Prepare for him
2. Welcome the new employee
3. Orientation for the job
4. Follow-up

R. Checklist for Orienting New Employees   Yes   No
1. Do you appreciate the feelings of new employees when they first report for work?   ___   ___
2. Are you aware of the fact that the new employee must make a big adjustment to his job?   ___   ___
3. Have you given him good reasons for liking the job and the organization?   ___   ___
4. Have you prepared for his first day on the job?   ___   ___
5. Did you welcome him cordially and make him feel needed?   ___   ___

			Yes	No
	6.	Did you establish rapport with him so that he feels free to talk and discuss matters with you?	___	___
	7.	Did you explain his job to him and his relationship to you?	___	___
	8.	Does he know that his work will be evaluated periodically on a basis that is fair and objective?	___	___
	9.	Did you introduce him to his fellow workers in such a way that they are likely to accept him?	___	___
	10.	Does he know what employee benefits he will receive?	___	___
	11.	Does he understand the importance of being on the job and what to do if he must leave his duty station?	___	___
	12.	Has he been impressed with the importance of accident prevention and safe practice?	___	___
	13.	Does he generally know his way around the department?	___	___
	14.	Is he under the guidance of a sponsor who will teach the right way of doing things?	___	___
	15.	Do you plan to follow-up so that he will continue to adjust successfully to his job?	___	___

S. Principles of Learning
 1. Motivation
 2. Demonstration or explanation
 3. Practice

T. Causes of Poor Performance
 1. Improper training for job
 2. Wrong tools
 3. Inadequate directions
 4. Lack of supervisory follow-up
 5. Poor communications
 6. Lack of standards of performance
 7. Wrong work habits
 8. Low morale
 9. Other

U. Four Major Steps in On-The-Job Instruction
 1. Prepare the worker
 2. Present the operation
 3. Tryout performance
 4. Follow-up

V. Employees Want Five Things
 1. Security
 2. Opportunity
 3. Recognition
 4. Inclusion
 5. Expression

W. Some Don'ts in Regard to Praise
1. Don't praise a person for something he hasn't done.
2. Don't praise a person unless you can be sincere.
3. Don't be sparing in praise just because your superior withholds it from you.
4. Don't let too much time elapse between good performance and recognition of it

X. How to Gain Your Workers' Confidence
Methods of developing confidence include such things as:
1. Knowing the interests, habits, hobbies of employees
2. Admitting your own inadequacies
3. Sharing and telling of confidence in others
4. Supporting people when they are in trouble
5. Delegating matters that can be well handled
6. Being frank and straightforward about problems and working conditions
7. Encouraging others to bring their problems to you
8. Taking action on problems which impede worker progress

Y. Sources of Employee Problems
On-the-job causes might be such things as:
1. A feeling that favoritism is exercised in assignments
2. Assignment of overtime
3. An undue amount of supervision
4. Changing methods or systems
5. Stealing of ideas or trade secrets
6. Lack of interest in job
7. Threat of reduction in force
8. Ignorance or lack of communications
9. Poor equipment
10. Lack of knowing how supervisor feels toward employee
11. Shift assignments

Off-the-job problems might have to do with:
1. Health
2. Finances
3. Housing
4. Family

Z. The Supervisor's Key to Discipline
There are several key points about discipline which the supervisor should keep in mind:
1. Job discipline is one of the disciplines of life and is directed by the supervisor.
2. It is more important to correct an employee fault than to fix blame for it.
3. Employee performance is affected by problems both on the job and off.
4. Sudden or abrupt changes in behavior can be indications of important employee problems.
5. Problems should be dealt with as soon as possible after they are identified.
6. The attitude of the supervisor may have more to do with solving problems than the techniques of problem solving.
7. Correction of employee behavior should be resorted to only after the supervisor is sure that training or counseling will not be helpful.

8. Be sure to document your disciplinary actions.
9. Make sure that you are disciplining on the basis of facts rather than personal feelings.
10. Take each disciplinary step in order, being careful not to make snap judgments, or decisions based on impatience.

AA. Five Important Processes of Management
1. Planning
2. Organizing
3. Scheduling
4. Controlling
5. Motivating

BB. When the Supervisor Fails to Plan
1. Supervisor creates impression of not knowing his job
2. May lead to excessive overtime
3. Job runs itself—supervisor lacks control
4. Deadlines and appointments missed
5. Parts of the work go undone
6. Work interrupted by emergencies
7. Sets a bad example
8. Uneven workload creates peaks and valleys
9. Too much time on minor details at expense of more important tasks

CC. Fourteen General Principles of Management
1. Division of work
2. Authority and responsibility
3. Discipline
4. Unity of command
5. Unity of direction
6. Subordination of individual interest to general interest
7. Remuneration of personnel
8. Centralization
9. Scalar chain
10. Order
11. Equity
12. Stability of tenure of personnel
13. Initiative
14. Esprit de corps

DD. Change

Bringing about change is perhaps attempted more often, and yet less well understood, than anything else the supervisor does. How do people generally react to change? (People tend to resist change that is imposed upon them by other individuals or circumstances.

Change is characteristic of every situation. It is a part of every real endeavor where the efforts of people are concerned.

1. Why do people resist change?
   People may resist change because of:
   a. Fear of the unknown
   b. Implied criticism
   c. Unpleasant experiences in the past
   d. Fear of loss of status
   e. Threat to the ego
   f. Fear of loss of economic stability

2. How can we best overcome the resistance to change?
   In initiating change, take these steps:
   a. Get ready to sell
   b. Identify sources of help
   c. Anticipate objections
   d. Sell benefits
   e. Listen in depth
   f. Follow up

II. Brief Topical Summaries

   A. Who/What is the Supervisor?
      1. The supervisor is often called the "highest level employee and the lowest level manager."
      2. A supervisor is a member of both management and the work group. He acts as a bridge between the two.
      3. Most problems in supervision are in the area of human relations, or people problems.
      4. Employees expect: Respect, opportunity to learn and to advance, and a sense of belonging, and so forth.
      5. Supervisors are responsible for directing people and organizing work. Planning is of paramount importance.
      6. A position description is a set of duties and responsibilities inherent to a given position.
      7. It is important to keep the position description up-to-date and to provide each employee with his own copy.

   B. The Sociology of Work
      1. People are alike in many ways; however, each individual is unique.
      2. The supervisor is challenged in getting to know employee differences. Acquiring skills in evaluating individuals is an asset.
      3. Maintaining meaningful working relationships in the organization is of great importance.
      4. The supervisor has an obligation to help individuals to develop to their fullest potential.
      5. Job rotation on a planned basis helps to build versatility and to maintain interest and enthusiasm in work groups.
      6. Cross training (job rotation) provides backup skills.

7. The supervisor can help reduce tension by maintaining a sense of humor, providing guidance to employees, and by making reasonable and timely decisions. Employees respond favorably to working under reasonably predictable circumstances.
8. Change is characteristic of all managerial behavior. The supervisor must adjust to changes in procedures, new methods, technological changes, and to a number of new and sometimes challenging situations.
9. To overcome the natural tendency for people to resist change, the supervisor should become more skillful in initiating change.

C. Principles and Practices of Supervision
1. Employees should be required to answer to only one superior.
2. A supervisor can effectively direct only a limited number of employees, depending upon the complexity, variety, and proximity of the jobs involved.
3. The organizational chart presents the organization in graphic form. It reflects lines of authority and responsibility as well as interrelationships of units within the organization.
4. Distribution of work can be improved through an analysis using the "Work Distribution Chart."
5. The "Work Distribution Chart" reflects the division of work within a unit in understandable form.
6. When related tasks are given to an employee, he has a better chance of increasing his skills through training.
7. The individual who is given the responsibility for tasks must also be given the appropriate authority to insure adequate results.
8. The supervisor should delegate repetitive, routine work. Preparation of recurring reports, maintaining leave and attendance records are some examples.
9. Good discipline is essential to good task performance. Discipline is reflected in the actions of employees on the job in the absence of supervision.
10. Disciplinary action may have to be taken when the positive aspects of discipline have failed. Reprimand, warning, and suspension are examples of disciplinary action.
11. If a situation calls for a reprimand, be sure it is deserved and remember it is to be done in private.

D. Dynamic Leadership
1. A style is a personal method or manner of exerting influence.
2. Authoritarian leaders often see themselves as the source of power and authority.
3. The democratic leader often perceives the group as the source of authority and power.
4. Supervisors tend to do better when using the pattern of leadership that is most natural for them.
5. Social scientists suggest that the effective supervisor use the leadership style that best fits the problem or circumstances involved.
6. All four styles—telling, selling, consulting, joining—have their place. Using one does not preclude using the other at another time.

7. The theory X point of view assumes that the average person dislikes work, will avoid it whenever possible, and must be coerced to achieve organizational objectives.
8. The theory Y point of view assumes that the average person considers work to be a natural as play, and, when the individual is committed, he requires little supervision or direction to accomplish desired objectives.
9. The leader's basic assumptions concerning human behavior and human nature affect his actions, decisions, and other managerial practices.
10. Dissatisfaction among employees is often present, but difficult to isolate. The supervisor should seek to weaken dissatisfaction by keeping promises, being sincere and considerate, keeping employees informed, and so forth.
11. Constructive suggestions should be encouraged during the natural progress of the work.

E. Processes for Solving Problems
1. People find their daily tasks more meaningful and satisfying when they can improve them.
2. The causes of problems, or the key factors, are often hidden in the background. Ability to solve problems often involves the ability to isolate them from their backgrounds. There is some substance to the cliché that some persons "can't see the forest for the trees."
3. New procedures are often developed from old ones. Problems should be broken down into manageable parts. New ideas can be adapted from old one.
4. People think differently in problem-solving situations. Using a logical, patterned approach is often useful. One approach found to be useful includes these steps:
   a. Define the problem
   b. Establish objectives
   c. Get the facts
   d. Weigh and decide
   e. Take action
   f. Evaluate action

F. Training for Results
1. Participants respond best when they feel training is important to them.
2. The supervisor has responsibility for the training and development of those who report to him.
3. When training is delegated to others, great care must be exercised to insure the trainer has knowledge, aptitude, and interest for his work as a trainer.
4. Training (learning) of some type goes on continually. The most successful supervisor makes certain the learning contributes in a productive manner to operational goals.
5. New employees are particularly susceptible to training. Older employees facing new job situations require specific training, as well as having need for development and growth opportunities.
6. Training needs require continuous monitoring.
7. The training officer of an agency is a professional with a responsibility to assist supervisors in solving training problems.

8. Many of the self-development steps important to the supervisor's own growth are equally important to the development of peers and subordinates. Knowledge of these is important when the supervisor consults with others on development and growth opportunities.

G. Health, Safety, and Accident Prevention
1. Management-minded supervisors take appropriate measures to assist employees in maintaining health and in assuring safe practices in the work environment.
2. Effective safety training and practices help to avoid injury and accidents.
3. Safety should be a management goal. All infractions of safety which are observed should be corrected without exception.
4. Employees' safety attitude, training and instruction, provision of safe tools and equipment, supervision, and leadership are considered highly important factors which contribute to safety and which can be influenced directly by supervisors.
5. When accidents do occur, they should be investigated promptly for very important reasons, including the fact that information which is gained can be used to prevent accidents in the future.

H. Equal Employment Opportunity
1. The supervisor should endeavor to treat all employees fairly, without regard to religion, race, sex, or national origin.
2. Groups tend to reflect the attitude of the leader. Prejudice can be detected even in very subtle form. Supervisors must strive to create a feeling of mutual respect and confidence in every employee.
3. Complete utilization of all human resources is a national goal. Equitable consideration should be accorded women in the work force, minority-group members, the physically and mentally handicapped, and the older employee. The important question is: "Who can do the job?"
4. Training opportunities, recognition for performance, overtime assignments, promotional opportunities, and all other personnel actions are to be handled on an equitable basis.

I. Improving Communications
1. Communications is achieving understanding between the sender and the receiver of a message. It also means sharing information—the creation of understanding.
2. Communication is basic to all human activity. Words are means of conveying meanings; however, real meanings are in people.
3. There are very practical differences in the effectiveness of one-way, impersonal, and two-way communications. Words spoken face-to-face are better understood. Telephone conversations are effective, but lack the rapport of person-to-person exchanges. The whole person communicates.
4. Cooperation and communication in an organization go hand in hand. When there is a mutual respect between people, spelling out rules and procedures for communicating is unnecessary.
5. There are several barriers to effective communications. These include failure to listen with respect and understanding, lack of skill in feedback, and misinterpreting the meanings of words used by the speaker. It is also common

practice to listen to what we want to hear, and tune out things we do not want to hear.
6. Communication is management's chief problem. The supervisor should accept the challenge to communicate more effectively and to improve interagency and intra-agency communications.
7. The supervisor may often plan for and conduct meetings. The planning phase is critical and may determine the success or the failure of a meeting.
8. Speaking before groups usually requires extra effort. Stage fright may never disappear completely, but it can be controlled.

J. Self-Development
1. Every employee is responsible for his own self-development.
2. Toastmaster and toastmistress clubs offer opportunities to improve skills in oral communications.
3. Planning for one's own self-development is of vital importance. Supervisors know their own strengths and limitations better than anyone else.
4. Many opportunities are open to aid the supervisor in his developmental efforts, including job assignments; training opportunities, both governmental and non-governmental—to include universities and professional conferences and seminars.
5. Programmed instruction offers a means of studying at one's own rate.
6. Where difficulties may arise from a supervisor's being away from his work for training, he may participate in televised home study or correspondence courses to meet his self-development needs.

K. Teaching and Training
1. The Teaching Process
Teaching is encouraging and guiding the learning activities of students toward established goals. In most cases this process consists of five steps: preparation, presentation, summarization, evaluation, and application.

   a. Preparation
   Preparation is two-fold in nature; that of the supervisor and the employee. Preparation by the supervisor is absolutely essential to success. He must know what, when, where, how, and whom he will teach. Some of the factors that should be considered are:
   1) The objectives
   2) The materials needed
   3) The methods to be used
   4) Employee participation
   5) Employee interest
   6) Training aids
   7) Evaluation
   8) Summarization

   Employee preparation consists in preparing the employee to receive the material. Probably the most important single factor in the preparation of the employee is arousing and maintaining his interest. He must know the objectives of the training, why he is there, how the material can be used, and its importance to him.

b. Presentation
In presentation, have a carefully designed plan and follow it. The plan should be accurate and complete, yet flexible enough to meet situations as they arise. The method of presentation will be determined by the particular situation and objectives.

c. Summary
A summary should be made at the end of every training unit and program. In addition, there may be internal summaries depending on the nature of the material being taught. The important thing is that the trainee must always be able to understand how each part of the new material relates to the whole.

d. Application
The supervisor must arrange work so the employee will be given a chance to apply new knowledge or skills while the material is still clear in his mind and interest is high. The trainee does not really know whether he has learned the material until he has been given a chance to apply it. If the material is not applied, it loses most of its value.

e. Evaluation
The purpose of all training is to promote learning. To determine whether the training has been a success or failure, the supervisor must evaluate this learning.
In the broadest sense, evaluation includes all the devices, methods, skills, and techniques used by the supervisor to keep himself and the employees informed as to their progress toward the objectives they are pursuing. The extent to which the employee has mastered the knowledge, skills, and abilities, or changed his attitudes, as determined by the program objectives, is the extent to which instruction has succeeded or failed.
Evaluation should not be confined to the end of the lesson, day, or program but should be used continuously. We shall note later the way this relates to the rest of the teaching process.

2. Teaching Methods
A teaching method is a pattern of identifiable student and instructor activity used in presenting training material.
All supervisors are faced with the problem of deciding which method should be used at a given time.

a. Lecture
The lecture is direct oral presentation of material by the supervisor. The present trend is to place less emphasis on the trainer's activity and more on that of the trainee.

b. Discussion
Teaching by discussion or conference involves using questions and other techniques to arouse interest and focus attention upon certain areas, and by doing so creating a learning situation. This can be one of the most

valuable methods because it gives the employees an opportunity to express their ideas and pool their knowledge.

    c. Demonstration
The demonstration is used to teach how something works or how to do something. It can be used to show a principle or what the results of a series of actions will be. A well-staged demonstration is particularly effective because it shows proper methods of performance in a realistic manner.

    d. Performance
Performance is one of the most fundamental of all learning techniques or teaching methods. The trainee may be able to tell how a specific operation should be performed but he cannot be sure he knows how to perform the operation until he has done so.
As with all methods, there are certain advantages and disadvantages to each method.

    e. Which Method to Use
Moreover, there are other methods and techniques of teaching. It is difficult to use any method without other methods entering into it. In any learning situation, a combination of methods is usually more effective than any one method alone.

Finally, evaluation must be integrated into the other aspects of the teaching-learning process.

It must be used in the motivation of the trainees; it must be used to assist in developing understanding during the training; and it must be related to employee application of the results of training.

This is distinctly the role of the supervisor.